Discovering Eve

Discovering Eve

ANCIENT ISRAELITE WOMEN IN CONTEXT

Carol Meyers

OXFORD UNIVERSITY PRESS
New York   Oxford

Oxford University Press

Oxford   New York   Toronto
Delhi   Bombay   Calcutta   Madras   Karachi
Petaling Jaya   Singapore   Hong Kong   Tokyo
Nairobi   Dar es Salaam   Cape Town
Melbourne   Auckland

and associated companies in
Berlin   Ibadan

First published in 1988 by Oxford University Press, Inc.,
198 Madison Avenue, New York, New York 10016-4314

First issued as an Oxford University Press paperback, 1991

Oxford is a registered trademark of Oxford University Press

Library of Congress Cataloging-in-Publication Data
Meyers, Carol L.
Discovering Eve : ancient Israelite women in context / Carol Meyers.
p.   cm.
Bibliography: p.
Includes index.
ISBN 0-19-504934-9
1. Women, Jewish—Palestine—History.   2. Women in Judaism.
3. Women in the Bible.   4. Palestine—Social life and customs—To 70
A.D.   I. Title.
HQ1172.M49 1988   83-31847
305.4'862—dc19   CIP
ISBN 0-19-506581-6 (pbk.)

6 8 10 9 7 5

Printed in the United States of America

for Eric

Preface

This book is truly a project of the university in several ways. The idea for studying women in ancient Israel grew not out of my own training and research but rather from the concern of my colleagues that "women in biblical tradition" receive curricular attention. Thus, as I began to teach that subject nearly a decade ago, I discovered how little really was known about women in the biblical world. Gradually, the investigation of that aspect of our western past did become one of my research interests. I became increasingly aware of how powerful the biblical texts dealing with women, especially the Eden narrative of Genesis 2 and 3, have been in shaping western attitudes about gender for two millennia. And I moved closer to realizing that the relationship of those texts to the women of ancient Israelite society needed to be explored.

The motivation for pursuing difficult issues, the process of coming to understand obscure texts, the very methodology employed, all emerged in significant measure from the classroom experience. The probing questions and insightful comments of students, both graduate and undergraduate, have given impetus to my own thinking in countless ways. The general support and encouragement of many colleagues has also been invaluable. In particular, the women's studies program at Duke has provided in its faculty seminars and colloquia a warm yet critical atmosphere in which many of the directions I have taken in this book were first explored.

The university grants leave time to its faculty; thus one is released from the normal demands on time and energy that are part of university life, in order to pursue scholarship more intensively. Twice in the past four years I have been the fortunate recipient of year-long research leaves without which I could not have brought this project to fruition.

My gratitude to the academy and especially to Duke University for the opportunity to have conceived, nurtured, and completed this work is thus enormous. I say this not only because of the direct and tangible ways in which I have benefited from my academic context but also because of the way this work, in its interdisciplinary nature, is representative of the university. As the academy brings together diverse disciplines, so does this account of women in ancient Israel traverse disciplinary borders. I have drawn from history, art, archaeology, anthropology, religion, sociology, language, and literature. There has been risk in this enterprise, for I do not pretend to be master of all the disciplines that have been essential to my task. Yet I have felt that it has been a risk worth taking, for it has allowed at least partial enlightening of a realm that otherwise would remain in the deep darkness of ages past.

Rooted in the academy as this work may be, it is meant to reach beyond the university. I hope that it will be of some use in the various disciplines from which I have taken materials and methods. But I also intend this for a broader audience, which consists of all those who are interested in the historical and biblical roots of present-day attitudes to gender relationships. As long as the Bible is quoted as justification for one or another belief or policy regarding women, the value of understanding the biblical texts involved and the social world from which they emerged is compelling.

In addition to my debt to the university, I owe much to sources outside its walls. In 1982–1983, a grant from the National Endowment for the Humanities enabled me to immerse myself in the study of social anthropology, particularly with respect to matters of gender. It had become clear, as I became involved in an investigation of women in Israelite society, that my training in biblical studies and archaeology, and in the disciplines ancillary to those fields, was not sufficient to the task. These disciplines could not tell me everything I needed to know. I discovered that analogies and theories provided by the social sciences were essential to my attempts to fill in the gaps left by the incomplete documentary and archaeological record of a past age. The opportunity to read in the social sciences for a year was thus enormously important for this project. I did this at Oxford University, as a fellow at Queen Elizabeth House, where Shirley Ardener was most gracious in including me in the women's studies research seminars.

In 1985–1986, the Howard Foundation at Brown University provided me with a grant that enabled me to carry out further research and to prepare a complete draft of this book.

Many individuals have helped along the way. Ernestine Friedl, in her position as dean of Duke University, nominated me for the Howard fellowship and assisted me in securing leave time; in her role as anthropologist, she encouraged me to use the insights of that discipline for research in biblical studies. Naomi Quinn, of Duke's anthropology department, helped me with bibliographical materials and an armload of readings as I set off for England. Jean O'Barr, director of women's studies at Duke, involved me in the many activities of that program;

such involvement gave invaluable reinforcement to the interdisciplinary nature of my research.

The staff of the religion department at Duke has been unfailingly cheerful and competent in taking care of the technical details of producing a book manuscript. At Oxford University Press, Cynthia Read, Paul Schlotthauer, and Stewart Perkins have contributed in countless ways with their expert advice and superb editing.

Finally, I can hardly imagine having completed this project without the deep interest, loving support, professional encouragement, and scholarly advice of my husband, Eric.

Durham, North Carolina   C.M.
June 1987

Note on Translations, Transcriptions, and Documentation

The scripture quotations contained herein, unless otherwise noted, are from the Revised Standard Version of the Bible, copyright 1946, 1952, 1971 by the Division of Christian Education of the National Council of the Churches of Christ in the U.S.A. and are used by permission. Translations of the Greek Bible (Septuagint) are taken from the Septuagint Version of the Old Testament (London: Samuel Baxter and Sons, Ltd., n.d.p.)

Since the Bible is an important source for this study, the reading of certain texts in the original Hebrew has been an essential part of the task. Discussion of certain Hebrew terms and phrases, especially those that lack exact English equivalents and those that have not always been accurately translated, is thus an integral part of several chapters. I have chosen to simplify the standard scholarly system of transliteration by omitting diacritical marks over vowels. In doing so, I have hoped to preserve the technical aspect of this enterprise while making it accessible to the non-specialist.

Similarly, with respect to documentation, I have tried to satisfy the needs of both the scholarly and the general reader. The notes contain full documentation of the sources from which I have gleaned data and insights. However, with few exceptions, the notes contain no additional discussion or technical details. Thus the text of this book can be read straight through without consulting the notes, except where the references I have used and cited might be of interest to the reader.

Contents

Discovering Eve

1

Eve as the Symbol of Women: Understanding the Task

Eve. We all think we know her and understand what she represents. Few come of age in the western world without having heard of Eden. It would be difficult to find anyone unfamiliar with the primeval couple, Eve and Adam. Nearly all of us have read, or have had read to us, the simple and powerful narrative of Genesis 2 and 3.

Portrayed as the first woman, Eve in fact symbolizes all women. She stands alone of her sex, signifying to all others in times to come the essence of female existence. Her story is so well known that it is somewhat surprising to find that in the rest of the Hebrew Bible, the story of Eden is not a prominent theme. Neither are the actions of Adam and Eve ever cited as examples of disobedience and punishment, although the long story of Israel's recurrent rejection of God's word and will provides plentiful opportunity for drawing such analogies.

Only in the literature of early Judaism and Christianity do Eve and Adam emerge into the mainstream of religious literature and theological discussion. By then, nearly a thousand years after the original shaping of the Eden story, Eve's role is recast by the beliefs and the needs of the nascent Jewish and Christian communities in the Roman world. So compelling are the views of Eve as reworked in the New Testament, in Rabbinic lore, and in the Apocryphal and Pseudepigraphical books, that it is difficult to examine the Eve story without being subtly influenced by the predominant Christian and Jewish interpretations of that story.

Nonetheless, biblical scholars in recent years have taken on the task of rediscovering the pristine Eve. The woman of Eden is being given her own voice, a voice radically distinct from the one heard through the unsympathetic, if not misogynist, words of influential figures such as Paul or Rabbi Yohanan or the anonymous author of the first-century Books of Adam and Eve. We will try to listen to that voice, to comprehend the place of the Eve story in Israelite literature, and to understand what it tells us about the Israelite conception of womanhood. Chapters 4 and 5 will deal directly with Eve and the story of Eden.

However, we must approach the Eve narrative in another way as well: its link with the experience of Israel in the ancient Near Eastern world. Not only does Eve represent Israelite women, she is also a product of the way of life of women in that world. The social realities of everyday life provided the raw materials from which the biblical narrator forged the now famous tale. The artful crafting of that simple yet powerful narrative is inextricably linked to the life experience of the Hebrew author. The world around him (or her?) contributed to his choice of words, characterizations, and motifs. It also constitutes the audience, the social group to be addressed by and moved in some way to respond to the multifarious messages of the story.

The grounding of the Eden account in the particulars of the ancient Israelite world can be seen quite easily when we look at the garden itself or at some aspects of its treatment of the male figure. The ready availability of water in Eden, for example, is a quality well suited for an idyllic tale in a land so poorly endowed with natural water resources as was ancient Palestine. Furthermore, two of the purveyors of life-giving water, according to the narrative, are the Mesopotamian rivers, the Tigris and the Euphrates. These abundant sources of water were known to the Israelites, whose ancestors came from Mesopotamia and whose cultural heritage included the land of those two rivers. The appearance in the Genesis story of the Mesopotamian rivers thus shows how the tale is rooted in the larger Israelite world. But the charge to Adam, with the description of the great difficulty he will have in eking out a living, is meaningful precisely for the conditions of agricultural life in the Palestinian highlands.

Similarly, the depiction of Eve must be treated as a reflection of and sanction for the lot of the Israelite woman. To become aware of women's way of life during the time the Hebrew Bible was written is to come to grips with the reality that determined Eve. In this sense, "Eve" is Everywoman—every woman who lived in ancient Israel. Before we can know either the Eve of Genesis or the Everywoman Eve, we must identify and describe her world. Chapter 3 will explore that world and identify the dynamics of Israelite life that would have determined the behavior and status of women.

At this point we must distinguish between "Israelite woman" and "biblical woman." Few could dispute the overwhelming orientation of the Hebrew Bible to the male world, a fact to which we shall return repeatedly in this work. Yet there is no dearth of female characters, and there are even a few fragments of women's writings. But, unfortunately, these tell us little about "ordinary" Israelite women. The women we glimpse in the Hebrew Bible are, almost to a woman, exceptional. They are women who rose to positions of prominence. As such, can they be seen as representative of their gender? Can generalizations about the parameters and dynamics of the daily existence of women be extracted from what we know about a Deborah or a Miriam, an Athaliah or a Huldah?

The Israelite woman is largely unseen in the pages of the Hebrew Bible. To presume to locate her in biblical narrative would be to commit a fundamental methodological error. To assume we can see nameless women in the activities of the named ones is to believe we can see an entire structure when only a fragment of it is visible.

In addition to examining the Eve of the Eden story, our purpose here is twofold: first, to promote an awareness among all who are affected by the Eden story—whether student or scholar, feminist or the faithful—of the very existence of the unseen life led by women in ancient Israel; and second, to begin to make that existence visible. These goals are interrelated: the idea that women's life experiences differed considerably from biblical depictions can gain credibility only if we can discover something about those lives. Chapters 6–8 will explore the world of Everywoman Eve.

An important corollary of our goal in setting out to discover Everywoman Eve lies in the relationship of that woman to biblical women. As we become able to envision the lot of an Israelite woman, so will we gain a better perspective on the unrepresentative material contained in the Hebrew Bible. Because of the fundamental role that the scriptural materials have played in the development of western religion, any information that can bear on passages that are difficult or controversial in the contemporary world becomes relevant to more than the company of academicians. For centuries we have looked at Eve through the distorting lenses of patriarchal, Judeo-Christian tradition. Now perhaps we can examine her in the clear light of her own world.

The motivation and the means for this quest to elucidate Eve come from two distinct directions: one is the recent involvement of feminist scholarship in many academic disciplines, including the study of religion; the other is the methodological potential in social scientific research for recovering woman's (or for that matter, man's) part in an ancient society. Since the advent of the new feminism in the 1960s and 1970s, feminist scholarship has become an important development in the field of religion. Also in the last two decades, the use of sociological and anthropological theory to categorize and comprehend the origins and development of ancient Israel as a socially distinct formation in the Near Eastern world of the late second and the first millennia has been established as the most important development in biblical studies since the contributions of such intellectual giants as Albright and Alt earlier in this century.[1] Each of these disciplinary developments has evolved far enough on its own that a study of Israelite women based on their intersection is now a possibility. At the very least, the enterprise can now begin; moreover, future developments in feminist scholarship and in social scientific biblical study will provide ongoing resources for increasing the visibility of Israelite women.

Feminism and the Study of Religion and Gender

The impact of feminism in recent decades on a variety of humanistic and social scientific disciplines can be well documented.[2] While many feminist scholars might find fault with the depth or breadth of that impact, few would deny that in many important ways the cultural contributions of women and their social, economic, and political roles are now part of both scholarly and popular consciousness. In short, the category of gender has entered the various disciplines, which recognize it as a distinct mode of experience and also as a system subject to analysis.

When it comes to religion, the matter of gender is more than a topic of academic concern. As in many fields, the presence of feminist research in religion has been intensified because there is more at stake than simple scholarly investigation. The institutional and theological crises in Judaism and Christianity that have been provoked by feminism have involved the interpretation of biblical texts dealing with women. What is the relationship of the biblical word to the traditional stance of church and synagogue on the role of women? In its broadest sense that question affects many important issues, such as the validity of leadership roles for women in the formal structures of western religion, and the nature of the relationship between men and women in the informal setting of home and family. It also involves the problem of general attitudes toward women engendered by the traditional understanding of biblical texts, and it affects the way in which decisions are made for continuing or changing tradition-based patterns in both formal and informal situations.

Hardly a week goes by without the appearance of a new publication dealing with "women and religion." The biblical foundation for western religion poses thorny questions for religionists in general, and feminist theologians in particular are forced to examine the relationship between the Bible and the modern world. The acceptance of the authority of the Bible as God's word, which is at the core of Judeo-Christian religion, is inevitably the sticking point. How can one deal with an authoritative text that asserts something apparently antithetical to feminist concerns? This fundamental question will be addressed, at least obliquely, in our discussion of approaches to biblical patriarchy in Chapter 2.

Feminist issues now occupy a focal position within religious traditions. Yet the concept of America as a secular society has kept religion as a feminist concern strangely separate from the consideration of various aspects of modern life that otherwise have attracted considerable feminist attention. Too often contemporary feminists misunderstand the fundamental religious modes and symbols that perpetuate the discriminatory dimensions of the political behavior they seek to abolish.[3] To ignore religion and the tenacious religious aspect of political life is to risk making superficial the quest for change. The emotional justification for the existence and continuation of present unacceptable gender roles is embedded in religious texts that shape the psyche of western humanity. Examination of those texts and their role in the ostensibly secular facets of modern life seems essential, yet conceptual and institutional difficulties have posed serious obstacles to such examination.

If feminism in combination with religion has failed to address political and other aspects of contemporary life, feminism on its own has made significant inroads in understanding the place of gender in cultural history and past and present forms of social behavior. The way in which feminism has influenced anthropology is a case in point. Anthropological research originated with the Victorian interest in understanding civilization as the product of evolutionary development. Cross-cultural studies of societies thought to represent various stages in this scheme were popular, and the place of women in societies seen as preceding the culminating Victorian ideal was given serious consideration (see Chapter 2, pp. 37–39).[4] Because the work of the nineteenth-century antecedents of modern anthropology as well as most of their twentieth-century successors has suffered from a range of masculine cultural biases, feminist anthropologists have had a double task. While recognizing the existence of sexual differentiation as a critical factor in analyzing any society, they also have had to deal with gender bias in the fieldwork that provides the hard data for anthropological research.

Feminist anthropological scholarship, in its insistence that gender differentiation is a salient feature of any cultural system, has opened the way for this study of the Israelite woman. Feminist inquiry has shown women to be significant social actors whose roles differ from those of men but are no less important. Furthermore, feminist scholarship has begun to develop valuable theoretical constructs. Despite their failure to explain completely the myriad patterns of gender distinction and valuation that occur throughout the world, such constructs provide valuable heuristic models. We may not be able to understand why women's roles in society tend to exhibit certain features largely not identified for men, but we can repeatedly test suggestions or theories against the data from one society after another, while admitting that the complexity of gender identity and behavior may preclude the applicability of any single explanatory mode.

The relationship of this study to feminist scholarship has yet another facet. Feminism, as it has entered the various disciplines, has necessarily been concerned with origins. The woman's movement has derived its strength and energy from the recognition of inequities in the position of women in the modern world. If the present situation with respect to gender is unacceptable, a search for the origins of that situation becomes compelling. Discerning the roots of an existing pattern may enhance the potential for change.

Effecting current social change is not central to our goals here, yet the search for origins has an important—though indirect—role to play. This search has brought to light a wealth of materials concerning a wide variety of differing social configurations. Our industrialized, technological society differs radically not only from many others in the world, but also from times past. The quest for an understanding of female–male differentiation has led the social anthropologist to preindustrial, pretechnological contexts that are relevant to the investigation of the ancient Israelite woman, whose world also was fundamentally distinct from our present experience of human behavior and gender identities. Despite the continuity between contemporary western religion and its biblical past, we must take into account the radical differences in the physical environment and the social configurations of biblical antiquity. The anthropological quest for premodern origins thus offers considerable comparative data for the investigation of ancient Israel as one example of a premodern society.

Contemporary Approaches to the Biblical Past

Although feminism and the study of the past are inextricably linked in the social sciences, biblical scholars have barely begun to utilize the information gathered by social scientists for the investigation of gender in the biblical past. Critical biblical scholarship has, however, ventured into the realm of social scientific analysis with the hope of explaining in nontheological ways the origins of the Israelite people and their beliefs. Similarly, particular cultural and sociopolitical forms found in ancient Israel have been subjected to sociological analysis. The results have been illuminating if not revolutionary in the field of biblical studies.[5] If not all biblical scholars are convinced by the results of these investigative methods, few are immune to the stimulation offered by the models that have been suggested.

After all, ancient Israel was first and foremost a community, a social entity. What we call religion was but one mode—albeit the most enduring and influential one—of its corporate existence. These facts underlie the fundamental premise on which social scientific appraisals of ancient Israel are based. To understand the living community of Israel, and the Israelite religion as an ideological expression of the communal life, we must examine Israel in the context of its own multidimensional environment. Important factors include Israel's social and political prehistory, as well as its ecological niche in the hill country of Palestine and the agrarian-pastoral economic base it offered to the nascent community.

Scholars have made enormous strides in reconstructing the social history of ancient Israel. In addition to the clues in the biblical record, they have utilized data from cross-cultural studies of other tribally organized societies as well as the information provided by archaeological findings about the cities and villages of ancient Palestine. Our knowledge of the people of the Book is thus no longer limited by the information contained in that Book.

The ideology-bearing narrations of the Bible were radically innovative in their time. They set forth humanitarian and egalitarian principles not found elsewhere in the ancient world. Those principles both reflected and affirmed the unique social system established by Israel upon breaking away from the existing sociopolitical systems of the Canaanites and the Egyptians, who dominated the biblical world at the time of Israel's formation as a distinct community.

Understanding ancient Israel as a social entity is not an easy task. Israel was acutely self-conscious about its distinct place in the world, but the biblical self-description does not appear in categories that can easily be translated into facts essential for social scientific analysis. For one thing, Israel's formation is documented in language appropriate to the cultic setting that utilized and preserved the basic themes of Israel's national experience. The language is thus theological; it describes human events in terms of God's actions. Furthermore, the language itself was in many cases formalized only several centuries after the events that gave rise to the sacred texts, with the result that the writings reflect later concerns intertwined with original materials. Also, the language used is highly selective, sometimes including apparently trivial or mundane matters, or omitting facts and personalities of great political or social importance.

Despite these methodological problems—perhaps because of them— social history offers a fresh approach in the attempt to understand and describe the social reality of ancient Israel. Sociology and anthropology have identified sets of social phenomena that can be linked to particular social settings. Insofar as those settings can be shown to be analogous to the conditions of Israel's existence, some of the gaps in our knowledge can be filled inferentially.

This procedure is not without its risks and has aroused its share of critical responses, yet there can be no doubt that it offers many valid insights that would not be otherwise possible. For example, research data on tribal groups, with their clan and family subdivisions and their characteristic uses of resources and establishment of leadership, have helped biblical scholars to understand the dynamics of Israelite beginnings. If the biblical record correctly indicates the tribal aspect of Israel in her early centuries, then extrabiblical information about tribal formations and structures constitutes a valuable research tool for biblical scholars. Similarly, cross-cultural studies of the forces leading to state formation and to the consequent growth of bureaucracies are relevant to an expanded appreciation of the Israelite shift from tribal self-rule to kingship. As we begin to recognize how centralized political forms can provide economic and political safeguards in a precarious environment, we can better understand the forces leading to the formation of the Israelite monarchy. We can also better comprehend why, despite the social and economic stratification it introduced, the monarchy is held in such high regard in the biblical record. Underlying all such analyses is acknowledgment of the sensitive relationship between economic-ecological factors and the adaptive nature of group behavior and organization.

The progress made in the social scientific investigation of ancient Israel has obvious implications for the study of gender in the biblical period. As our conception of the social world of the biblical past becomes clearer, we can more effectively investigate the function of gender in that world; thus do the social actors—the men, women, and children of Israelite society—also become more discernible as figures on the ancient landscape.

Resources for the Task

The developments in feminist scholarship and in sociohistorical analysis of ancient Israel constitute the methodological potential through which we hope to discern the outlines of Eve, the Israelite Everywoman. How can we move from the desire to see her, fired by the conviction that she can become more visible than she currently is, to the actual task of delineating female life in the biblical world? The process is complex, for it requires that we integrate the results of separate disciplinary inquiries. Even then, we shall probably never possess more than a small though significant fraction of the data we should ideally have in order to reconstruct any aspect of ancient Israelite life.

The discipline of biblical studies, especially in its goal of historical reconstruction, has suffered from the increasing uncertainty surrounding the reliability of its data bases. Even while social scientific methodology has stepped in to help rescue biblical scholarship from the weakening of its traditional foundations, the overall inferential aspect of the task has caused much concern. An intriguing recent attempt to describe the complex nature of biblical studies suggests that the simile of a hologram can help with the whole/part dilemma of the biblical scholar. The technology of holography can offer models for integrating different kinds of evidence used for interpreting the past: "Literary, archaeological, and comparative sociological interpretations interact in ways similar to the three laser beams used to create a holographic image [which] is analogous to the interpretations offered as hypotheses by biblical historians."[6] The difficulties caused by incomplete evidence are, according to this simile, not insuperable.

The *biblical text* itself remains the major source of information about the population of the biblical period. The usefulness of this body of literature for the task of investigating the people whose lives are reflected in it is, however, nearly offset by the problems involved in extracting ethnographic data from it. A number of serious obstacles arise when we analyze female roles via the Bible.

The Hebrew Bible is for the most part the result of the literary activity of a small segment of the Israelite population that is likely unrepresentative. Those parts of the canon that seem to contain the most useful materials for our task are by and large the products of a literate elite. Much of the Pentateuch (the first five books of the Bible) is derived from priestly activity or from priestly editions of more broadly based materials. The priesthood, of course, was an all-male, hereditary group

with its leadership based in the Temple, which was located in the capital
city of Jerusalem. In addition, virtually all of the historical writings—the
so-called Deuteronomic history, which runs from Joshua through 2
Kings and constitutes the core of the Hebrew Bible—were probably
based on court records or traditions circulating in royal circles. Again, a
largely male group, based in the precincts of the royal palace in Jerusalem, was responsible for formulating the narrative of Israel's national
existence. The second narrative account of Israel's existence, 1–2
Chronicles through Ezra and Nehemiah, echoes the Deuteronomic account and follows it into the postexilic, postmonarchic period. It also can
be located, with respect to authorship, in the male leadership circles of
Jerusalem in the postexilic period.

Consequently, those portions of the Hebrew Bible that contain most
of the few fragments of information about women come from sources
removed both hierarchically and demographically from the lives of most
women. This social distance between the shapers of sacred tradition and
females is reflected in the androcentric orientation of the Hebrew Bible.
Women were never included in the priesthood, nor were they ever a
regular or direct part of the ruling elite. Yet the exclusion of women
from these elite segments of the population that were responsible for
much of the canon is not necessarily or by itself the source of bias in the
biblical materials. The priestly, royal, and gubernatorial establishment
was not only unrepresentative of women; it was also unrepresentative of
the population as a whole. Priests, kings, officers, and bureaucrats were
elite groups; as such, they were removed from the masses of the population, both male and female.

We must therefore identify one other factor that separates the shapers
of tradition from many of their fellow Israelites. As residents of Jerusalem or of other major cities, they participated in an urban pattern of life
not shared by most of the population. The urban location for the formation and formulation of a large portion of the Hebrew Bible is of more
than passing consequence for the study of female roles and status in
ancient Israel. If most of Israel remained rural, even after the growth of
urban centers, then most women lived in the nonurban settings that are
underrepresented in the Bible. Images of the countryside abound in the
Bible, but the daily life of the countryfolk remains mostly obscure. One
of the contributions social science can make is to elucidate the dynamics
of gender relations in premodern rural or agrarian life, in contrast to the
urban environment that produced the cultural documents and also the
physical monuments most readily available to the researcher.

The Bible as a source presents problems of omission in its treatment of women as individuals or as a group. Its androcentric bias and also its urban, elite orientation mean that even the information it contains may be a distortion or misrepresentation of the lives of women removed from urban centers and bureaucratic families. Similar difficulties face almost any research endeavor concerned with past time: *empirical* observation of various social circumstances and relationships is not possible. The cultural and material products of societies that existed in the past inevitably fail to give a true picture of all facets of those societies. Cultural statements or texts may be idealized or may stand in some other disjunctional relationship to the social realities that underlie them. To put it another way, the biblical text is essentially a public document and as such does not necessarily provide an accurate source for learning about the private lives of the nameless men and women who inhabited the villages and hamlets of ancient Palestine.

Ethnographic research as a source for examining social behavior—as distinct from ideology—is thus a vital resource in any attempt to deal with this problem. Yet even there, pitfalls abound. Sir Edmund Leach's warning to anthropologists is relevant to biblical scholarship:

> The observer must distinguish between what people actually do and what people say that they do; that is between normal custom as individually interpreted on the one hand and normative rule on the other. When they come to write up the results of their research different anthropologists will, for doctrinal reasons, give very different weight to those two major aspects of the data, but in the field, the anthropologist must always pay attention to both sides. He . . . must distinguish behavior from ideology.[7]

The biblical scholar does not have the methodological option of observing behavior. Only the ideology is available. Hence there is danger in equating ideology with daily reality, which can diverge from the normative expression contained in the biblical text.

Working with the biblical text is also hindered by the Bible's complex literary history and its status as literature, albeit sacred literature. Israelite society underwent fundamental changes over time, as its tribal organization shifted to a monarchic one, as its rural orientation gave way to an urban one, and as its economic horizons moved from local subsistence to international markets. In theory, one cannot make statements about gender in ancient Israel without specifying time as well as place. But the biblical sources do not readily lend themselves to this requirement. The chronological span of the Hebrew Bible covers about a millennium, from the earliest of its passages to the latest. While the broad outlines of its total literary history from a chronological perspective are fairly well established, individual passages can be notoriously hard to date. Consequently, their value as clues to conditions in any given period is diminished.

The patriarchal narratives of Genesis provide the premier example of the methodological problems one encounters in using biblical materials. Those tales are virtually the only ones concerned with domestic matters, and they are the only materials with sustained narrations about family life, if one excludes the stories of the royal household as being atypical of the Israelite domestic scene. Yet their social and chronological location are the subjects of ongoing and unresolved debate. The historicity of the individual figures in the patriarchal stories cannot be established. The highly stylized literary characteristics of Genesis 12–50 render questionable the validity of using the material in these chapters as mirrors of social reality. While they are not simply figments of the creative imagination of their author or authors, and surely derive their enduring value from the way they draw upon familiar life situations, nonetheless they are not firmly anchored in an identifiable setting. They telescope time, place, and personalities to suit the author's purposes. In short, the literary stylization of such narratives and the chronological imprecisions of others create further obstacles to our attempts to see the Israelite woman.

What can be done in the face of the profound problems surrounding the use of the Hebrew Bible as a source? One cannot ignore it, since it contains the symbolic portrayal of what we wish to see in reality. The biblical depictions of women and of womankind are the very essence of that which we would like to compare with the average Israelite woman, who is neither named nor described in the biblical text.

Our strategy will be to concentrate on that period of Israelite existence which is best known in terms of its social configurations. Work on the sociology of the monarchic period and the transition to monarchy is well under way in biblical studies, as are investigations of later periods. Still, the most thoroughly investigated period to date is that which preceded the monarchy, the period of Israelite origins.[8] The greater attention given to the premonarchic period is logical, for that was clearly the formative era in the long story of the biblical people. In order to understand the dynamics of subsequent periods fully, one must begin with the time of Israel's emergence into the arena of world history as an identifiable people with an organizational structure and at least a rudimentary ideology.

This formative period of Israel's history is called by various terms. We have already used "premonarchic," which, like "tribal," is descriptive of the sociopolitical character of the period. Another designation, "period of the Judges," relates the era to the biblical book that most scholars consider a product and reflection of the experience of Israel when it first established itself in the central hill country of Palestine. The word "Judges" represents not only the biblical book by that name but also the biblical term for the tribal and supratribal figures who provided some approximation of national leadership during a time when a formal, centralized government had not been established.

The terms "settlement period" or "conquest period" are sometimes used to denote the time of Israelite origins with reference to the manner in which Israel established a political and demographic presence in the eastern Mediterranean. The phrase "settlement period" indicates that Israelites populated an area either formerly unpopulated or at least formerly unpopulated by Israelites. A closely related designation is "pioneer period," which presumes that Israelite origins involved the taking hold of previously undeveloped territory. The designation "conquest period" has a specifically military nuance, which long seemed appropriate on the basis of narratives found in the Book of Joshua. However, the term "conquest" does not adequately represent what we now know to have been a complex and drawn-out period of populating virgin territories, as well as taking over ones previously occupied by Canaanites. Archaeology and sociological reconstruction have ruled out, or at least greatly qualified, the long-held notion of conquest as an adequate or appropriate description of Israelite beginnings.

One final designation is the archaeological one, which expresses the position of early Israel on the continuum of time with a taxonomic term that somewhat arbitrarily imposes the concept of an evolutionary movement in material culture upon a variety of contemporary societies that were, in fact, at very different stages of technological development. The archaeological terms Bronze Age and Iron Age were linked to chronological parameters on the basis of what now appear to be unrepresentative sequences in the use of those two metals. Nonetheless, the designations endure, for they are inextricably bound up in the literature dealing with Near Eastern antiquity. For the period of Israelite origins, the relevant term from an archaeological perspective is the Iron I period; this encompasses the approximately two centuries that transpired between the time of Moses and the foundation of the monarchy, that is, the period when the Judges ruled. Since neither of those events can be precisely dated, however, the exact chronological limits remain vague, though less so for the end of the period than its beginning. A working set of dates for the Iron I in Palestine would be 1200–1000 BCE.[9]

The fact that the social organization of Israel is better known for the earliest period of its national existence than for any subsequent era is not the only reason that the Iron I period constitutes our chronological focus. Because it was the first period, it saw the rise of patterns of life that probably persisted well into the monarchy, which began at the end of the eleventh century and continued for more than four centuries, until the Babylonian destruction of 587 BCE. To be sure, the inception of the monarchy meant the beginning of urban development and a ruling elite; yet the bulk of the population remained rural. Our modern concept of the city as a large and distinct economic unit, pulling population away from the countryside into its giant machinery of production and service, is not appropriate for the preindustrial world. Cities were small units, albeit influential; in most cases they were barely more than walled villages. An estimated 90–95 percent of the people continued to live in rural settings.

Observing the nature of rural (i.e., agrarian) life is critical to a reconstruction of family life and to our task of examining the woman's role in that setting. We shall explore the features of rural existence in Palestine in some detail in Chapter 3; for now, it is well to emphasize that, despite radical shifts in the political structure toward the end of the period of the Judges, Israel's rural patterns of existence persisted to some extent at least until the great disruption of the sixth-century exile, if not until Alexander's late fourth-century conquest of the east introduced western (Greco-Roman) political forms. The additional economic burdens created for farmers by a centralized government surely caused immediate adjustments and gradual changes; yet social groups are innately conservative, so established modes of everyday life and behavior in the small hamlets of Israel probably remained the same in more ways than they changed. In short, we cannot impose upon Near Eastern antiquity the rapid social change common to our modern world.

Archaeological materials are also an important resource for dealing with past time. We have already alluded to instances in which archaeology has contributed to our understanding of Israelite history by providing an independent witness to the selective details contained in the biblical narrative. Until recently, "biblical archaeology," a misleading but popular designation for Syro-Palestinian archaeological projects potentially able to shed light on the Bible, concentrated disproportionately on the urban sites most likely to provide verification or illumination of the political history recorded in the Bible. Such sites also possessed the greatest likelihood for yielding the monumental architecture and distinctive artifacts that make good museum pieces and good press. Archaeology, enamored of and elated by its intimate contact with objects and structures of the biblical past, felt itself in possession of the key to that past.

If archaeologists had looked beyond the material relics they uncovered and the political history with which they were preoccupied, they might well have been correct in their self-assessment. However, until the last decade or so, archaeologists working in Palestine at sites dating from the biblical period have suffered from the same urban, elite bias that characterized the document, the Bible, which in nearly every case determined their choice of sites in the first place and their strategy in excavating those sites in the second place. Except for salvage work, in which the prior selection of an excavation site was not a factor, nearly every place selected for fieldwork was a site with a biblical pedigree. Normally, the mere geographic mention of a site in the Bible, apart from a historical discussion, was not sufficient cause to choose it for excavation. Archaeological remains that could be identified as places associated with key events or important persons documented in the biblical record were by far preferable.

Consequently, the sites chosen tended to be major cities, those assumed to have been cultic and administrative centers. Palestinian or biblical archaeology became practically synonymous with *tell* archaeology, the excavation of the city mounds that dot the Palestinian landscape and that derive their characteristic shape—a truncated cone—from the fact that they were surrounded by fortification walls or ramparts. Fortification walls tended to prevent the debris of destroyed levels from being washed away and in the process created the layer-cake effect that requires careful stratigraphic excavation, that is, the peeling away of layers, one by one. W. F. Albright, perhaps the greatest of Palestinian archaeologists, gave the first chapter in his classic book on Palestinian archaeology[10] a revealing title. He called it "The Art of Excavating a Palestinian Mound" (*tell*), thereby virtually excluding from the archaeologist's purview the investigation of villages and hamlets, of farmsteads and country estates.

The focus on cities rather than rural settlements was detrimental enough to the potential of archaeology for recovering all dimensions of the human past. Yet the typical strategy for excavating a Palestinian city mound contributed even further to the failure of archaeology to provide material that might be relevant to those interested in nonpolitical—to say nothing of nonurban—aspects of ancient life. Archaeologists working on city mounds concentrated on fortification systems (walls, towers, and gates), palaces and villas, and public buildings, notably temples. In so doing, they chose features of urban life related almost exclusively to a select and tiny proportion of the population. They uncovered architectural and artifactual materials related to the military, to the governing elite, and to the cultic establishment. They focused on the most visible public structures and in so doing contributed further to the lack of visibility of the middle and lower echelons of society, and of all those whose realm of social activity was oriented to private or domestic affairs. Insofar as women's lives characteristically are associated with the domestic realm, a supposition that we shall discuss below, their visibility through the archaeology even of the unrepresentative urban settings is precluded. In short, almost nothing that archaeologists set out to do until recent years was directed specifically to a balanced understanding of the social history of early Israel, beyond the fact that some people lived in urban centers. Consequently, it offered virtually nothing that could be used to reconstruct the social role of women or anyone else belonging to the nonurban, nonelite, or nonspecialist segments of the population.

Since the 1960s, however, the "new archaeology" as developed and conceptualized largely in the new world has influenced the development of Palestinian archaeology. According to the pioneering work of L. R. Binford[11] and others, archaeology should seek to illumine basic processes of cultural change and not simply the high points of culture from a material perspective. Such goals mandate attention to archaeological remains on the microlevel rather than the macrolevel. Small settlements and the minute details of diet, economy, and domestic structures that comprise such settlements provide the data base congenial to the new archaeology. The impact of this perspective has caused Palestinian archaeologists to become interested in village life and its agrarian economic foundations. Uncovering domestic structures is seen as a source of information about the lives of the inhabitants of those structures. The archaeology of the fundamental unit of society, the family and the household it occupied, is now possible.

Within certain limits, the archaeology of the family offers good potential for the study of gender. Features of the domestic economy and therefore of social structures can surely be elucidated through analysis of floral and faunal remains, study of architectural accommodations to the stabling of animals, and attention to technological artifacts such as grinding stones, loom weights, and potters' wheels. The mode of life of the domestic unit can then be reconstructed to some degree, and the contributions of women to life in that unit can be determined. In addition, for the period of Israelite origins in the Iron Age, archaeology has been able to identify the technologies that had to be implemented in order for settlement in the hill country to be a viable possibility. The basic ecological determinants—lack of a year-round water supply and an extremely varied topography—brought specific technological responses that required varying degrees of individual and community labor. Such projects critical to survival, along with the everyday domestic tasks, contributed to the shaping of family structure and the roles of individuals within the families.

This description of the archaeological potential tentatively assumes that the products of archaeological fieldwork can be considered "gender noisy." But can one really assume that the mute walls and artifacts of a bygone age will reveal the roles and relationships of the men and women who lived within the walls and used the artifacts? Can the silent bones and seeds of remote antiquity speak to the question of how those remnants of ancient subsistence were taken from field or pasture and transformed into food? Such questions are germane to any analysis of the lives of women, since the division of labor between men and women in the basic operations of domestic life is intrinsically related to the place of women in society. Regretfully, the answer to these questions has been largely negative. Without some ancillary pictorial or textual evidence, the gender of the hands that shaped and used the material recovered by archaeology cannot be specified, and so no distinction can be made about the domestic tasks performed by men and women in ancient villages.

Nonetheless, the recent involvement of the new archaeology in Palestinian archaeology allows us to answer the question of whether archaeology might address the matter of gender with a tentative yes. As the archaeology of Palestine turns to villages, it identifies certain patterns of domestic architecture that dominated Israelite settlements and provides data about the economic life of the inhabitants. Interpretation of the dynamics of the social life of these rural settlements can then proceed with the help of the social sciences in general and with the aid of comparative ethnography in particular. The latter, for example, can suggest some probabilities as to which roles always fall to men and which to women in similar societies. Clues in the biblical record, as we have already suggested, likewise contribute to this interpretative task.

It should be clear from the above discussion that *social scientific research* is another important resource for investigating the lives of Israelite women. Recovering the social history of ancient Israel is, to reiterate, a major concern of contemporary biblical studies. Like biblical studies in general, the investigation of women's participatory roles in the formation and continuation of Israelite society must draw upon the theoretical formulations and also the examples from analogy that the social sciences provide. Indeed, precisely because the traditional sources for examining Israelite gender behavior are relatively empty with respect to information about females, filling the vacant spaces cannot take place without recourse to interdisciplinary study.

The need for social scientific models may seem obvious, but in fact this need has not been readily recognized with regard to feminist issues in biblical studies. The strong impact feminism has had on most practitioners and interpreters of religion today has not yet been complemented by the establishment of a sound methodology for investigating the historical roots of contemporary sexism in religion—that is, in the place of women in the biblical period. Surely the biblical roots of the sexual politics of today cannot be ignored, and any feminist critique of western-based religion must properly begin with biblical scholarship. The seemingly extensive influence of feminism in biblical studies exists only in its contrast to the situation of barely a decade ago, when the investigation of gender-related matters in biblical studies was virtually nonexistent.

Feminist inquiry has thus far failed to take an interdisciplinary approach in biblical scholarship in large part because the motivation and energy required to develop an essentially new aspect of most any discipline in order to address issues of gender lies with female scholars. Many male scholars support and even applaud research with a feminist perspective; relatively few engage in such research. This division of labor along gender lines has put feminist concerns in biblical studies at a distinct disadvantage in comparison with many other fields of humanistic or social scientific research. Biblical studies have long been dominated by men and traditionally pursued more in seminaries, which were almost exclusively male institutions, than in universities. Consequently, relatively few female scholars have been equipped with the requisite tools to deal with biblical texts and the biblical world. As late as 1970 women accounted for only 3.5 percent of the members of the Society of Biblical Literature, the major scholarly organization in the field of biblical studies.[12] Most of those were faculty members of women's colleges, where a lack of graduate programs often precludes active research programs. Furthermore, the published articles of those women who participated in the Society showed no evidence, until quite recently, of a feminist interest.

Working with the Hebrew Bible in any of its dimensions requires not only a knowledge of biblical languages but also a familiarity with ancient Near Eastern history and at least an acquaintance with the archaeological recovery of Syria-Palestine. The ready availability of good English translations is seductive and misleading. Translations are themselves interpretations and subject to the bias of the translators. Serious researchers must go back to the Hebrew original lest they fail to comprehend or rectify the mistakes of centuries of Bible translators. For example, the generic word for "human," which permeates the creation tales of Genesis and which appears elsewhere in the Hebrew Bible, is frequently if not universally translated "man." In most cases, the gender-specific potential of the English word "man" is thereby erroneously attached to a Hebrew word that almost always functions as a collective singular noun designating *human* life as a category to be distinguished from God on the one hand and the animals on the other. Additional examples of misleading translations will emerge in the course of our examination of various biblical passages.

In addition to training scholars, mostly men, competent to examine the Bible in its original languages, seminaries also imposed a masculine interpretative bias that has proved even stronger than that found in other quarters of academic life. The very scholars equipped to deal with feminist concerns were working in the service of religious institutions, which tend to be conservative in matters of gender. Open investigation of the texts that have traditionally been used to promulgate beliefs, and to preserve the power structures based on those beliefs, was not likely to take place within the confines of church- or synagogue-related institutions.

Consequently, because biblical studies has been a male-dominated field and because theological institutions have predominated in biblical studies, a feminist perspective has been generally slow to emerge. Even where the recent demand of feminist considerations has brought significant response, the rather too hasty biblical scholarship on gender matters has tended to be impressionistic if not sloppy. It has also been vulnerable to apologetic tendencies and biases of its own, some of which will be explored in the next chapter.

The traditional location of biblical studies in settings attached to institutional religion has not only hampered the emergence of scholars qualified to deal with matters of gender in the biblical world; it has also obscured the methodological usefulness of social scientific research for such endeavors. Biblical studies in universities have always been considered part of the humanities curriculum and as such have involved less exposure to or awareness of the potential benefit of social scientific approaches. Furthermore, most university departments of religion have drawn their faculties from the company of individuals whose training has included a divinity degree.

The lack of openness to an interdisciplinary methodology lies to a great extent in these sociological conditions surrounding biblical studies, but more profound impediments exist as well. Biblical scholarship, until well into the second half of this century in some circles and until today in many more, considers religion to be an independent, albeit crucial, aspect of social life. Like political organization or social structure or economic development, religion is thus perceived to be analyzable as a separate facet of human existence, even though it may well interact with or even determine the course of other aspects of community life.

In opposition to this approach, social scientists place religion under the rubric of ideology. Even the term propaganda is probably appropriate in describing religion, although its exceedingly negative connotation tends to impede rather than facilitate a conceptualization of religion's role. Besides, religious ideology and ritual played a more fundamental role in complex societies such as ancient Israel than merely an informational one. Religion was not merely an epiphenomenon, devoid of causal significance of its own.[13] In archaic societies, which ancient Israel also was, religious ideology reflected and sanctioned mundane as well as lofty aspects of group behavior. Religious belief served to legitimate and stabilize social and political structures, especially adaptive forms that would have been difficult to establish without the compelling and authoritative force of religion.[14] To cite one obvious example, the Israelite monarchy, which created a cumbersome bureaucracy and a growing tax burden—both of which increased social stratification—was viewed positively through most of its history because the prevailing ideology affirmed that God's will had mandated this political form, even though that form represented a radical change from the preceding and more egalitarian tribal orientation.

The conceptualization of religion as an integral and integrative part of society rather than a discrete cultural expression, and as a component of sociocultural identity rather than as its sole foundation, has been slow to penetrate the scholarship of biblical religion. This is particularly so in a secular society such as the United States, where the principle that religion is a feature that can and should be separated from the rest of formal American life is so rigorously upheld in many quarters. The idea of religion as an inseparable part of national, social, and political institutions is therefore difficult to entertain. The Bible's own rhetoric provides the concept of theological primacy, that is, that events and ideas originated in God's command. A social and political understanding of those events and ideas for that reason appears to be sacrilegious. Never mind that a social scientific approach might rescue ancient Israel from the ultimately destructive notion that this people was specially chosen and ultimately cast aside.

Despite this inherent reluctance of biblical scholars to follow a contextual approach, the value of examining Israel as an archaic society in its entirety has been recognized by a significant minority and has produced fruitful results, as we have noted earlier. Thus we are now in a position to use those results for exploring gender behavior. The ability to identify the physical and social landscape of ancient Israel makes it possible to distinguish time-bound texts from universally valid ones. From the perspective of women's studies, it should allow for the discovery of the place of women in the biblical world apart from the place of women in the biblical text. This essentially functionalist approach is, I think, the only legitimate way to deal with the thorny problem that plagues the feminist interest in biblical studies—namely, the issue of an authoritative text in which are embedded perspectives uncongenial to present values and situations. I assume that the essential characteristics of Israelite gender roles were established, along with many other features of Israelite life and belief, during the early period. As we shall see in Chapter 3, in that period primary survival needs were a crucial issue. The functional aspects of any system appear most salient in precisely such situations. Patterns of gender behavior were established to meet the needs of the existing demands of life and must be understood in that context.

2

The Problem of Patriarchy

Those who are concerned with the relationship between men and women in the biblical world tend to assume that a hierarchical situation existed. The apparent domination of females by males is seen as reflecting the patriarchal orientation of Hebrew scripture. The inferiority of woman is inferred from a multitude of texts, both by those who accept the androcentric tendencies in the Bible as authoritative and normative and also by those who are made uncomfortable or are outraged by them. Liberal feminists and conservative traditionalists share a perception that the Bible portrays women as secondary or inferior to men in fundamental ways.

The term "patriarchal" inevitably and properly surfaces in feminist discussions of both biblical texts and Israelite society. However, the value attached to that term sets feminist critiques apart from conservative positions that find in scripture validation for the exploitation or restriction of women. Feminist consciousness uniformly assumes negative connotations for the word patriarchy. An examination of the literature of feminist biblical interpretation reveals a wide range of attitudes toward biblical patriarchy—all of them negative. Mildly critical stances give way at times to strong condemnation.

A recent anthology of essays by prominent theologians, biblical scholars, and historians of religion is illustrative. Each of the contributions to this volume, entitled *Feminist Interpretation of the Bible,*[1] explicitly in most cases and implicitly in others, grapples with what is viewed as a central problem, namely, the patriarchal bias of Hebrew or Christian scripture. L. R. Russell, the editor of the volume, sets the tone in the introductory piece:

> As the contributions to feminist interpretation have continued to grow in volume and maturity, it has become abundantly clear that the scriptures need liberation, not only from existing interpretations but also from the *patriarchal* bias of the texts themselves. . . . Thus the issue continues to be

whether the biblical message can continue to evoke consent in spite of its *patriarchal* captivity [emphasis mine].[2]

Another biblical scholar, K. D. Sakenfeld, describes in her essay the challenge posed to all feminist critics dealing with the Bible:

> Their beginning point, shared in common with all feminists studying the Bible, is appropriately a stance of radical suspicion. . . . Feminists recognize in common that *patriarchy* was one of the most stable features of ancient biblical society over the thousand-plus years of the Bible's composition and redaction. Thus, in studying any biblical texts, feminists need to be alert not only for explicit *patriarchal* bias but also for evidence of more subtle androcentrism in the world view of the biblical authors. Only such a frank and often *painful* assessment of the depth of *patriarchal* perception in the text provides an honest starting point [emphasis mine].[3]

She also points to several options in feminist biblical study, including one in which "the explicit emphasis on the depth and continuity of *patriarchy* simply highlights the many *painfully oppressive* portions of biblical material. . . . No feminist use of biblical material is finally immune to the risk of finding the Bible hurtful, unhelpful" [emphasis mine].[4]

In another essay in this volume, J. C. Exum deals with strong female figures, who emerge despite the "admittedly *patriarchal* context of biblical liberation." She finds evidence of stories that "undermine *patriarchal* assumptions and temper *patriarchal* biases," although even her heroines are seen as "*victims* of a *patriarchal* society" [emphasis mine].[5]

Perhaps the strongest language of all comes from the noted and influential feminist theologian, Rosemary Ruether. She equates patriarchy with enslavement and chastises biblical prophecy for failing to address the existence of class and gender hierarchies:

> The prophets are oblivious to or justify that *enslavement* of persons within the Hebrew family itself: namely, women and slaves. At most, their vision of justice for these people extends to an amelioration of the *harshness* of one system under which they *suffer,* rather than a real critique of that system itself [emphasis mine].[6]

These statements share the assumption that patriarchy exists in the biblical record and in the society which that record reflects. They also share some biases of their own, biases that originate in misunderstandings, or at least vagueness, in their conceptualization of patriarchy. While broadly correct in associating patriarchy with ancient Israel, their assessment of patriarchy as a limiting, harsh, enslaving, or oppressive

system, or as a fact that is painful to consider, reveals a serious methodological flaw. They are misusing the term patriarchy as a synonym for
male dominance or for a system in which male traits are valued over
female ones. Worst of all, their judgmental response to biblical patriarchy unfairly uses contemporary feminist standards (which hope for an
elimination of sexist tradition by seeking to promulgate equality between the sexes) to measure the cultural patterns of an ancient society
struggling to establish its viability under circumstances radically different from contemporary western conditions.

Underlying the bias in the statements quoted above is the difficulty in
defining patriarchy. The term itself is a controversial one, and feminist
scholars have subjected it to intense scrutiny. Feminist social science
has, in its ongoing methodological discussions and reviews, produced
critiques of the basic assumptions involved in the concept of patriarchy.
A working vocabulary that is useful in analyzing the patriarchal aspect of
societies has emerged. Those who use the term patriarchy in describing
the biblical world should consider how much progress has been made
toward understanding patriarchy and also the controversy that has
arisen about its origins and function. But the realization that the concept
of patriarchy must be approached carefully has not yet become apparent
to most feminist theologians or biblical scholars. These examples are
just several of many egregious misuses of the word patriarchy that appear in the writings of feminists in the field of religion.

Defining patriarchy in a way that satisfies all its usages is not really
possible. Its meaning varies considerably, depending on the discipline in
which it is used. Some critics even suggest that it has hindered rather
than helped our understanding of the relationships between men and
women. The variety of definitions attached to the term indicates the
confusion involved in using it:

> Patriarchy has been discussed as an ideology which arose out of men's
> power to exchange women between kinship groups; as a symbolic male
> principle; and as the power of the father (its literal meaning). It has been
> used to express men's control over women's sexuality and fertility; and to
> describe the institutional structure of male domination. Recently the
> phrase "capitalist patriarchy" has suggested a form peculiar to capitalism.[7]

The applicability of any of these definitions to Israelite society, or to
any premodern society for that matter, is questionable. Yet, as we have
seen, the term patriarchy is freely used in consideration of biblical materials. In our opinion, this is a serious matter and calls for an examination
of the research on patriarchy.

Patriarchy and Feminist Research

However imprecise or erroneous it may be, the current use of the term patriarchy in feminist theology and biblical studies is as an ideological or structural designation. Analysis of patriarchy originates in earlier feminist movements, particularly those tending to Marxism; and patriarchy as a dimension of human experience to be confronted, understood, and challenged belongs to a recent expansion of feminist consciousness. Contemporary feminist discourse has appropriated the concept of patriarchy in its struggle to deal with feminist feelings of oppression and exclusion. In dealing with this oppression, the use of the concept of patriarchy has political value for feminists. The understanding of patriarchy is a necessary step in opposing it.

Feminists, in their need to understand and explain patriarchy, have given it powerful theoretical significance by raising profound questions about the relationship of ideology, economics, and society. The passions surrounding the political motivations have, however, clouded the theoretical quest. Statements in feminist expositions about the development of modern patriarchal structures are often polemic or misleading because of enormous disagreement generally about female and male role relationships in contemporary cultures the world over.

Two aspects of patriarchy have emerged as central in feminist assessments: implications for power relationships and relationship to modes of economic production.

Power Relationships

Radical feminism (which has been very influential in the intellectual development of nearly all feminist circles) focuses the analytical discussion on the power relationships by which men dominate women. This essentially political approach is represented by Kate Millet's *Sexual Politics*,[9] which was among the first serious efforts to deal head-on with the specific nature of the oppression of women. The radical feminist movement introduced the term patriarchy into contemporary feminist discourse. Millett and her successors have been most successful in dealing with patriarchy descriptively, because they have highlighted the division that exists between males and females, and have established that it involves female subordination. They have documented the institutionalization of power relationships.

Drawing attention to male domination and its inequity has not been accompanied by an ability to provide a satisfactory explanation of the origins of patriarchy. For the most part, radical feminism has rejected biological determinism or reductionism, that is, the notion that biological differences between men and women are directly responsible for variations in temperament, social behavior, and prestige; however, it has not put forth alternate theories about the foundations of patriarchy.

Furthermore, radical feminism's political orientation to patriarchy has precluded dealing with cultural and nonpolitical variants. For example, Millett failed to account for the wide variety of forms the male domination can take, which anthropological research has convincingly documented. Radical feminism also has not properly considered the relationship between patriarchal social forms and economic structures.

Modes of Production

Marxist feminist theory has taken on the challenge of formulating both descriptions and explanations of the interaction between patriarchy and the economic organization of society. A Marxist-oriented framework maintains that the systems of production in a given society are related causally to hierarchical structures and that those patterns of domination are manifest in gender classes as well as social classes. This approach has its roots in the nineteenth-century theories of Engels, notably in his *Origin of the Family, Private Property, and the State.*[10] Appearing in 1884, this work linked the privatization of economic surplus with the subjugation of women.

The issues are so complex and involve the intersection of so many modes of inquiry that a great variety of models has emerged, even within Marxist feminism; furthermore, besides the general issues of Marxist analysis, these feminists must deal with theories of patriarchy relating specifically to feminist concerns. Consequently, no adequate theory about the relationship between female subordination and the organization of economic productivity has yet been established, although the discussion continues in a lively and increasingly insightful way,[11] particularly as it draws attention to the importance of economic structure as a powerful determinant of social structure.

The orientation of Marxist feminism to the classic Marxist critique of capitalism lends to it an attitude toward patriarchy that is difficult to divorce from its consideration of capitalist society. Marxist feminists are correct in going beyond Marx by asserting that inequality between males and females is not an invention of capitalism. However, the existence of at least some sexual differentiation with hierarchical characteristics in most if not all societies for which we have reliable information is a matter of debate. Furthermore, the bias against capitalism, in which female subordination is equated with oppression, has an implicit message that patriarchy in all settings is a static condition in which women are oppressed or exploited.[12]

Feminist analyses based on modern western capitalism have a tendency to be transhistorical. That is, they do not look carefully enough into the seemingly hierarchical features within the specific dynamics of a particular community. Like the politically oriented theories of radical feminism, Marxist assessments often unconsciously tend to superimpose contemporary standards on groups that existed in the past as well as on contemporary nonwestern or nonindustrial societies. A classic example of the problem of applying values universally is in the matter of family size.[13] Whereas feminists today would demand autonomy in the decision whether or not to have children, or of how many to have, many societies like ancient Israel valued large families for vital political and economic reasons. In such situations, large families brought status and honor as well as material benefits to both parents. Can one legitimately talk about male exploitation of female reproduction in such situations?

The dynamics of gender hierarchy, as I understand them, are historically specific. The concept of patriarchy is thus misleading unless it recognizes and deals with variations across time. If the idea of patriarchy is not fluid or flexible, then it may not be applicable to other or ancient modes of social life. As part of the critique of western capitalism, patriarchy is often a value-laden and rigid term, which interferes with an openness to understand the position of women in cultures removed from our own.

Critique of Patriarchal Models

The problems of understanding and utilizing the concept of patriarchy go beyond the specific difficulties that lie within the various approaches found in the contemporary women's movement. The relevance of patriarchy to premodern or pre-industrial societies remains at the core of any discussion. But certain other issues of gender asymmetry affect the effort to examine the position of women in any particular society with a minimum of bias.[14] Included among these are the assumption of universals, the dualistic modeling of gender differentiation, and the valuation of one gender over another.

Universals

One should be wary of any system of explanation that deals in universals. As we have already noted, radical and Marxist feminists tend to characterize patriarchy without the variation that might exist in other cultures. Both the political and economic approaches have generalized about patriarchy because of the way they interpret the evidence from ethnography and comparative sociology. Human culture and the social forms it takes may always have been male dominated. Although some feminist anthropologists might insist that they can identify a few societies in which women were equal or even dominant,[15] the overwhelming consensus is that no society truly egalitarian with respect to gender has ever existed. Furthermore, the notion of a primitive matriarchy, popular at one time among nineteenth-century evolutionists and their intellectual heirs, has been shown to be dubious at best.[16] The putative matriarchal past, as it is now conceived, is more a product of the wishful thinking of its protagonists than the result of objective anthropological and historical inquiry.

Patriarchy is related to ideas of male dominance, but what does male dominance mean? It may always be present, but it is not always the same. Cross-cultural studies show that male dominance does not have a universal content or shape. Furthermore, male dominance cannot be equated with female passivity or lack of autonomy. Nor does the existence of some dominant males mean that all males dominate all females. Women may exert their wills and prevail over male members of society in ways that are of consequence for all members of their society. Yet the formal configurations of the society might easily give the appearance that males dominate. In other words, overt cultural patterns may accord prestige to males rather than females, but social reality may present a rather different picture.

Anthropologists have only very recently become sensitive to the existence of powerful undercurrents in the gender-ordered life of many groups. Some are even willing to use the designation subsystem for female control mechanisms that can be identified in societies for which there is little or no cultural or outward recognition of the importance of the female contribution to group life. Everyone within such a community would be well aware of the autonomy of female activity; but they probably would not readily admit it to outsiders, and outside observers would have great difficulty in discerning it on their own.

This disjunctive situation has been observed, to cite just one instance, in Sicilian villages. Men are accorded great public recognition and privilege. Legal authority to make decisions that affect families and the community resides almost solely with males. Yet, in practice, the apparently low status of women paradoxically is accompanied by

> a freedom not available to men that permits women to move, operate, and manipulate the daily exigencies of life so that they become not only skilled . . . but absolutely indispensable to the normal maintenance of affairs. This idea may come as a surprise to many social scientists but not to the Sicilians, who were almost universally in agreement that this is how things are.[17]

In these agrarian Sicilian villages, still relatively untouched by industrialization in the early 1960s when this study was made, women were almost totally isolated from public life. Yet the extreme gender segregation visible to external observers did not mean that men had all the power and that women were passive and subservient or felt exploited. On the contrary, a complex situation of female participation in and even control over vital aspects of group life could be identified. The researcher, in trying to explain the disjunction between overt value systems and actual practice, suggests that the extraordinary requirements of agriculture on the largely barren and dry island is at the root of the subsystem of female activity. In other words, female behavior in this case is adaptive to the circumstances present in the particular constellation of physical environment, traditional culture, and social patterns.[18]

The premise of universal male dominance hence must take into account the possible existence of subsystems as well as the variety of overt forms that male dominance can take. Yet none of these qualifications can ignore the fact that no matter how much autonomy women have, or how many prerogatives women may enjoy, or how dependent men are on their expertise in certain areas, there always seem to be one or more facets of community life that males control.[19]

Male dominance of some sort or to some degree is connected with biological facts by many researchers.[20] Sexual or biological asymmetry—with men having greater physical strength and with women bearing children—can partly explain male dominance, but the relationship between the female role in reproduction and male dominance is complex. Biological reductionists who would argue for a direct causal connection between biological constraints and social patterns have been called to task. Cross-cultural variation is too great to allow for such a simple explanation. While the role of biology is universally present, its way of surfacing in social fact is infinitely varied. The particular ecological and historical conditions in which a community lives temper the role of biology and shape the extent, form, and relative importance of male dominance.

Dualistic Modeling

Much of the feminist discussion of male dominance or patriarchal patterns draws upon the recognition that society operates on two different levels, the public and the private.[21] These two arenas of life are equated with a general division between two kinds of activity. The private or domestic sphere revolves around the home and the reproductive processes that originate there. The public sphere is everything outside the home: collective behavior, legal or judicial regulation of supradomestic matters, and responses to conditions that transcend the needs or problems of individual families. In this domestic–public scheme, female identity is linked with the domestic sphere and male identity with the public sphere. Females are said to be closer to the "natural" functions taking place in the domestic contexts; males are then more closely identified with supradomestic "cultural" life.

The value of this dualistic model for analyzing gender differentiation has its limitations.[22] While it may have great descriptive validity, it is unsatisfactory as an explanation for patriarchy, or male dominance. Its theoretical formulations, as with many feminist analyses, are not sufficiently cognizant of historical variants. The gross domestic–public distinction is simply inadequate to describe most social action in many societies. The dichotomous view makes sense in compelling ways, yet it places the private in opposition to the public so as to blur the essential integration of domestic with public life in many prestate societies,[23] of which emergent Israel was surely one.

The public–private dichotomy is rooted in the nineteenth-century tendency to view the world in "essentially gendered spheres."[24] The dualistic way of looking at spheres of gender behavior does not always or easily transcend its origins in modern western ideology. Our present-day values give primacy to the public sphere, but can we legitimately translate those values to societies in which matters of kinship and family (the domestic realm)—cannot be so easily separated or distinguished from economic and political matters (the public realm)? At best, it is a risky business to apply these distinct spheres and attendant values known from modern experience to societies that are smaller and less complex than our own. At worst, doing so means failing to grasp the important position of women in such societies.

If ancient Israel in its formative period fits the description of being small and relatively undifferentiated, as we shall argue below, then the public–domestic opposition as an analytical tool must be used with great caution. Identifying certain public spheres of activity in ancient Israel as closed to women, or as only exceptionally occupied by them, cannot be equated with the patriarchal control observed in more recent societies that exclude women from the public sphere.

Gender Valuation

Recent critics have pointed out that social science itself tends to be "patriarchal." From Marx and Durkheim to present research, the burgeoning literature purporting to analyze dominance and subordination makes assumptions of value. By and large, those assumptions are androcentric. They assume that male prerogatives and responsibilities are innately better than female ones.[25] In dealing with the division of labor according to gender, for example, they look at the tasks performed by males as having inherently more value in the eyes of everyone than do tasks performed by females. But are such assessments drawn from a balanced investigation of both male and female views of relational value? Is it not possible that an ideology of male domination or male supremacy is one held by men and not necessarily by women?

Again, in the matter of gender valuation, we may tend to superimpose contemporary ideas on societies different from ours in fundamental ways. Certainly the measure of female success or worth in most ancient societies cannot compare with what it is for most western women in the final quarter of the twentieth century. Consider the reflections of one feminist scholar dealing with classical antiquity:

> Is it really fair to imply, as some of us have done, that ancient women would have wanted to live differently had any had the opportunity? What if any evidence can be found to support such a claim? For many years I doubted whether intelligent women took pleasure in leading an anonymous life of service to husband and family, but now I wonder if I have not been judging ancient women as I judge myself, by male standards of accomplishment?[26]

This personal and informal statement is similar in its conclusions to the analytical statements that anthropologists have begun to make as the result of recent gender-sensitive fieldwork.

This problem of gender valuation in ancient Israel is based on the information gleaned from biblical texts. As stated above, the Hebrew Bible is largely a public, urban document. It contains some statements that appear to value men more highly than women or to give men certain legal privileges that are not extended to women. From our contemporary perspective, these texts give incomplete evidence of biblical patriarchy. They do not tell us how Israelite women felt about differential treatment. In the context of the specific social and economic structures that characterized ancient Israel, the existence of gender asymmetry, with men accorded a set of advantages apparently unavailable to most women, must not automatically be perceived as oppressive. In objecting to the tendency to label as discriminatory texts that favor men, we do not intend to be apologetic but rather to sensitize the reader of scripture to the antiquity of the texts, the otherness of the society that produced them, and the lack of evidence that the Eves of ancient Israel felt oppressed, degraded, or unfairly treated in the face of cultural asymmetry. Gender differences that appear hierarchical may not have functioned or been perceived as hierarchical within Israelite society. Again, the biblical record is a cultural document that emerges from, but does not necessarily mirror, social reality.

A related problem of interpretation consists of generalizing from limited information about women's position, or female status. The more remote a society is, the more likely observers are to form opinions on the basis of a small number of highly visible conditions. Ethnographic research has been particularly susceptible to this methodological hazard. Consider the results of an anthropological study that subjected to comprehensive analysis a large number of factors thought to signify gender status. This effort, published in a book called *The Status of Women in Pre-industrial Societies* (by M. K. Whyte),[27] produced some surprising and informative results.

Whyte set out to examine a number of issues surrounding the status of women relative to men in society. Although status is a vague term, its very imprecision lent itself to the broad scope of his study. Whyte collected information on the status of women from ninety-three different cultural groups. Included were the distinctions of "differential power, prestige, rights, privileges, and importance of women relative to men."[28] The cultures were all preindustrial, and more than one-third were peasant communities with complex agrarian economies. This emphasis on the investigation of variations in the status of women prior to the large industrialized nation-states makes his study and conclusions relevant to ancient Israel in its formative period.

The primary goal of Whyte's study was to determine whether the status of women has any regularity cross-culturally. He identified fifty-two status items (e.g., participation of women in religious ceremonies, dwelling ownership, relative ease of divorce, final authority over children) and set out to determine whether clustering of the items existed. Hypothetically, the existence of "the status of women" would be reflected in a statistically identifiable pattern of associations among the fifty-two status variables. This study also addressed an important corollary question about the relationship of one area of social life to another in the status of women. For example, would a relatively low status in one area, such as political life, imply a similarly low position in all the areas, including economic, domestic, sexual, and religious spheres of life?

Whyte's strategy for collecting and analyzing the data was well designed, and his conclusions[29] deserve serious attention. He failed to discover a *pattern* of universal dominance, which agrees with what most comparative ethnographers have already noted. That is, there exist wide variations among groups in nearly every aspect of the relative position of women to men. Although he found no society in which women totally dominated men, he warned that the absence of evidence of female dominance did not automatically mean absolute domination of women by men.

Many scholars assume that discrete aspects of the status of women vary in relationship to each other. If women appear to be discriminated against or devalued in one item of consideration, it follows that they will be widely devalued also in other areas of social life. Whyte's study revealed that such a common supposition on correlations is neither obvious nor necessary. The various indicators of the status of women do not interrelate automatically.

Thus, the correlation between low status in one area of life and low status in other areas is negative. Access to religious roles, for example, may be more available to males and so appear to indicate higher male status. But this presumed higher status for men cannot be seen as automatically implying an overall low status for women. Similarly, unfavorable consequences for women in divorce does not mean much more than that; it merely indicates how women fare in divorce cases.[30] These two examples are relevant because an all-male priesthood and divorce as a male-initiated procedure existed in ancient Israel. These conditions are often removed from the total cultural context that gave rise to them and are taken as signs of biblical "patriarchy," and of the inferior status of women generally in Israelite society.

Whyte's cross-cultural investigation has shown, however, that it would be erroneous or misleading to assign gender value to such instances of apparent discrimination against women. The concept of a reliable set of indicators pointing to a definable status for women appears to be unacceptable. Without a set of conditions that might predict women's status, it is clear that a single instance can be of little use in determining the way women are valued in any or all aspects of a society. Furthermore, focusing on any instance of gender differentiation tends to wrest it from its context and hence preclude an understanding of its possible functional role in any specific cultural setting. We shall entertain below, for example, the possibility that the exclusion of females from the Israelite priesthood had functional value in meeting demographic needs and is not in and of itself a sign of belief in female inferiority.

Although Whyte does not deal directly with the relationship of gender to other social categories as a reason for variation of female status, other researchers have pointed to this interaction. For example, age is a variable that encompasses other aspects of social position and hence may have significant bearing on the relative status of women.[31] However, a women's age is not an absolute indicator of her status. In some instances, as probably with ancient Israel, gender differentiation may decrease in importance with age, whereas advancing age may bring about little or no change in female status in other cultures.[32]

The problem of assigning uniform cultural values to an independent item is related to the unreliability of generalizing female value. The matter of menstrual taboos, whereby during menstruation women are separated completely or are isolated from some areas of activity, has normally been interpreted as an example of institutionalized discrimination and as a feature of patriarchal society. Millett, for example, asserts that menstrual taboos are a sign of male dominance.[33] One of the most balanced discussions of women in the Hebrew Bible considers the treatment of menstruating Israelite women to be explicitly discriminatory.[34] However, these beliefs concerning female biology can be interpreted in other ways. M. Douglas, for example, asserts that it is only when women are powerless that notions of female impurity are absent. Conversely, menstrual taboos, involving the avoidance of contact with menstrual blood, are present when women constitute a challenge to male authority because of their social or economic position.[35] Another view of sex-related taboos is that they are not related at all to the dynamics of gender relations.

Clearly, the existence of an apparently discriminatory practice is at best only a variable indicator of female social and economic status. Each case must be investigated on its own terms. There is no wish to imply that biblical menstrual taboos cannot be interpreted as discriminatory. Yet, because these sex-related taboos in the Hebrew Bible are linked with other physical conditions, some linked to males and some sexually neutral, we can at least call for a reassessment of menstruation and impurity (see especially Lev 12–15).

Patriarchy and Patrilineality

The discussion thus far has revealed that patriarchy is a value-laden and diffuse term and that its applicability to any society must be individually evaluated. If one uses the term to indicate the dominant/subordinate position of men relative to women, then it is necessary to identify the specific areas of hierarchical arrangement in the community's life. Furthermore, the possibility of a discrepancy between legal or political domination on the one hand and psychological or social control value on the other must be taken into account. Using the term patriarchy in reference to any society is problematic. The remoteness in time and the limited nature of the available source materials makes scrutiny of ancient Israel especially difficult. Again, the public, political, and masculine orientation of most biblical materials creates a one-sided record of the complex interweaving of male and female social patterns.

Despite the possible technical accuracy of the term, the difficulties inherent in calling ancient Israel patriarchal leads one to consider using instead the term patrilineal. Ironically, this suggestion comes from the imprecise way in which the concept of matriarchy was used by nineteenth-century writers when describing certain primitive societies discovered by Victorian explorers. Information published by Bachofen and Morgan and later used heavily by Engels noted that in these societies kinship was reckoned from the mother's lineage.[36] Furthermore, the mythology of these groups tended to emphasize female figures or deities, and the language describing family relationships had unexpected female characteristics. Perhaps because these characteristics were so alien to their own experience, these scholars designated them as matriarchal. They concluded that primitive matriarchy was part of an evolutionary sequence culminating in patriarchy, and suggested that the status of females in such putative matriarchies exceeded that of males.

The nineteenth-centuries ideas of primordial female supremacy have not held up well under subsequent scrutiny. The groups labeled matriarchal are in fact matrilineal. That is, group membership is reckoned from female rather than male lineage, or the descent group is traced by the line of females. Accordingly, the social identity of a male also derives from his mother rather than his father. Closely related to the matrilineality of some simple societies is matrilocality, in which a newly married couple will live near or with the wife's family.[37] In neither matrilineality nor matrilocality does a corresponding high status for women or female control of significant aspects of political life exist.[38] The apparently matriarchal nature of such groups derives from their simple structure. Without developed suprafamily political or economic structures, the family orientation gives the impression of female dominance. The observers of these primitive societies, had they not been hampered by their Victorian context, should have concluded that the power of women in family situations deserves special attention.

If matrilineal groups were erroneously labeled matriarchal, patrilineal groups might also—though for different reasons—be inaccurately called patriarchal. In fact these two terms (patrilineal and patriarchal) are sometimes found used interchangeably in loose, and technically incorrect, parlance. Patrilineality refers to the tracing of group membership through the father's line. Patrilocality, in which newlyweds take up residence near or in the home of the husband's family, normally accompanies patrilineality. In addition, the inheritance of property is through the male line, as it often is even in matrilineal groups. The orientation of descent, dwelling location, and inheritance through males is characteristic of societies, such as ancient Israel, adopting intensive cultivation systems.[39] (Intensive cultivation is defined as farming that involves one or more of three agricultural techniques: irrigation, fertilization, and plowing.) The land base for agrarian societies is of primary importance, and regulating access to productive lands is a critical dimension of family structures.

How does ancient Israel fit into the scheme of marriage patterns and family structures outlined by anthropologists? Investigating Israelite marriage has been a frustrating task for all the same reasons that make the study of Israelite women a complicated business. The Bible contains no systematic marriage laws. Information about marriage practice comes obliquely from a few legal statements that deal with marriage or divorce, and from scattered narrative accounts that as often as not contradict each other or are at odds with legal materials. The wide time spread of the texts in question no doubt gives rise to some of the confusion. Difficulty in reconstructing normative Israelite practice also occurs because of the normal disjunction between societal ideals, as expressed in laws, and actual practices that the laws may seek to alter but which persist in reality and surface in narrative.

Influenced by the theories of Bachofen and other scholars such as J. F. McLennan,[40] earlier generations of biblical scholars trying to understand the characteristics of Hebrew marriage assumed that a matriarchal regime underlay the androcentric order visible in nearly all relevant biblical texts. W. Robertson Smith, for example, amassed a body of evidence from which he concluded that matrilineal descent was once the norm in ancient Israel or at least among pre-Israelite Semites.[41] He seized on such passages as the marriage of Samson in Judges 14, in which Samson's Philistine bride remains in her own family following her marriage to Samson, as evidence of matrilocality if not matrilineality. Later generations of scholars have readily pointed out, however, that Samson's behavior was dictated by its own peculiar circumstances, involved a non-Israelite, and is no more normative than would a man living with his wife's parents in our society be judged a vestige of an original Anglo-Saxon matriarchy.

Robertson Smith's theories have been substantially discredited,[42] and a more probable picture of Israelite marriage and lineage patterns has emerged. The recent social scientific approach to Israelite society, especially for the formative period, has brought new attention to family life and structures. As we shall see in Chapter 6, the family was the organizing feature of Israelite society. Consequently, the position of women relative to the family, as much as to men, provides a key enabling us to open at least a crack in the door of time and distance that hides the lives of Israelite women from the modern observer. A delineation of what might be seen through that crack appears in Chapters 7 and 8. Suffice it now to point out that early Israel was a lineage-based system with group membership established by tracing descent established along patrilineal (male) lines.[43]

The enormous emphasis on geneology in the biblical record is testimony to the importance of patrilineage. Similarly, the very terminology for the basic family unit, known as the *bet 'ab,* which literally means "house of the father," establishes the patrilineality of Israelite society. References to the "father's house," which we shall examine closely in Chapter 6, are scattered throughout the biblical text and leave no room for any possibility of evolutionary shift or change in the fact of male-determined descent. While patrilocality and patrilineality are not always cross-culturally interconnected, the intensive agricultural base of the Israelite economy throughout the Iron Age involved territorial imperatives associated with patrilocality and with principles of male inheritance, or patrimonalism.

Thus there can be no doubt about the existence of a system of lineage reckoned through male ancestry and regulating the transmission of property through the male line in ancient Israel. This system predominated during the formative or tribal period. The rise of the monarchy probably brought about the demise of the lineage system as the determining social and political pattern, but the patrilineal and patrimonial aspect of it continued unabated. Rather than review the many biblical passages that reveal the functioning of a patrilineal and patrimonial system, we point to an instance in which the system falters. What happens in a patrilineal, patrimonial system when male heirs are lacking? Numbers 27:1–11 presents the famous case of the daughters of Zelophehad:

> Then drew near the daughters of Zelophehad the son of Hepher, son of Gilead, son of Machir, son of Manasseh. . . . "Our father died in the wilderness . . .; and he had no sons. Why should the name of our father be taken away from his family, because he had no son? Give to us a possession among our father's brethren." Moses brought their case before the LORD. And the LORD said to Moses, "The daughters of Zelophehad are right. You shall give them possession of an inheritance among their father's brethren and cause the inheritance of their father to pass to them."

The text goes on to stipulate what might happen if Zelophehad had no daughters either, or no brother, or no uncles. Clearly the passage is concerned with retaining the territorial integrity of certain family units. Likewise, the related passage in Numbers 36 stipulates that Zelophehad's daughters should arrange their own marriages, but that they should do so within closely aligned families, and that they should not go outside their tribe. Again, the protection of lineage property rights is at stake. Females can inherit property, but even this breach in the normal pattern is handled in such a way as to preserve the principle of transferring name and property to succeeding generations according to the father's line.

The Zelophehad incident provides information about Israelite social structure and also about marriage possibilities. In-group marriages were apparently preferred. But the nature and function of marital alliances is far more complex than this one story alone suggests, and we shall consider the matter of endogamy and exogamy (patterns of marriage within and outside the group) in Chapter 8.

Patriarchy and Power

For Israel in its earliest period of national existence, the reckoning of descent and the accompanying transfer of property through male lineage were central and organizing features of the community. In an environment with limited water and usable land, the establishment of fixed and theologically sanctioned patterns for family land tenure was an essential component of societal stability. But the patrilineality of early Israel cannot simply be equated with patriarchy, if the latter implies the absolute control of males over females, or of the male head of the family over his wife and other family members, or of the subservience of women to men. Certain biblical texts or features of biblical language may give that impression and will be examined in due course, but the social reality did not necessarily coincide with what appears in the official canonical document.

The distinction between authority and power is relevant to an assessment of the extent or even the existence of patriarchal dominance in early Israel. Social scientists whose research is sensitive to feminist concerns have stressed the importance of distinguishing between these two aspects of social behavior when it comes to analyzing the position of women in any society, from the most egalitarian to the most stratified of gender relationships. The distinction between power and authority is especially important in revising the notion that sexually stratified arrangements leave women helpless, which does not seem to be the case. Women in such arrangements play out their parts as social actors in less visible or less official but nonetheless equally vital ways.

In his classic work on *The Theory of Social and Economic Organization*,[44] Max Weber distinguished between power and authority. Feminist theorists have since adapted and used his definitions. In her theoretical summary of the articles in the landmark anthology of feminist scholarship, *Women, Culture, and Society*,[45] Rosaldo defines *authority* as the culturally legitimated right to make decisions and command obedience. With respect to male–female relations, it is seen formally as male dominance and female compliance. *Power* refers to the ability to effect control despite or independent of official authority. Regardless of legal status, power is the influence that females have in gender-related behavior. Female power typically involves informal and unofficial modes of behavior that may never receive male acknowledgment but through which females may exert considerable and systematic direction over a range of circumstances. Authority is basically a hierarchical arrangement that may be expressed in formal legal or juridical traditions. Power has no such cultural sanctions but nonetheless can play a decisive role in social interaction.[46]

Many of the essays or case studies in *Women, Culture, and Society* provide discussion or documentation of the issues to which Rosaldo draws attention. In addition to establishing working definitions, Rosaldo also asserts that the distinction between power and culturally legitimated authority, between the ability to gain compliance and the recognition that it is right, is crucial to our study of women. Social scientists by and large have taken male authority for granted; they have also tended to accept a male view that sees the exercise of power by women as manipulative, disruptive, illegitimate, or unimportant. But it is necessary to remember that while authority legitimates the use of power, it does not exhaust it, and actual methods of giving rewards, controlling information, exerting pressure, and shaping events may be available to women as well as men.[47]

The functional distinction between authority and power is not simply a theoretical position. Important recognition that women can exercise power and influence significant decision-making even with legally sanctioned subordination has come from recent ethnographic research. Authority structures, being formal and public, are of course more visible and therefore easier for social scientists to record. When anthropologists limit their investigations to the observable structures, men will inevitably appear to dominate a society and women will appear helpless. But should this be taken at face value? A number of feminist anthropologists say no and have set about to clarify the situation.

One notable example is the work done by S. C. Rogers on a peasant society in southern France.[48] The village that she chose for her study is a tiny agricultural community of about 350 people. The structure of village life was, at least at the time of the fieldwork, still untouched by industrialization. Her investigation of the male monopoly of authority showed that men in fact wielded relatively little power. Consequently, she calls the visible or symbolic superior status of men a myth: the "myth of male dominance." Her use of the term "myth" is not casual. Following the work in mythology of the anthropologist Leach,[49] Rogers understands myth to be a significant part of the belief system of its adherents, but one that expresses a truth not literally reflective of day-to-day reality. Male dominance is thus a public attitude of deference or of theoretical control but not a valid description of social reality. Incredible as it may seem at first consideration, both men and women in this peasant society actually work to maintain the idea of male dominance while not subscribing to it as a reality. Women's power is culturally muted but functionally active. The result, according to Rogers, is a situation of *functional* absence of hierarchical relationships alongside the structural and symbolic presence of gender stratification: "the 'myth' of male dominance paradoxically serves to order social relationships in a nonhierarchical system."[50]

The implications of Rogers' findings for a study of gender relationships in any community are clear. One might even say that her description of the configuration of male and female behavior and ideology challenges the very core of the idea of patriarchy as a system of male dominance. The parameters of male dominance, at the very least, must be examined more closely than has been the norm. Rogers lists characteristics of a system in which the myth of male dominance is operative. These characteristics can be identified in a wide variety of peasant and even nonpeasant societies. Their value in cross-cultural analysis is therefore legitimate, and hence they can be used appropriately in considering another social group—tribal Israel—for which direct observation is not possible.

What then are the features of a community in which the "myth" of male control is superimposed on a condition of functional nonhierarchy? The components are as follows:[51]

1. Women are primarily associated with domestic matters.
2. The society is domestic-oriented; life centers around the home, and what happens in the home has implications for life beyond the home.
3. Formal rights may disadvantage females; but the day-to-day informal interactions in which females can exert power in a small community are at least as important a force as authorized rights.
4. A corollary and prior condition of item 3 is that males do have greater access to jural, political, and other formal aspects of community structure.
5. Men are occupied with activities that are culturally valued.
6. Males and females experience mutual interdependence in important ways, e.g., politically, economically, and/or socially; males may appear autonomous, but in fact can no more act or survive on their own than can females.

According to Rogers, the last point is particularly critical, for it means that both men and women will tend to perpetuate the system of social balance: of male authority offset by female power.

This model is readily suggestive of a potential method for evaluating gender relationships in formative Israel. Items 3, 4, and 5 require no investigation. The "patriarchal" stance of the biblical canon establishes the androcentric nature of ancient Israel with respect to legal rights, formal positions in society, and prominent activities in the community.

Item 1 can also be assumed in that females are all but invisible in the Bible with its public orientation. Viewed from another angle, those biblical books least overtly concerned with public and corporate life are the very ones in which females are, relatively, most visible. For the so-called "patriarchal" legends of Genesis, the social setting of family life and female characterizations in the persons of the "matriarchs" are essential parts of the narratives. Skeptics might argue, on the basis of literary analysis,[52] that the females serve only to underscore the importance of certain male figures. Be that as it may, the dominant actions of the patriarchs cannot fully mask the active roles of their female counterparts. Other examples of biblical books with a nonpublic orientation and a concomitant prominence of females are the Song of Songs and Proverbs, although the latter involves glimpses of female qualities in opposition, with women both highly valued and also treated as sources of danger or objects of contempt. We shall examine below female portrayals in the Song of Songs (Chapter 8) and in Proverbs (Chapter 7).

What about items 2 and 6? Can the combined resources of archaeology, the biblical text, and comparative sociology and social anthropology provide us with sufficient evidence for an evaluation of domestic orientation and mutual interdependence? My opinion is that, for Israel's formative period, an analysis of female and male interaction as a function of these two points is possible. The second part of this book (Chapters 6–8) will argue for the domestic orientation and gender interdependence of earliest Israel. Insofar as we are successful in doing so, we shall be able to conclude that there was a functional lack of hierarchy in Israelite gender relations.

Even if a substantial amount of female power exists in any society, the accompanying lack of female authority is in no way to be condoned from a contemporary perspective. Rogers does not intend to be apologetic, nor do I. The ancient or peasant configurations may indeed be functional and adaptive, although anthropological theory has yet to produce fully explanatory analyses. Clearly the maternal role of women in preindustrial societies is related to gender asymmetry, but any set of fundamental and predictable consequences of that relationship has eluded scholars. The great variation in the patterns of gender asymmetry that we have already noted is the norm and hence is part of the problem. Subtle nuances in the environment and history of individual societies create an infinite number of cultural and social forms that defy attempts to understand origins and establish typologies.

The matter of apologetics deserves further comment. Functional nonhierarchy of at least some peasant societies is not synonymous with equality, because gender asymmetry is an intrinsic feature of such situations. Yet the balance between female and male power is not a trivial matter, even from the perspective of contemporary feminist ideology. The ability of women to determine the shape of important aspects of personal and group life, and the concomitant hidden value attached to the female persona, make the notion of legal or jural equality a moot point.

Feminists who condemn or bemoan the apparent patriarchy of ancient or other societies may be deflecting their energies from what should be the real focus of their concern: the transformation of functional gender balance to situations of real imbalance. In other words, what happened to change the myth of male dominance to the reality of male dominance? What is there in the nature of urban and/or industrial life that alters the model of balance that exists for some peasant societies? If our position with respect to biblical or Israelite patriarchy is revisionist, this is not to idealize ancient Israel but rather to free feminist critics from a misplaced preoccupation with biblical androcentrism and allow them to search for the dynamics that led to the dichotomizing of gender attributes by early postbiblical times.

A Note on Terminology

In subsequent chapters we shall deal directly with the earliest period of ancient Israel and with some of the literature produced then. Our exploration of theoretical problems and models has already involved the use of some technical language. The discussion has included terms such as patriarchy, patrilineality and matrilineality, power and authority; other social science terms used throughout this text merit some explanation.

Peasant, for example, will be used to denote independent farmers working on their own lands. "Free agrarian," "free citizen," or "free producer" might be more accurate terms, but they are also more cumbersome. We mention them, however, because in Marxist circles, "peasant" is part of the vocabulary describing feudal and other societies in which the farmer lacks full control over the products of labor. In such situations the peasantry is subject to exploitation in the forms of taxation and conscription, and political hierarchies and social stratification also are present. Technically, therefore, peasantry would refer to ancient Israel's farm families during the monarchy as well as during the pre-Israelite period of Canaanite dominance. However, the general meaning of the term of peasant refers to the agrarian economic base of a society and is commonly found. We use it in that sense, with no political overtones intended.

Another term, or set of terms, requiring clarification is "sex" and "gender." Although these words are sometimes used interchangeably, they actually have distinct though related meanings. The definitions suggested by M. Gould and R. Kern-Daniels are helpful. The use of the word "sex," according to their analysis, should be limited to that which refers to "the biological dichotomy between female and male, chromosomally determined, and for the most part unalterable."[53] Consequently, sex roles would be behaviors, such as sexual intercourse and childbearing, that are determined by biology. "Gender" has a social dimension. It is that which societies recognize as masculine or feminine, and consequently it can vary from group to group. True, with great consistency certain behaviors or identities are cross-culturally associated exclusively with one sex or the other. But unless the behaviors or identities are thus associated only because of biological identity, then they theoretically can be—and in occasional instances are—associated with the sex other than the one in which they are most often present. Gould and Kern-Daniels propose, therefore, that "gender" be perceived "as a continuum of human attitudes and behaviors, socially constructed, socially perpetuated, and socially alterable."[54]

Obviously one can expect a high degree of congruency between gender and sex, particularly in traditional societies. Yet much of the behavior that some would loosely label sex roles could be exhibited by either sex. The patterns within an individual society determine whether males or females perform certain tasks or play certain roles. In light of this situation, we use "gender" in reference to all behavior other than the sex act so as to take into account the inherent sociality of the term.

3

Setting the Scene: The Highland Environment of Ancient Israel

Many of the biases interfering with an evaluation of any aspect of life in antiquity stem from our temporal distance from that life. Time alone is the symbol but not the substance of the problem. We live today in a postindustrial and highly technological society. The weather may be a recurrent item of news and conversation, but for the majority of people the ecological milieu rarely impinges directly and regularly on the central aspects of daily life. An early frost may destroy our flower beds and disrupt the aesthetics of our neighborhood landscapes, but it hardly threatens our survival as individuals. Can we ever understand what it means to live in a world in which existence is intimately, immediately, and inextricably bound up with environmental features?

Many of us are concerned with the natural world. We want to protect it from contamination, and we want to reverse the policies and practices that have allowed pollution to occur. We hope to survive earthquakes and hurricanes. We want to vacation on clean beaches and in fresh air. But do we look at the sky in the morning and wonder if today is the day that the first rains of winter will fall, awakening life in the seeds we have placed in the parched ground, seeds that will become the grain for feeding our families in the long months ahead, or seeds that will crumble into the dust around them, leaving our children faint with hunger and our storehouses lacking the seeds for the next planting?

The psychological distance between our time and ancient agrarian life and its vicissitudes is vast. Hence it is important to be familiar with the constraints of daily life in ancient Palestine so as to transcend the barriers separating our world from the world of our biblical ancestors. In the context of this study, and with the importance of economic and environmental circumstances for determining the pattern of gender relations in any given society, examination of the features that determined early

Israel's agricultural system becomes a compelling dimension of our task. As we have shown, ethnographers have documented an enormous variety of roles available to both sexes and in the degree to which males appear dominant. What causes this variety? In our own society we would look to historical contexts. We would first consider traditional patterns and then set them against the impact of economic changes and political developments. But can we use that approach to examine a preindustrial, agrarian society?

This question is particularly acute in reference to traditional patterns as a starting point for analysis of gender relations. Ancient Israel, to borrow a model from psychobiology, was the offspring of the high civilizations of the ancient Near East. Though a participant in the general matrix of Babylonian, Egyptian, and Canaanite culture, Israel was also radically different. The difference in Israel's identity is to some tantalizingly immeasureable extent the product of Israelite self-establishment on a previously unsettled landscape: the Palestinian highlands. The ideology Israel formulated and promulgated was conditioned by the exigencies of the new environment along with the inherited thought patterns of the component populations.

The Bible as a primary source is unreliable in reconstructing Israel's history, which means that a multidisciplinary approach is necessary, the results of which are social history rather than the more conventional political history attempted by past generations.[1] Scholars have learned that they must integrate archaeological data (including historical geography) and sociological approaches with traditional literary and textual analyses. Only then can they reconstruct Israel's character and understand the role of ideology in that community. Likewise, the setting of ancient Israel provides information crucial to the investigation of one particular aspect of Israelite society, the differential roles played by males and females and the value placed on those roles.

Feminist and biblical scholarship both recognize the necessity of contextual approaches. Feminist anthropology has largely succeeded in exploding the old myth of biological determinism. The great range of female behaviors shatter the notion that genetic factors underlie some theoretical set of traits that inexorably determine the pattern of female activities. An environmental or contextual orientation has superseded the erstwhile biological one, although even the environmental approach must begin by considering the anatomical and physiological differences between the sexes. Friedl's useful handbook[2] on the anthropological approach to gender differences in a range of societies takes its very structure from the economic and environmental variables that she has found critical for understanding patterns of gender interaction. One of her basic propositions is that

> the subsistence technology of a society and its social and political organization have crucial consequence for (1) the sexual division of labor, (2) the differential allocation of power and recognition of men and women, and (3) the quality of the relationship between the sexes. Therefore modes of subsistence, that is, the types of energy used by members of a society to procure its food, are used . . . as the base for the examination of sex [*sic*] roles.[3]

Friedl reasons further[4] that because males and females everywhere have the same psychobiological potential, the specific pattern of male–female interaction must depend on the allocation of labor. With rare exceptions, all men and all women work. Beyond childbearing, what else do women do? That question cannot be answered in an environmental vacuum. Other questions follow: what else *can* women do? How *much* do they do? The range of possibilities is influenced by the subsistence technology (by what the societal tasks are), which in turn is determined to great measure by the natural resources at hand. The answers to these questions are important in evaluating women's position, because both the nature and level of female participation in the basic tasks of a group affect the status of women. In short, Everywoman Eve can become visible to the extent that her contribution to the group effort can be discerned.

The task of discovering Eve thus begins with an examination of the material conditions that were the basis of Israel's existence and hence integral to Israel's distinct social and cultural formations. Religious ideology became the encompassing cultural expression and motivation of Israelite life; gender relations constituted the core of Israelite social structures. Gottwald stresses the materiality of Israel's life and thought as essential to understanding her religion: "The basic tenet for future research and theory is clear and commanding: only as the full *materiality* of ancient Israel is more securely grasped will we be able to make proper sense of its *spirituality*."[5]

The technoeconomic characteristics of Israel are essential to understanding the smallest unit of that society, the female or male individual. Most analysis of social history stops at the smallest corporate level, the family. Getting to know Eve means realizing that the females within the family can emerge only through appropriate consideration of the material world that not only sets strictures but also offers potentials for family and national survival. For early Israel, three broad aspects of the material world must be considered: Israel's status as a pioneer society, the particular demands of agricultural subsistence in the Palestinian highlands, and the demographic situation in the early Iron Age.

Pioneers in the Land

Where did Eve live with her husband, sons, and daughters, near kin, close neighbors? Biblical tradition gives a wide scope to the Israelite inhabitation of the Promised Land. The territorial allotments recorded for the twelve tribes included a large tract of east Mediterranean lands. The second half of the Book of Joshua delineates boundaries that stretched from Mt. Hermon in the north to the uninhabitable Negev wilderness in the south. The classic phrase "from Dan to Beersheba" (e.g., 2 Sam 3:10) reflects a similar conception of Israelite territory, stretching from the headwaters of the Jordan in the north to the arid area, east and west, at the southern end of the Dead Sea in the south. The breadth of the land is not directly indicated by the "Dan to Beersheba" designation, but the lists of tribal portions signify the Mediterranean Sea as the western border and the Transjordanian highlands as the eastern extent.

The Deuteronomic account of Moses' leadership provides a similar inclusive view of the "Holy Land." Moses' words to the Israelites, urging them to begin the process of entering their destined country, suggest an extensive land base: "Take your journey, and go to the hill country of the Amorites, and to all their neighbors in the Arabah, in the hill country and in the lowland, and in the Negeb, and by the seacoast, the land of the Canaanites, and Lebanon, as far as the great river, the river Euphrates. Behold, I have set the land before you" (Deut 1:7–8). Likewise, from a vantage point at Mount Pisgah east of the Jordan River, Moses is told what land will accrue to the Israelites: "Go up to the top of Pisgah, and lift up your eyes westward and northward and southward and eastward, and behold it with your eyes . . . and he [Joshua] shall put them in possession of the land which you shall see" (Deut 3:27–28). All told, despite the mood of great expanse created by the language of such passages, the "Promised Land" was a rather small area in the whole scope of the Fertile Crescent: at its greatest national extent, ancient Israel occupied a territory no more than about 145 by 257 kilometers (90 by 160 miles).

Even so, such dimensions are a deceptive ideal. The texts designating a greater Israel reflect the rather brief span of time during which Israel actually exercised sovereignty over the lands from Dan to Beersheba and from the coast to the highlands east of the Jordan. But for most of Israel's existence, the territorial ideal was not realized. By the end of Israel's national life, its geography had been reduced to the tiny southern kingdom of Judah, consisting of the slowly eroding territory of only two tribes. Likewise, at the beginning of national life, in the epoch where our search for Eve begins, the tribal groups held only a fraction of what was eventually to be greater Israel.

That Israel's territorial resources were restricted at the outset is apparent from the terse summary of the situation in the Book of Judges. Repeatedly, the text bluntly records that the Israelites failed to occupy large portions of the coastal plain, most of the broad Jezreel Valley in the north, and significant urban centers (including the Shephelah stronghold of Gezer and the Jebusite fortress of Jerusalem) in the highlands. Without the plains, the Jezreel, and also most of the broader intermountain valleys, a rather circumscribed area remained as the setting for early Israel. Its geographic core was the highland area: the mountainous spine west of the Jordan, from the Beersheba basin in the south into the Galilean uplands in the north. To use the Bible's own terminology, Israel's national existence is identified in its first centuries largely with the "hill country" of Judea, Samaria, and Galilee.

Archaeological data as well as biblical narrative point to the mountainous areas of Cisjordan (west of the Jordan River) as the actual extent of early Israel. The Israelites could secure a territorial base in the central highlands at the beginning of the Iron Age because, as excavations have revealed, most of that territory was unoccupied at that time. The Israelites were unequipped to face the chariot armies of the Canaanites, who held the plains and valleys by virtue of their superior military technology as well as by dint of the greater economic resources provided by the relatively less arid and more arable lands they controlled.

There were important environmental reasons for the fact that throughout most of the preceding Bronze Age, only occasional, and usually minor, settlements had been established in the highlands. The soils in the mountainous areas are rather poor. Perennial sources of water are virtually nonexistent except for a few relatively minor springs. The greatest obstacle to settlement was probably the difficult topography: an irregular configuration of hills and valleys.

After over a century of extensive and intensive archaeological excavation and exploration of the Holy Land, scholars can now plot accurate maps of the settlement patterns during all the periods of human habitation of Palestine. Those maps indicate that the highlands were virtually empty during most of the periods preceding 1200 BCE.[6] In the millennia before 1200, dramatic developments in the history of civilization were taking place in other parts of Palestine: the construction of what may have been the world's first city at Jericho; along the Phoenician coast, the invention of the alphabet; the construction of one of the world's oldest "superhighways," the Way of the Sea, connecting Egypt and Mesopotamia, the superpowers of the ancient world. The highlands remained remote and isolated, not far in distance from the successive spurts of urban life and intercontinental traffic to the east and west, yet relatively untouched by the passing of armies and merchants, diplomats and kings.

This isolation ended during the Iron Age. The Israelites altered forever the settlement patterns that had characterized the narrow strip of land at the eastern end of the Mediterranean for thousands of years. One of the great historical geographers and archaeologists of Eretz Israel (the Land of Israel), the late Yohanan Aharoni, called the Israelite occupation of the hill country "the greatest habitational revolution that had ever taken place in the history of this country."[7]

As we have already suggested, both archaeological survey and excavation corroborate the information the Bible gives about Israelites moving into the highlands. In the Late Bronze Age (1550–1200), the last of the periods preceding the emergence of the biblical people, only twenty-three sites were recorded for an area of 4200 square kilometers (1622 square miles), representing the highland zone of Palestine. At the beginning of the Iron Age, 114 sites were inhabited, with almost 100 of those being entirely new settlements. The pattern is striking: most of the scattered Bronze Age towns were abandoned, and an enormous number of new and permanent villages were established. In short, Iron Age Palestine witnessed a dramatic growth in the number and density of occupied sites in the hill country.[8]

Why the Israelites should have ventured into uncharted territory is a question for which no decisive answer has been given. Traditionalists tend toward the theological, echoing the Bible's claim that divine promise and election brought displaced Israelites to a homeland. Social historians now see the beginning of widespread settlement in the hill country as in fact constituting a social or even a political revolution. They identify Israelite tribes as social formations composed of disaffected peasants who were rebelling against or escaping from Canaanite and Egyptian exploitation and vowing en masse to establish an alternate and egalitarian society, answerable only to their god Yahweh and not to any human master.[9] The hill country offered a location for their venture, a place to establish settlements of their own, a territory where farmers could work the land and retain the hard-won products of their own labor. This reconstruction of the situation does not actually contradict the biblical view; rather it sees the biblical view as the theological description of a sociopolitical process.

One sociologist who recently offered a critique of the social-revolutionary model of the origins of Israel has suggested that a frontier model should be used to characterize Israel's early experience in the hill country.[10] Whether or not one accepts the proposed synthesis of the theological and social-revolutionary models, certain features of a frontier society were present in Israel's formative period. Identification of these characteristics aids in the understanding of Israel's emergence.

The availability of territory affected the origin of Israel because the potential for expansion into unsettled lands allowed disaffected peoples to leave (or rebel against?) their old homes to find new ones, and to form new life-styles and accompanying belief systems. To put it another way, could Israel have succeeded in breaking away ideologically if there did not exist the actual geographic space in which to break away socially and politically? Frontier societies, like early Israel, feel themselves set apart in fundamental ways from traditional centers of population. The American experience, while vastly removed in fundamental ways from that of Iron Age Israel, nonetheless offers certain value as analogy. The American political revolution combined with expansion into largely unoccupied territories brought about the birth of a new society on the North American continent. The American Colonies, like early Israel, continued certain aspects of the urban centers (as in Europe) while at the same time transforming critical social, political, economic, and ideological dimensions of the old landscape.

Israelites were "frontierspeople," regardless of the theories of social change. Israelites[11] moved into a heavily wooded region and built their new homes in an ecological setting that lacked substantial year-round water supplies. The early generations of Iron Age settlers in the hill country faced tasks far more demanding and extensive than the normal annual cycle of activities of an agrarian people. One brief passage in the Book of Joshua comments directly on the situation of land reclamation. In high antiquity Palestine was covered with woodlands. Stands of evergreen, oak, and terebinth, oi Jerusalem pine and cypress, formed a continuous arboreal mantle.[12] In his charge to the groups to which the highlands were allotted, Joshua tells them "the hill country shall be yours, for though it is a forest, you shall clear it and possess it to its farthest borders" (Josh 17:18).

This Joshua passage deals with the the problem of the wilderness for pioneer farmers. It does not mention the water problem, but the Hebrew Bible is replete with allusions to the difficulty of securing adequate water supplies. Springs are rare, and perennially flowing streams are virtually nonexistent in the hill country. The major supply of water was rain, as the Deuteronomist recognized: "the land . . . is not like the land of Egypt . . ., where you sowed your seed and watered it with your feet, like a garden of vegetables; but the land which you are going over to possess is a land of hills and valleys, which drinks water by the rain from heaven" (Deut 11:10–11). But this rainfall is seasonal, with precipitation concentrated in the winter months. Furthermore, the intensity of the seasonal rainfall as well as the high evaporation rate mean that much of the rain that does fall in winter is lost to agriculture.[13]

The system of dry farming that predominated in the highlands developed primarily in response to water constraints. The villagers selected crops with water requirements that could be met in most years by the winter rains and by the summer dew. But the water needs of the highland farmers were not only those connected directly with agriculture. The human and animal populations required year-round supplies, which nature does not provide in large areas of the hill country. The dearth of perennial water created a problem that could be solved only by human intervention. The solution was the carving of deep cisterns into the bedrock that lay close to the surface of the hilltops where most of the early villages were located.

The introduction of the cistern into the inventory of Iron Age technologies was perhaps the *sine qua non* for the Israelite settlement of the highlands. Water runoffs in the rainy season were channeled into cisterns so that water was available during the long summers when no rain fell. The cisterns therefore augmented the meager water supply available from springs. But more important, they made possible settlements in places far from natural sources. In short, the use of cisterns, lined with slaked-lime plaster to render them water impermeable, greatly improved the water supply. The widespread use of cisterns constituted a technological factor that opened up the highlands as a viable frontier. There were other such factors, but none so singly important.

Archaeologists do not agree about whether or not the Israelites should be credited with the development of the cistern. Albright's classic statement that the Israelites were able to open the highland frontier "thanks to the rapid spread of the act . . . of constructing cisterns and lining them with waterproof lime plaster"[14] is still compelling for many. Others point to earlier Bronze Age cisterns that apparently were lined with slaked lime or to some highland villages built on rock that was nonporous enough to make waterproofing unnecessary.[15]

The role of the Israelites as inventors of technology is a moot point. What stands out as innovative is the presumably unprecedented and widespread use of cisterns in the pioneer period. Several settlements just north of Jerusalem provide good evidence of the plenitude of cisterns at sites associated with Israelites. For example, more than fifty cisterns, most associated with individual houses, were discovered at Tell en–Nasbeh.[16] The excavations at ʿAi found one or more cisterns for every Iron Age I dwelling, and the same appears to have been true at the nearby site of Raddana.[17]

The cutting of cisterns and clearing of forests were among the most immediate challenges facing the highland pioneers. Both tasks required monumental expenditures of labor in terms of time and energy. Many scholars believe that the introduction of iron tools at about this time must have facilitated both enterprises. The very fact that the beginning of hill country settlement coincides with the beginning of the archaeological period called the Iron Age certainly adds to the impression that this was so. However, archaeology has not substantiated such a claim, because the number of implements made of iron in proportion to bronze does not rise significantly in the Iron I period.[18]

Whether with iron or bronze tools, the physical effort involved was substantial. At the outset, the unique challenge of the frontier environment augmented and intensified the amount of human labor necessary for achieving subsistence. The pioneer tasks facing early Israel were of such a magnitude that they were certainly accomplished in ways that affected the lives of all. Our interest, however, lies in how the Israelite response to the new environment particularly affected the lives of women. Countless details of their daily existence must have been determined by the nature of the work load that the group as a whole had to shoulder, and those details for the most part are lost to the modern observer. Yet the constraints of pioneer life would have had an impact on women's lives in some ways that can be suggested.

We have cautioned that with the division of labor along gender lines, no single societal task can be universally assigned to one gender. Nonetheless, strong evidence from cross-cultural studies reveals that certain tasks tend to be performed by men rather than women and vice versa. A case in point is the clearing of land. In horticultural societies at least, men have what might be considered a monopoly in the clearing of fields.[19] There seems to be no convincing argument that the same is not true for agricultural societies, of which ancient Israel was one. Israelite women therefore would not have been involved in the felling of trees and the clearing of undergrowth. Males probably performed these arduous tasks, along with the equally difficult and tedious job of hewing out cisterns.

That men were responsible for tasks specifically associated with the frontier environment in the Palestinian highlands has implications for women's lives. This becomes apparent by considering first the primary activities of any society. Group survival is dependent on the involvement of its members in three basic kinds of activities: reproduction, defense, and the production of subsistence goods.[20] The interrelationship of these activities is meaningful with respect to gender in societies like tribal Israel in which state mechanisms do not interfere with the distribution and use of the products of any of these activities. That is, we can reconstruct the extent to which females and males took on the tasks associated with each activity and in that way begin to estimate their relative contributions to society.

Reproduction, of course, was an exclusively female contribution to Israelite society. Similarly, defense matters fell largely to the males; in the militia system alluded to in the stories of the Judges, the men of the various tribes respond, and in some cases fail to respond, to a call to arms (Judg 4:10; 6:34–35; 7:24; 12:1). The subsistence activities of ancient Israel, as for most social groups, were therefore those in which a shifting balance of female and male participation could take place. We will return in Chapter 8 to a discussion of what the proportions of female and male subsistence labor might have been in ancient Israel. For the present, we suggest that, with men clearing the land, digging cisterns, and performing other pioneering tasks, the labor of Israelite women in subsistence activities would have had to increase. The move to a new agricultural zone created an intensification of subsistence tasks generally, including both pioneer tasks and those necessary for the normal production of food and clothing. Females would have had to perform certain regular productive tasks that otherwise might have been relegated to males alone.

Frontier life meant more work for everyone. It also, no doubt, had its impact on the maternal imperative. The number and spacing of children, like the productive activities that women perform, are related to total societal needs. While the biological potential of women for motherhood is a fundamental factor in the establishment of family size, the variety of family configurations that ethnographers report strongly suggests that environmental and social constraints figure prominently in the way families take shape.[21]

Classic examples of this premise can be found in all types of societies: hunters and gatherers, horticulturalists, plow agrarians, industrialists. Among nomadic foragers, for example, it is advantageous for population size to be limited.[22] Children must literally be carried during much of the year, and women involved in foraging cannot care for a large brood. Extended lactation practices along with the reduced maternal body fat in women who are physically active and who have a diet of grains and fruits apparently contribute to reduced female fertility in such settings. Children few and far between are an adaptive aspect of the economic pattern.

Economic and environmental pressure from the opposite direction—to increase family size—is present in a wide variety of societies and among a range of conditions. Our hypothesis that the demands of pioneer work would have created an impetus for women to bear more children suggests a possible influence on the importance of maternity in pioneer Israel. But it would have been neither the only influence nor the enduring one. The basic economic structure of Israelite life surely affected concepts of ideal family size. The agrarian circumstances of Palestinian farmers throughout the Iron Age shaped the dynamics of family life, including the maternal imperative. Thus we turn now to examine the agricultural economic base of life in the Palestinian highlands.

A Nation of Farmers

Just as an interplay of environmental influences and technological responses characterized Israel's pioneer period and helped shape social structures and values, so too did the hill country environment or ecosystem determine the nature of the agricultural system that the highland farmers established. The settlers chose crops suitable to the land and climate, and they developed technological strategies essential for making the land productive. The combination of environment and technology determined the needs and rhythms of agrarian life and thus the structure and size of the villages and their constituent families. In other words, the agricultural system that best met the particular conditions of the highland setting affected the social organization of the settlers on both the community and family levels. Therefore, examination of the agricultural system becomes necessary.

In *Peasants,* a book analyzing peasant economies throughout the world, Eric Wolf classifies the range of agricultural systems that can be found in the preindustrial world. Under his classification, the Palestinian highland mode of farming would be listed as a Mediterranean variant of a general Eurasian grain farming "ecotype."[23] Wolf's basis for distinguishing ecosystems is by the intensity of cultivation, that is, the relationship between the amount of time the land is planted and the amount during which it lies dormant. While these distinctions are derived from the comparison of fallowing practices, Wolf does consider other critical variables such as land use, farm implements, growing season, and labor. Even this list of variables hardly exhausts the possible determinants.[24] Yet Wolf's and other similar analyses[25] are valuable because of their emphasis on the interrelationship of environmental, technological, and demographic features. The mere consideration of crop selection is not adequate in describing an agricultural system. It is also critical to examine the labor variant, or the demographic variable, which is directly relevant to our interests because it affects family size and gender roles.

Crop selection in the ancient Mediterranean area is easily determined from information contained in the Bible, as well as from analysis of paleobotanical remains and from observation of traditional farming patterns still existing in the less modernized parts of contemporary Mediterranean lands. The primary products of Israelite farming were grain, wine, and oil, and they appear together in a multitude of biblical texts. The blessings of Deuteronomy, for example, involve the promise that God will respond positively if the people obey the commandments: Yahweh will bless "the fruit of your ground, your grain and your wine and your oil" (Deut 7:13). Through the prophet Hosea, Yahweh addresses wayward Israel as a people who "did not know that it was I who gave her the grain, the wine, and the oil" (Hos 2:8). And the future promise in Joel has Yahweh assuring the suffering people: "Behold, I am sending to you grain, wine, and oil, and you will be satisfied" (Joel 2:19).

However, agriculture in the highlands was not limited to this triad. The famous seven species of the Promised Land include four other products: "For the LORD your God is bringing you into a good land . . ., a land of wheat and barley, of vines and fig trees and pomegranates, a land of olive trees and honey" (Deut 8:7–8). This basic variety of fruit trees and cereals was further supplemented by animal husbandry. Untilled hillsides provided abundant pasturage for livestock; besides providing a protein source, animals were also an insurance against starvation in the face of the constant risk of drought and consequent crop failure. Although the total variety of locally produced foodstuffs was not large, it was certainly adequate to sustain the nutritional needs of the population.

The development of the Israelite crop system was not easily achieved.

Besides the fluctuating pattern of annual rainfall, the Israelites faced a number of serious environmental obstacles. The biblical words describing a "land flowing with milk and honey" create an image that belies the paltry resources available to the highland farmers. A detailed discussion of the environmental constraints on agriculture in the hill country is beyond the scope of this book, but we must describe at least those difficulties that relate most clearly to issues of demography, and hence of gender.

The lands controlled by the early Iron Age settlers were for the most part mountainous. The Israelites failed to gain a foothold in the traditional breadbaskets of Palestine: the coastal plain, the adjacent Shepheleh and Sharon lowlands, and the broad Jezreel Valley. The pioneers had access to only a few narrow valleys. Yet cereal crops were at the core of the ancient economy; for the Israelites as for so many others, bread was the staff of life. Palestine may have even been one of the places where the earliest domestication of the wild progenitor of durum wheat took place some time during the Neolithic period (about 8000 years ago).[26]

The most efficient planting and harvesting of wheat and barley takes place on level ground, where draft animals can pull plows to turn the soil, rows can be planted, and rainwater can penetrate. The scarcity of level ground led to the construction of terraces. Terracing creates narrow tiered strips of land for grain growing as well as an area for planting olive trees and grapevines. Without terracing, self-sufficient agriculture in the highlands might not have been possible.

Although the remains of terraces are notoriously difficult to date, archaeologists have identified a number of systems dating to the period of earliest Israelite settlement. Terracing has been found in the Iron I villages of ʿAi and Raddana north of Jerusalem, and evidence of grain cultivation in these terraces has also been discovered.[27] Along with the archaeological corroboration of the early Israelite use of terracing, the biblical record mentions terraced fields at an early date. The Song of Deborah (Judg 5), which is one of the oldest pieces of literature in the Hebrew Bible, and thus dates to the period of earliest Israel, apparently contains a reference to terraces. A verse (Judg 5:18) normally translated "heights of the field" (RSV) is more accurately rendered "terraced fields."[28] Similarly, an ancient elegy from the end of the premonarchic period (2 Sam 1:21) should be translated "O mountains of Gilboa, O terraced fields" rather than by the awkward "fields of offerings" or "upsurging of the deep" found in many English translations.[29] In addition, many later biblical contexts using the word *śadeh,* usually rendered as "field," probably describe not fields but terraces.[30] In summary, it is clear from both textual evidence and archaeological remains that the introduction of terrace systems to Palestine coincided with the settlement of the highlands.

This deceptively simple technological device, hillside terracing, made all the difference. It allowed the creation of fields, orchards, gardens, and vineyards on slopes otherwise too steep or rocky for anything but thorns and scrub oak to grow. Some scholars would have terraces be the *sine qua non* for the ability of the Israelites to settle the highlands, while others suggest that the settlers turned to terracing only after they had established small villages and needed to expand their productivity.[31] If the Israelites did not invent terrace agriculture, they surely developed it in an unprecedented way. The Palestinian landscape still bears the marks of their terracing, and some of these terraces, probably dating back to Iron Age antiquity, are in use today.

From a functional viewpoint, terracing is an ingenious solution to a range of problems besetting highland farmers.[32] It not only provided level surfaces for crops, but the removal of stones needed for the terracing exposed a layer of cultivable soil. Furthermore, it made dry farming (farming without irrigation) possible. While the cisterns solved the water problem for humans and animals, they did not meet the agricultural needs. The farmers learned to plant their crops, especially the grains, in coordination with the rainy season. But without a device that could cope with the rapid runoff of rainwater on the hillside inclines, the meager soil would not have absorbed enough water even during the wet months to sustain a grain crop. Because the precipitation is often very heavy in the winter, terraces that reduce the speed of water's downflow not only increase its chances of penetrating the soil but also protect the soil and crops from erosion.[33]

Extensive terracing required a huge output of human energy. Though simple in concept, the construction of terracing was a "complex operation demanding a staggering investment of time and labor."[34] Furthermore, the initial construction of terraces did not mean the end of labor requirements. Terraces need to be maintained. Regular attention to the dry-laid stone enclosure walls was essential to correct and forestall the potential destructiveness of driving rain and rushing water. It is noteworthy that agencies of governments that promote development often hesitate to introduce terracing into certain communities because of the high labor costs involved.[35] Without a large initial output of human energy and an ongoing vigilant maintenance effort, terraces cannot fulfill their multifunctional potential.

With terracing, the highland settlers thus became dependent on a markedly labor-intensive agriculture. So costly were the making and maintaining of terraces that, as one analyst of ancient Israel's agriculture suggests, a suprafamily collective labor system would have been necessary in order for terracing to succeed.[36] Collective responsibility for dealing with terrace systems may well have developed; but the labor demands of terracing, like those of clearing forests and cutting cisterns, would still have put pressure on individual members of the society. For women, the increased labor needs had a double impact: more work meant women became more involved in production; in addition, increased labor needs required a larger work force, which in turn called for larger families.

The relationship between pressure to increase family size and the concomitant increase in the amount of food and goods needed to maintain larger families is not easy to reconstruct. Perhaps some sort of spiral effect can be suggested to account for the general population growth and extended land use that were evident as the decades of the Iron I period passed. The overall process of intensification of agriculture involves the complex interweaving of demographic and economic needs. The difficulty in balancing these needs may underlie in part the eventual shift in Israel to a monarchic government, which provided centralizing mechanisms to organize labor, to spread the risks of highland agriculture, and to secure additional territorial or market resources. But in the early centuries of Israel's existence, responsibility for meeting the extraordinary labor requirements of highland dry farming lay with local communities and rested ultimately on the shoulders of both women and men and on the reproductive capacity of women.

Technological aspects of highlands agriculture were clearly important; but other influences also played a part in the kind of labor force that was needed. The very nature of the crops, climate, growing season, and harvest times created special labor needs. Israel's Mediterranean ecotype did not allow for an even spread of agricultural tasks throughout the year. Rather, some seasons of the year required concentrated efforts. The sowing of the all-important grain optimally took place within a rather limited period of time at the beginning of the rainy season. Even more critical than the time of sowing was the need to harvest the crops within the few weeks or even days between their ripening and the onset of the "latter rains"—sudden downpours coming late in the spring after a short period of dry weather. Because these cloudbursts could rot or destroy the fully matured grain, the harvest had to take place before these late rains began.[37] Similarly, ripened fruit had to be gathered and sun-dried before the fall rains.

Given the climate and the geomorphology of the highlands, there was little that the farmers could do to stagger sowing or to spread out the harvest schedule. Production cycles determined by the crop selection and the seasonal weather patterns inevitably created labor-intensive periods. It is possible that community efforts reflected in some biblical passages were initiated to accommodate the labor demands at particular times in the agricultural calendar. For example, the village threshing floors mentioned in several biblical texts (e.g., 1 Sam 23:1; Ruth 3:2–6) should be understood as examples of communal cooperation at harvest time.[38] These cooperative efforts only partially offset the demands of the labor-intensive agricultural system, which involved all able-bodied workers and made it necessary to increase the number of such workers.

The survival and success of the farm villages involved the hard work of all and the creation of an adequate labor supply. One wonders whether, under such conditions, there existed tension between the need for women to contribute labor and the need to bear many children. Social scientists suggest that such possible tension would have been more apparent than real. The idea of motherhood and work as competing alternatives for women is a product of recent history and is not normally applicable to ancient or preindustrial societies. And even for industrial societies, where child-care systems must be more consciously shaped, these two aspects of women's lives can coexist in continuity with patterns known from past times. Alice Rossi comments explicitly on the combination of labor and motherhood:

> In the long evolution of the human species, women have always engaged in productive labor along with childbearing and -rearing. Hence women in industrial societies are not departing radically from the past when they combine childrearing and employment. All women work, and they always have—sometimes as producers of goods and services on the land and in the household, sometimes for wages in the marketplace.[39]

The picture that emerges of Israelite women in highland villages is of hard-working women who also gave birth to many children. At first glance such a pattern contradicts the picture that economists such as Ester Boserup have drawn. In her classic book, *Woman's Role in Economic Development,* Boserup rightly points to the increase in labor specialization and division of labor according to gender that characterize developing agricultural systems.[40] She investigated female and male participation in productive tasks in a variety of traditional farming systems ("traditional" meaning not based on scientific methods or involving mechanization or modern technologies). Boserup then made a series of generalizations about gender roles in farming:

> In very sparsely populated regions where shifting cultivation is used, men do little farm work, the women doing most. In somewhat more densely populated regions, where the agricultural system is that of extensive plough cultivation, women do little farm work and men do much more. Finally, in regions of intensive cultivation of irrigated land, both men and women must put hard work into agriculture in order to earn enough to support a family on a small piece of land.[41]

If the Israelite highlands are identified as a moderately populated area and cultivated by plow agriculture, such a pattern might lead to the assumption that Israelite women did not perform much farm work. However, Boserup's conclusions must be considered carefully. Most of the radical changes that she observed in female participation in agriculture came about as the result of agricultural intensification, notably, the change from a horticultural to a truly agricultural economy through the introduction of the plow. She also observed the male predominance in agricultural work in long-established farming communities, where adaptive shifts had taken place centuries if not millennia earlier. Her work describes patterns found today in Arab villages in the Palestinian highlands, for example, but it cannot be expected to fit the situation that would have existed when that territory was *first* occupied. In fact, the amount of female participation in agricultural work can either increase or decrease in relation to the relocation to new village sites and to the adoption of new technologies. For formative Israel, there is good reason to suspect that, initially at least, the new environment and also the agrarian and technological response to it brought increased female participation. In Chapter 5, our close reading of Genesis 3 will provide some biblical evidence for the intensification of female labor in early Israel.

Boserup's study concentrated on farming chores in and of themselves, but these chores are hardly the full complement of labor needs. The processing and preparation of the foods along with other tasks not directly part of childrearing were also part of the labor demand in an agricultural society. To the extent that Iron I Israel consisted of self-sufficient families in self-sufficient villages, female participation in subsistence work as a whole must be considered. We shall examine the characteristics of self-sufficiency and household management in Chapter 7.

Survivors in the Land

Both the highland environment and the agricultural system affected the demographics of the settlers in the hill country. During the pioneer period, an opening frontier created conditions in which labor would have been in short supply. As important as the ecosystem and the economic base were in exerting pressures to increase the number of workers, these influences do not tell the whole story. We must look also to the demographic situation as a whole in the East Mediterranean world as the Bronze Age ended and the Iron Age began.

The waning of the Bronze Age throughout the Mediterranean basin was marked by disruptions and turmoil in lands that had survived with some measure of stability for centuries. But the causes of that disruption are not easy to determine. Perhaps a microclimatic change severely curtailed food supplies in regions to the north of the Mediterranean Sea. This would have had a ripple effect, displacing large groups of people and weakening the political structures of the city-states and nation-states that were invaded by outsiders or that found their own economies suffering.[42]

One of the most devastating and dramatic features of the demise of the Bronze Age was the widespread depopulation of many traditional centers of population. The threat of plague played a role in the weakening of Late Bronze Age civilization, whether as cause or effect. Biblical passages clearly show that disease along with famine and warfare could cause even mighty cities to collapse. The prophets believed that these ills were sent by God as punishment to wayward people. "The LORD said to me: 'Do not pray for the welfare of this people. Though they fast, I will not hear their cry, and though they offer burnt offering and cereal offering, I will not accept them; but I will consume them by the sword, by famine, and by pestilence [*deber*]' " (Jer 14:11–12). Similarly, the curses at the end of both Leviticus and Deuteronomy provide the hideous details of how the Lord would bring about the destruction of a wayward people. Along with famine and warfare, dreaded disease would bring to a painful end the lives of those who disobeyed God's word.

The spread of disease and its treatment in the modern world is radically different from the experience of our ancestors. In a fascinating reconstruction of the course of pestilential infections among human populations, the historian W. H. McNeill emphasizes how difficult it is for us to appreciate the ubiquitous presence and consequences of infections in the ancient world. Our concerns with public health tend to focus on chronic illness, mental disorders, or problems of aging: problems that have always existed but have become prominent because of increased longevity in the western world. But in the past, health concerns were centered on the dramatic effects of pestilential disease.

> The sporadic outbreak of pestilence, in any of its dread forms, was a terrifying and ever-present possibility. Although statistical and clinical data allowing precise definition of which infections killed how many people, when and in what places are unattainable before the nineteenth century—and remain spotty even then—we may still observe major changes in patterns of pestilential infection.[43]

McNeill goes on to chart the course of infections in humans and makes some surprising and compelling claims. For example, the extraordinary success of relatively few Spaniards in converting a continent of South American Indians to Christianity was due in part to the relative immunity of the Spaniards to smallpox, which they brought to the New World, where it ravaged the native population. The God of the Spaniards, in sparing the white man, appealed to the demoralized Indians who survived the lethal epidemic.[44] McNeill also recounts other examples in which the outbreak of disease brought about major political changes. The examples are instructive in that they also alert us to ways for culling information from nonmedical texts about disease among premodern peoples.

In ancient sources, references to disease tend to appear in the guise of theological language. Deaths from sickness, especially when concentrated in time and place, are recorded as divine action. How else could the ancients deal with the apparently inexplicable spread of lethal illness? And even in more recent times, the onset of disease (such as AIDS) is perceived by some as God's doing, even as God's punishment. Written texts as old as Gilgamesh or Atrahasis provide evidence of the human attempt to deal with the problem of disease. In Gilgamesh, the gods debate the value of the deluge just brought to the world. Ea suggests such total devastation was not necessary. Famine or pestilence would have been preferable:

> Instead of thy bringing on the deluge,
>   Would that a famine had risen up to lay low mankind!
> Instead of bringing on the deluge,
>   Would that pestilence had risen to smite mankind![45]

For the hero Atrahasis, too, the disastrous flooding he witnessed on the Mesopotamian plains was the greatest devastation the gods could send. But famine, drought, and plague were only a few degrees lower in their severity. The gods resorted to one of these calamities when "the peoples multiplied" and the "noise of mankind" became intense, that is, when the land became overpopulated and concomitant political strife erupted, disturbing the repose of the pantheon.[46]

Our biblical ancestors likewise attributed the devastation of disease to God's actions. The theological explanation for the widespread and sudden loss of human life is often couched in language describing the movements of one of Yahweh's angelic messengers, those heavenly beings found throughout scripture as the divine carriers of God's word and will to the human world. When God's will meant death by plague, the phrase "angel of death" or "angel of the LORD" appears. Perhaps the most dramatic example is the biblical account of the miraculous delivery of Jerusalem from destruction by the Assyrian war machine in the eighth century BCE: "and that night the angel of the LORD went forth, and slew a hundred and eighty-five thousand in the camp of the Assyrians" (2 Kgs 19:35). The text does not mention disease, but years later Herodotus (II: 141) recalls this event and records a tradition apparently linking it with plague. Disease has always been more lethal than enemy weapons among premodern armies.[47]

Having acknowledged the nonmedical language in ancient documents that describe waves of deadly disease, we can recognize the diseases in the premodern world. The Bible itself has a modest vocabulary in dealing with various illnesses and diseases. Like all people, the ancient Israelites were subject to the periodic outbreak of endemic parasitic disease, that is, infections which occur in a community more or less all the time without much alteration from year to year or even century to century.[48] The biblical word *deber,* usually translated "pestilence," probably refers to recurrent and devastating outbreaks of endemic disease (see the quotation from Jeremiah, p. 64).

Another term, *maggephah,* is normally translated "plague" in English and refers to epidemics, to the abnormal occurrence of acute infectious disease. In such awful instances, the death rate can be extraordinary. Epidemiological statistics for periods when records were kept reveal the enormous loss of life that plagues can cause. One-third to one-half of the population of Europe is thought to have died in the thirteenth century CE from virulent bubonic infection.[49]

Several lines of evidence point to an equally devastating outbreak of plague in another thirteenth century, the thirteenth century BCE, which marked the end of Bronze Age civilization in the ancient world. Disease may or may not have played a causal role in the collapse of national powers and in the destruction of leading urban centers; but disease surely accompanied and exacerbated the calamitous decline in population and polities in the Late Bronze II period. The reconstruction of the deadly epidemics of this time is possible by looking at the biblical evidence, at extrabiblical texts, and at archaeological data.

First, let us look at the biblical sources that reflect the trauma of deadly epidemics. The word "plague" appears in several places in the Pentateuch, chiefly in the nonpriestly passages of the Book of Numbers and also once in Exodus. These texts, despite layers of later explanation, contain narratives rooted in Israel's experience with plague and pestilence in the period preceding settlement in the Palestinian highlands. One such episode is Korah's rebellion, recounted in Numbers 16. Associated with a violent power struggle within the Israelite camp is a devastating plague. The 250 leaders of the rebellious Korahites were consumed in a fire coming forth from the Lord. Before Moses could perform efficacious acts of atonement, another 14,700 people lost their lives to the plague. The number is large and probably symbolic, because it contains multiples of the holy Semitic number seven; yet an outbreak of disease that decimated the Moses group underlies the literary elaborations.

Numbers 21:6 recounts another population loss. The actual word for plague does not appear in that story, but the language reflects a plague situation: "Then the Lord sent fiery serpents among the people, and they bit the people, so that many people of Israel died." Numbers 14:11 is still another text recording disease: only Joshua, who brings back a favorable report, survives a plague that strikes down the others sent ahead to reconnoiter the land of Canaan.

Again, in Numbers 11:1–3, the actual words for plague or pestilence do not appear; the text nonetheless records in other language the outbreak of deadly disease as the effect of God's punitive anger. At a place called Taberah, which means "Burning,"[50] God's "anger was kindled, and the fire of the Lord burned among them, and consumed some outlying parts of the camp." The burning fever of serious illness apparently underlies this statement, which is a theological description of the mysterious onset of disease. Divine anger is associated with the punitive, consuming heat of fire and fever.

The unfortunate incident at Beth Baal Peor, recounted in Numbers 25, also is set in the wilderness period. A number of Israelite men are reported to have participated in an orgiastic rite in connection with the Baal of Peor (Peor is perhaps derived from a Hittite word for fire).[51] God's anger was kindled and turned on all the people. How did they know God was angry? At least 24,000 people are said to have died in an epidemic that broke out at Beth Baal Peor.

Exodus 32 is an additional text dealing with death by plague. The famous story of the Golden Calf is linked with an outbreak of disease: "And the LORD sent a plague upon the people, because they made the calf which Aaron made" (Exod 32:35).

This clustering of texts dealing with the period immediately prior to the settlement of the highlands reflects the spread of epidemic disease in the East Mediterranean at the waning of the Late Bronze Age. The very exodus of the Moses group from Egypt is also associated with plagues, although it is difficult to comprehend what sort of historical experience underlies the highly formalized recounting of the Ten Plagues. Despite the stylized language and the inflated or symbolic numbers associated with those biblical texts mentioning plague, there is every reason to believe that they reflect an authentic experience of the ravages of epidemic disease. Not only do they come from a period of general cultural decline, which a priori may be associated with population decimation; they are also not the only textual evidence for plague at the end of the Late Bronze Age. Extrabiblical textual sources also refer to rampant disease.

The Amarna letters, from the period immediately preceding the Exodus, have been extremely valuable to scholars attempting to reconstruct the social and political world in Palestine at the dawn of Israelite existence. The Amarna archive—so called because of its discovery at Tell-el-Amarna in Middle Egypt—consists of nearly 300 letters. Almost all of the letters were written by Canaanite scribes in Egypt-controlled cities of Palestine, Phoenicia, and southern Syria. Most of the letters complain to the Egyptian overlord about the deteriorating conditions in Palestine. In the process of describing uprisings and battles, some of the letters almost incidentally report the existence of disease. The prince of Megiddo, for example, asks for military aid against the raids of the Shechemites. He justifies his request for "one hundred garrison troops to guard the city" partly on the fact that already, "verily, its city is destroyed by death from pestilence and disease."[52]

From Anatolia at about this time comes the moving testimony of the Plague Prayer of Mursilis. Mursilis was a Hittite king, the son of the powerful monarch Supiluliumas. The plague to which he refers seems to be one which Mursilis' father and his soldiers picked up in a battle against Egyptian forces in southern Syria. The returning army carried the disease back to Hatti land, where it spread among the populace with devastating effects for decades thereafter. Mursilis appeals to the gods to remove the plague from his country and give it to other lands:

What is this ye have done [ye gods]? A plague ye have let into the land. The Hatti land has been cruelly afflicted by the plague. For twenty years now men have been dying. . . . As for me, the agony of my heart and the anguish of my soul I cannot endure any more. . . . The few people who were left to give sacrificial loaves and libations were dying too. . . . The Hatti land, all of it, is dying. . . . O gods, take ye pity on the Hatti land! . . . Look ye upon the Hatti land with favorable eyes, but the evil plague give to [those other] countries![53]

Mursilis' poignant words reveal the widespread loss of population and his belief that the gods are responsible. And the persistence of the plague has grave implications in his way of thinking: with so few people left, the sacrifices to the gods will diminish in quantity and quality, and the anger of the gods cannot be appeased. This is surely a Catch-22, ancient style.

If we take the combined testimony of the Bible and extrabiblical documents, the Late Bronze Age was a period of widespread epidemic disease. Archaeological evidence offers further corroboration. The excavation of the Canaanite city-states reveals the startling fact that most of them suffered severe destruction, marked by a thick layer of ashes. The cities were burned, that much can be said. But archaeology cannot tell us how or why. Scholarly wisdom of past decades attributed these conflagrations to the Israelite invaders, but the present generation of biblical scholars realizes that such an attribution tends toward the speculative.[54]

We have suggested elsewhere[55] that the widespread burnings that marked the end of many Late Bronze cities are not necessarily, in any or all cases, the result of military action. Note that the biblical language prescribing the *herem,* the total destruction of cities (e.g., Josh 6:17–19), is related to the awareness that fire can be used as a drastic measure to halt plague. At the end of Numbers, the Beth Baal Peor incident is recalled and the Israelites are instructed to destroy all the inhabitants of Peor, with the exception of one small part of the population. Everything is to be burnt, except "the gold, the silver, the bronze, the iron, the tin, and the lead, everything that can stand the fire, you shall pass through the fire, and it shall be clean" (Num 31:22–23). Furthermore, all the Israelites who had come into contact with the slain Peorites were instructed to quarantine themselves for seven days and also to purify all their clothing and whatever could be washed (Num 31:19–20). These procedures reveal a primitive awareness of medical matters, an attempt to stop disease by eliminating a diseased population and all the material objects associated with the infected people. The staggering death tolls associated with plague aroused great fear, and measures to deal with communicable disease were accordingly drastic. Documentation for such extreme and seemingly cruel actions taken to restrict the inexorable spread of plague can all too readily be found in European history.[56]

Another kind of archaeological study provides evidence not of plague itself but of a population loss for which plague could easily be a cause. Estimations of population growth and decline for antiquity are extremely difficult to make. Nonetheless, experts have attempted to chart population fluctuations in antiquity on the basis of a large number of variables, including number and size of cities and concentrations of burials in tomb groups. Anthropologist J. L. Angel's study of the East Mediterranean suggests a dramatic population decline in the transition from the Late Bronze Age to the Iron Age. He estimates a population density of thirty people per square kilometer (km^2) at the end of the Bronze Age, a high point for all the Bronze Age. That number had shrunk to a density of nineteen per km^2 or less at the beginning of the Iron Age.[57] In other words, the Iron Age begins with a marked reduction in population in the East Mediterranean, which includes Palestine; some scholars suggest as much as a four-fifths reduction.

In light of all this evidence for widespread population loss, the Israelites who ventured into the highland wilderness at the beginning of the Iron Age were survivors. They were a people who emerged from the upheavals that had brought the Bronze Age to an end. The disease and destruction that had decimated the peoples of the East Mediterranean thus constituted another influence on the demographic character of the Israelites. The severity of the population loss was so dramatic that one wonders if the early Israelites themselves were conscious of the implications of underpopulation for the labor needs of their pioneering agrarian mode of life.

A clue to the Israelite awareness of a serious demographic problem can be found in the biblical passage narrating the infamous Beth Baal Peor incident. One small group of the conquered Midianites was singled out to survive the divinely ordained *herem* (destruction). Who were the individuals who were so important that the Israelites would risk contamination from them while putting all others to death and everything else to the fire? The answer comes in Numbers 31:18: "But all the young girls who have not known man by lying with him, keep alive for yourselves." The extraordinary exception in this case is a population of females suitable to become wives of Israelite men. The sparing of nubile females in the face of the possibility that they might carry the dreaded infectious disease (see the discussion of Numbers 31:19–23) must mean that the Israelites were conscious of the need to replenish or increase their numbers.

Israelite attitudes toward exogamy, the taking of wives from outside their group, varies throughout the biblical period. Sometimes exogamy is implicitly condoned, as when heroic figures such as Moses and David take non-Israelite wives. At other times intermarriage with non-Israelites is explicitly condemned. This problem of Israelite gender relations will resurface in Chapter 8. For the moment, we suggest that in this instance the fluctuating Israelite attitude toward exogamy was tipped in the direction of condoning marriage with outsiders. For serious pragmatic reasons, women from outside the group were considered suitable mates. The pressure on all wives, foreign or native, to bear children must have been considerable.

Recovery from an extended period of plague and population loss was thus a direct demographic factor, as were the indirect ones brought about by the environmental context and the shape of the agrarian economy, inpinging upon the lives of Israelite men and women. Establishing a new life in the corporate sense in the central hill country meant increasing new lives on an individual level. The birthrate in traditional societies is to some degree a strategy that emerges, sometimes unconsciously, to deal with the complex interweaving of societal needs and resources.[58] For ancient Israel, a value system or an ideology encouraging women to have large families—while simultaneously contributing their own productive labor—would have been an effective adaptive mechanism, at least in the early part of Israel's national existence. The Bible is the ideological record of ancient Israel, and we turn now directly to the biblical text to identify traces of an ideology sanctioning such a role for women in the highland villages. In the next two chapters we shall scrutinize Eve in her biblical setting of the garden story of Genesis 2–3; in Chapter 8 the communal needs and motivations for urging procreation become topics for discussion.

4

The Genesis Paradigms for Female Roles, Part I: Genesis 2–3

The early chapters of Genesis challenge our ability to be open-minded in dealing with biblical texts relevant to gender. Perhaps more than any other part of the Bible, those chapters have influenced western notions of gender identity and roles. But we must remember that Genesis 2–3 antedate by a millennium or more the religious traditions that have appropriated those texts as normative statements about human nature. That is, the earliest Jewish and Christian communities used the Genesis stories, as they used many other parts of the already ancient and sacred literature of Israel, to help them deal with their own sociological and theological concerns.

The leaders of nascent postbiblical religion interpreted and emphasized certain features of Genesis 2–3 as they established their own views of creation and gender, of sex and sin. The church fathers and the early rabbis were interpreters of new religious developments emerging from the biblical past, and their views became authoritative and normative. Consequently, we tend to see those pivotal texts of the Hebrew canon through the interpretive eyes of the early Jewish and Christian sages. So fixed in our minds are the explanations of postbiblical tradition that we are hardly aware that the commonly accepted translations and expositions of Genesis 2–3, among other biblical passages, may not accurately or fairly represent the meaning and function of these texts in their original contexts.

No book that was to become part of the canon of the Hebrew Bible was composed after the second century BCE. The authoritative early Jewish and Christian texts—such as the Apocrypha and Pseudepigrapha, the New Testament and the Mishna—nearly all postdate the material in the Hebrew Bible. They are, of course, important in a consideration of any biblical passage. Yet, as we have already suggested, the exegetical contributions of early Judaism and Christianity tend to tell us more about the particular needs of the latter groups than about the meaning of a text at the time when it first emerged as an authoritative statement destined to be included in the sacred literature of western religious tradition.

Consequently, to be truly open-minded we must consider the possibility of differences between the meaning of texts in ancient Israel and their meaning in post-Israelite biblical religion. The rabbis and fathers of the early Christian era were an extremely active and prolific group of people. They accorded the Hebrew Bible a place of central importance in their search for religious values during the turbulent times in which they lived. The hermeneutic perspective of the faithful has often been obvious and self-consciously achieved in recent epochs, but the extent to which the ancient commentators were themselves aware of how the challenges of their own world affected their understanding of a past world is debatable. While the ancient sages may have been quite unaware of how they reshaped earlier meanings, it is incumbent on us to identify their exegetical shifts.

When it comes to matters of gender (for which certain biblical texts have held such a powerful place in the millennia following their formulation), the imperatives for identifying viewpoints not inherent in the texts become especially compelling. The function of the passages for ancient Israel is assumed to have been the same as for the later observers, so all-pervasive has been the force of those later authorities. The attitudes engendered by the Judeo-Christian tradition are so well entrenched in contemporary religion that they constitute powerful barriers to an understanding of the antecedent functions of certain texts in Israelite life. We are simply not aware that we often look at Israelite texts with post-Israelite eyes.

An analogy from the natural sciences is apt in helping us comprehend how powerful the barriers of religious doctrine can be. Historians of science have long wrestled with the problem of why it took so long for scientists to discover certain aspects of the physical world. Why was there such a dearth of scientific discovery in the centuries between the early awakening of scientific inquiry in the classical world and the breakthroughs of modern science in the Renaissance? The answer, at least in part, lies in recognizing the constraints of Christian theology on the inquiring scientific mind in the Byzantine and medieval periods. Arthur Koestler, in describing the enormous breakthrough of a scientist such as Kepler, asserts that "some of the greatest discoveries . . . consist mainly in the clearing away of psychological road-blocks which obstruct the approach to reality; which is why, *post factum,* they appear so obvious."[1]

The barriers caused by the Judeo-Christian tradition must be identified and removed before the original force of the texts can speak in a voice uncomplicated by later voices. The theology of later generations had access neither to historical tools nor to a social scientific awareness necessary for understanding and therefore were susceptible to creating misrepresentations of the past. In some ways, the problems of misrepresentation caused by the views of later authorities is akin to the obstructionist role of theologians in their opposition to the scientific endeavors of Galileo and others. Galileo bravely criticized the church authorities with the observation:

> Let us grant then that theology is conversant with the loftiest divine contemplation, and occupies the regal throne among the sciences by this dignity. But acquiring the highest authority in this way, if she does not descend to the lower and humbler speculations of the subordinate sciences and has no regard for them for they are not concerned with blessedness, then her professors should not arrogate to themselves the authority to decide on controversies in professions which they have neither studied nor practiced. Why, this would be as if an absolute despot being neither a physician nor an architect, but knowing himself free to command, should undertake to administer medicine and erect buildings according to his whim.[2]

The ancient Jewish and Christian commentators on the Hebrew Bible stand at times as unwitting and unintentional despots by lending the authority of their religious positions to their statements and commentaries, which thereby achieve canonical form or force of their own. These statements did not, could not, use the methodology of the "lower and humbler speculations" of philology, archaeology, anthropology, or historical criticism; and so the ancients are to be forgiven. But contemporary research can use the "subordinate sciences," and in so doing, hammer away at the enduring psychological barriers developed in the early centuries of the Christian era and perpetuated until the last few centuries. An example of these psychological barriers is the way Eve appears in religious literature postdating Genesis 2–3.

Apart from the early chapters of Genesis, there is in the Hebrew Bible no mention of Eve. Other figures or events, such as the Patriarchs or the Exodus, are often mentioned subsequent to the original narration of their stories. But Eve does not resurface at all in Hebrew scripture and is certainly not a dominant figure in the Israelite canon.

Eve finally appears in extant literature in the second century BCE, when she figures in a work that is not part of the Hebrew canon. After Genesis 2–3, the earliest writing that refers to Eve is probably Ecclesiasticus, or the Wisdom of Ben Sira, which is part of the canon in Catholic but not in Jewish or Protestant Bibles. Ben Sira apparently is alluding to Eve when he says, "From a woman was the beginning of sin, / And because of her we all died."[3] In associating sin with Eve, Ben Sira was probably taking a minority position because his contemporaries tended to ascribe sin either to Adam or, on the basis of Genesis 6:1–4, to the fall of evil angels and their cohabitation with women.[4] Nonetheless, as the first known author to state that sin and death are the negative results of a woman's act, this early sage provided one of the most extraordinarily tenacious interpretations of a biblical narrative.

A century later, the unknown author of a work called the Books of Adam and Eve picked up on Ecclesiasticus' reading of the Adam and Eve story. Written in part as if Eve herself were the author, this pseudepigraphical book leaves no doubt as to the role of Eve in bringing about all the sin and suffering in the world. In passage after passage, Eve recounts and confesses her awful deeds. One sample indicates the tone of Eve's words, as she seeks to relieve the suffering that Adam experiences when God begins to punish him for disobedience. " 'O Lord my God, hand over to me his pain, for it is I who sinned.' And Eve said to Adam: 'My Lord give me a part of thy pains, for this has come to you from fault of mine.' "[5] A related composition also dating to the early first century BCE, the Apocalypse of Moses, similarly underscores the causality of Eve with respect to sin. The anonymous author of that work has Eve proclaim: " 'I have sinned, O God, I have sinned, O God of All, I have sinned before Thee. . . . I have sinned before Thee and all sin hath begun through my doing in the creation.' "[6]

Such attitudes as these, current in the Jewish world in the last few centuries before Christ, entered Christian tradition and can be found in the New Testament in such passages as 1 Timothy 2:13–14: "For Adam was formed first, then Eve; and Adam was not deceived, but the woman was deceived and became a transgressor." Not only is Eve associated with sin; her creation is viewed as secondary and, by implication, of lesser importance.

By the early centuries of the Christian era, instances of such attitudes toward Eve become common in religious literature. The association of Eve and sin with sexuality and lust, already present in texts such as the Books of Adam and Eve and the New Testament, is expanded in both Christian and Jewish postbiblical sources, with the serpent playing an increasingly satanic and phallic role. And of course the more Eve is

identified as the source of sin, the more urgent becomes the need to
control, subdue, and dominate her. Eve is seen as representative of her
sex, and thus all women are regarded as requiring subjugation to wiser
and superior male figures.

As if this situation were not already problematic enough, it led to still
another kind of interference with our vision of the Eve of Genesis: the
problem of translations. That is, most of us read about Eve in texts that
are not in their original language. While translations can and do often
accurately represent the texts they render, they can also—often unconsciously—subtly change and distort the original meaning. Because the
process of translating the Hebrew Bible began in the same centuries that
the interpretive literature just described was being composed, the ancient
translations also suffer from the possibility of bias and distortion.

The antifeminist views of St. Jerome, for example, subtly influenced
the way he dealt with passages about women in his extremely influential
translation of the Hebrew Bible, known as the Vulgate. Commissioned
by Pope Damasus in 382 CE, the Vulgate became the authoritative Bible
of the Catholic Church. Jerome was a highly competent Hebrew scholar,
yet his hostility toward women and his fear of them constituted "such a
powerful and all-pervasive influence upon him that the accuracy of his
vulgate translation itself has been affected."[7] The Vulgate is the standard Roman Catholic Bible and an influence on much of the western
world through the influence of Latin on Romance languages. The smallest and most subtle examples of antifemale bias in the Vulgate can have
far-reaching consequences. This is not the place to deal with Jerome's
antifeminism, but it is the place to emphasize the existence of bias in
translation. The matter of such bias will figure in the discussion of the
Eve story in this chapter and will be prominent in the exposition of
Genesis 3:16 in the next chapter.

In both religious texts and standard translations dating to the centuries following the formation of the Hebrew canon, interpretations of the
Hebrew narrative of Genesis 2–3 became common. The themes of female sin and inferiority were introduced, although they were not, as we
shall see, part of the original text. Thereafter, variations on those
themes became endless. Western literature and art are replete with
expressions of the Eve story cast so as to express the author's or artist's
own social views. Perhaps the most influential of all has been John
Milton's *Paradise Lost,* which developed the Eden tale so strongly that
many of our present recollections of the biblical story are more faithful
to his portrayal of Eve or Satan than to the original Hebrew narrative.

Milton no doubt did not intend to distort the biblical material with which he worked. Yet his own world view worked its way into the characterizations in his poetry: "[Milton's] hierarchical world view led him to assume that every creature had its proper place in an elaborately descending order from God who is pure spirit, to angels, men, women, plants, and finally non-living creatures. Even within human society, this hierarchy was necessary."[8] Consequently, Milton saw both political rulers and husbands as God's deputies, controlling the state and the family, respectively. Although both Adam and Eve were created in God's image, Eve was somehow less in God's image: Adam's "perfection far excell'd Hers in all real dignity" (*Paradise Lost* 10:150–51).

Eve indeed has "fallen." But the term "Fall" in relation to the Eve–Adam narrative does not occur in the Hebrew Bible, and its widespread use is a good example of how an interpretive concept has become so familiar that no one notices that it does not belong to the Genesis story itself. In fact, the idea of a "Fall" came into the Christian world through Orphic thought. Classic expression of this idea is found in the *Phaedrus,* where Plato describes heavenly perfections shedding their wings and *falling* to the earth to be implanted and born as humans.[9] It can only apply if one begins with the notion of an originally perfect human. But that point is debatable for the Hebrew Bible, where the first pair are creatures of earth and not of heaven. Thus, it is more appropriate to drop the term "Fall" from any reference to the story in its Hebraic context. It is used only ironically at the beginning of this paragraph, to highlight the perceptions of Eve as having changed radically—from the perceptions embedded in the ancient Genesis narrative to the clearly derogatory ones that appear almost a millennium later.

The later, derogatory perceptions of Eve thus constitute major barriers to our ability to see the function of the Genesis 2–3 narrative as it existed in Israel before the "fall of Eve," that is, before the emergence of the influential expositions of Jewish and Christian antiquity. The barriers are considerable but not insurmountable. With the realization that the ancient biblical texts were both responsive to and reflective of their own late second or early first millennium world, and with some knowledge that conditions in that world were different from those in later times, we can discover the Eve that existed before the time of her linkage with sin and suffering. We can recover the pristine Eve. We now set about to do that in this chapter by examining the Eden narrative as a literary piece and as a reflection of the particular conditions of highland life, as described in the previous chapter, to which the agrarian Israelites had to adapt. Then, in Chapter 5, we will take a close look at perhaps the most troublesome verse of all, Genesis 3:16.

A New Look at Eden

Since the very beginning of their awareness of the need for feminist hermeneutics, feminist biblical scholars have been particularly concerned with the powerful and, to their mind, detrimental impact of the traditional postbiblical interpretations of the second creation story. With their focus on Genesis 2–3, they join the ranks of the enormous group of scholars[10] who have commented on various aspects of Genesis, including the Eden narrative. The pioneer in modern feminist research of the creation stories is Phyllis Trible, of Union Theological Seminary of New York. Her methodology involves an analysis of the literary construction and characteristics of the Genesis 2–3 text. Employing what is known as rhetorical criticism, she has explored certain stylistic features that have been overlooked or ignored by earlier critics but that provide the major clues to the meaning of the text.[11]

In the first of a series of analyses of various biblical texts, Trible's study of Genesis 2–3 is a landmark achievement among her efforts to reclaim the Bible for feminists and to provide fresh perspectives on difficult passages. Originally published in 1973,[12] the Genesis 2–3 material appeared five years later in a more developed form as a chapter in *God and the Rhetoric of Sexuality.* At the outset she exposes the misogynist references that have dominated our understanding of the text over the centuries. Both the opponents of an androcentric order and its advocates have misunderstood the tale because of the power of traditional interpretations such as those cited earlier in this chapter. Feminists unwittingly rejecting the authority of Genesis 2–3 and acknowledged traditionalists invoking it have together subscribed to at least a dozen gender-related dogmas that they assume to be set forth by the creation account.

What are some of these interpretive readings—or misreadings—that have almost achieved a canonicity of their own? The following[13] are among the most tenacious and also the most erroneous:

    1. A male God creates a man first, which makes the man superior, and the woman second, which automatically means she is inferior.

    2. Woman is created as a helpmate, a lower-order companion to stave off male loneliness.

    3. Woman tempted man and is thus responsible for all human sinfulness.

    4. Woman is cursed by pain in childbirth.

These and other similar assumptions about women and men and gender relations are based on the familiar Genesis story. But careful analysis shows that such statements are not intrinsic to the text. On the contrary, they violate its integrity, rhetoric, lexical choices, and cultural setting.

This is not the place to examine in detail the ways in which feminist scholars have challenged these nearly sacred suppositions. Trible deals with many of them in great detail, and J. Higgins' work is to be recommended especially in reference to the popular misconception of Eve as temptress and source of sin.[14] However, we shall summarize some of the major points that emerge when the barriers of traditional perspectives are removed, and make some observations that place the Eve and Adam tale in the context of ancient Israelite life. Also, in the next chapter we shall examine in detail the troubling verse (3:16) that contains God's punitive charge to the woman and that, erroneously translated and understood, underlies item 4 above, namely the notion that childbirth is painful and cursed. More important, it forms the scriptural basis for the powerful assumption that God mandated male dominance over females. By correcting the translation and explaining the syntax, we shall challenge the traditional androcentric interpretations and offer a more accurate understanding of the text.

To begin with, let us consider the literary identity of the Eden account. Broadly speaking, Genesis 2–3 belongs simultaneously to two genres of folk literature: "creation myths" and "etiologies." Genesis 3 also contains fragments of a third genre, that of "wisdom parable" (see below, pp. 91–92). The simple tale clearly operates on many levels and conveys profound messages about human existence.

The "creation myth" genre represents the tale on its most overt level. The use of the word "myth" does not mean either that these two chapters of Genesis are false or that they are recounting some quaint and antiquated story. Rather, "creation myth" suggests that Genesis 2–3 is a tale dealing with origins; as such it is a tale meant to help human beings come to grips with the nature and meaning of their own existence. In this sense, the biblical creation stories differ fundamentally in purpose from scientific explanations or theories of origins. At the same time, the biblical accounts share with the creation stories of other ancient peoples the quest for an understanding of their own present reality rather than of their actual human origins. Genesis is perhaps technically nonmythological in that it does not relate the escapades of superhuman beings. Yet, it does belong to the genre of ancient mythology in its ultimate concern with the nature and meaning of human existence. It is a true *mythos,* a parable of the human situation. The ancient Hebrew writers, along with their counterparts in Babylon, Memphis,* Athens, and Rome, crafted tales about people and god(s) that would help them conceptualize their own place in the cosmos.

It follows from this fundamental characteristic of ancient tales of creation that they tend to have a strong etiological flavor. In trying to deal with the realities of their own lives and societies, the largely anonymous contributors to mythic literature understood their present order to be the result of divine actions. From them, the etiology, or "explanation" of how things got to be the way they are, functioned as a sanction for the present order. Etiology helped prescientific people answer the perennial questions about how they fit into the natural and social worlds; and it also helped them to accept the answers. Etiologies thus cannot be read as statements of historical or scientific causality. The Roman historian Sallust, in the first century BCE, aptly characterized such products of the human struggle for understanding: "A myth has never happened. It happens every day."[15]

In considering the biblical narratives in Genesis 2–3 as myths of origin and as etiologies, it is helpful to recognize their archetypal value. Archetypes, according to one useful definition, "reveal and define form, showing how a truth of a moment has the same structure as an absolute or eternal one."[16] Prototypes, in contrast, are formative events that happen in time and influence subsequent generations. In the Bible, the Exodus looms large as the ultimate prototypical event: it is reenacted and recounted so that the inheritors of the Exodus traditions can experience the values and meanings inherent in the original event.

The problem for the biblical creation stories is that they contain archetypes but are cast as prototypes by virtue of their place at the fore of what is the first great historical tradition ever recorded. The Eden narrative probably circulated as an independent and "pungent description" of every woman and every man. As the Pentateuch took shape, that description was placed at the beginning of Israel's national history.[17] But the distinction between archetype and prototype should not thereby be blurred. To grasp the value of having stories about origins or "first" anything, one must appreciate the literary and conceptual value of "first" meaning "all" or "always."[18] The characters in the creation story present the *essential* (archetypal) features of human life, not the *first*

---

*Memphis was an important city in ancient Egypt. Located just south of modern Cairo, it was the capital of the oldest Egyptian dynasty and is associated with one of the oldest creation stories, the "Memphite Theology of Creation," which goes back to the third millennium BCE.

(prototypical) humans in a historical sense. The features depicted for the "original" couple are the features thought by the ancient author to be shared by all: our differentiation from God on the one hand and from plant and animal life on the other. The Genesis tale is couched in temporal language because it presents human life, which exists in time, and not because the specific characters existed in time. In a sense the characters are symbolic of their kind.

With this understanding of the nature and role of Genesis 2 (and 3) as a creation story, we can turn to more specific and interrelated aspects of its language and message, notably as they deal with gender. It is important to remember in any analysis of gender in the Bible, with respect to God or human, that Hebrew is a gendered language. To take at face value the gender of a noun or of a verb inflected according to gender is to ignore or preempt those instances in which an inclusive, neutral, or general meaning may be intended. That is, certain words may be rendered as masculine in places where they are not meant to specify gender.

Perhaps the best example is the generic word for "human," *'adam,* which permeates the creation tales and appears frequently elsewhere in the Bible. This word is usually, if not universally, translated as "man." In most cases the gender specific value of the word "man" is thereby erroneously attached to a collective singular Hebrew word designating "human" life, as a category to be distinguished from God on the one hand and animals on the other.[19]

To translate *'adam* as "man" in the creation stories is to imply a priority for male existence and also to ignore a magnificent Hebrew wordplay. The word for the stuff from which the first human being is formed is *'adamah,* usually translated as "ground" or "earth." The words for "human" and for "ground" are thus connected phonetically and perhaps also etymologically. Texts such as Genesis 2:7, in their traditional renderings, do not communicate either the generic nature of "man" or the integral connection of humanity with its earthly matrix. Consider the Revised Standard Version's rendering:

> Then the LORD God formed man of dust from the ground and breathed into his nostrils the breath of life and man became a living being.

In order to capture the flavor and meaning of the original text, such verses ought to be rendered something like:

> Then God Yahweh formed an *earthling* of clods from the *earth* and breathed into its nostril the breath of life; and the *earthling* became a living being.

Alternately, "human" might be substituted for "earthling" and "humus" (fertile soil) for "earth" in order to capture the pun and the assonance of the Hebrew:

> Then God Yahweh formed a *human* from clods of the *humus* and breathed into its nostrils the breath of life, and the *human* became a living being.

After all, English "human" is not the combination of *hu* with *man* but rather is derived from a theoretical Indo-European root (*ghum*) meaning "earth" or "ground" from which comes Latin *humus* (earth) and Old English *guma* (man).

The obvious play on words should not, however, be taken as mere punning.[20] Names or substantives were not simply labels; they were also indicators of the very essence of the thing or creature designated. It is highly significant that the first creature is not inherently gendered, even though such distinctions were readily available. The term *'adam* tells us that the essence of human life is not its eventual classification into gendered categories but rather its organic connection to the earth. And the earth in this case is not general, vague, unspecified soil or ground but rather *'adamah*, that reddish brown substance, or humus, that is capable of absorbing water, being cultivated, and supporting life.[21]

At the very outset, human existence is thus portrayed as inextricably related to that which makes life possible, arable land. The agrarian orientation of the Israelites is at work in the shaping of the narrative of creation. Other imagery is present, namely the anthropomorphic idea of a creator God taking lumps of earth and fashioning them into a life form which then is vivified by the divine breath. Yahweh the sculptor is a metaphor drawn from another function served by the malleable clods of earth; such clods, or clay, served as the raw materials for making the ubiquitous and indispensable ceramic vessels and bricks of the ancient world. Yet the primacy of the agricultural imagery is apparent from the very positioning of verse 7 in the narrative.

The creation of the earth creature in verse 7 is the centerpiece of a longer passage (Gen 2:4b or 5 to 2:9) that is full of language of plant life.[22] Indeed, let us not forget that Genesis 2 and 3 have a garden as their setting. Perhaps we are so familiar with the designation "Garden of Eden" that we fail to appreciate the role of growing things—plants and trees—in its organization and meaning. Scholars have long noticed the distinction between the opening of Genesis 1, with primal chaotic water everywhere (Gen 1:2, 6–7, 9–10), and the beginning of the second creation account in Genesis 2, without rain but with orderly rivers lying to the east. The watery chaos of primeval existence in the first account is just one of several features Genesis 1 shares with Mesopotamian epics of creation.

But the second account bespeaks a Palestinian setting and a yearning for a place where waters flowed continuously: an "Eden," a place or an environment in which the constant fear of drought would be lifted from the anxious shoulders of the Israelite farmers. Life was not possible, according to Genesis 2:5, without two critical elements: rainfall and human labor. Let us look more closely at that verse.

> a. No *bush of the field* was yet on the *land*
> b. Nor had any *grains of the field* yet sprouted
> c. For God Yahweh had not sent *rain* upon the *land*
> d. Nor was there an *earthling* to work the *earth*.
> [emphasis and translation mine]

The vocabulary of these lines is grounded in the agricultural world of ancient Israel. In line a, "bush of the field" is a phrase that reflects all growing things. While "fields" can mean either a cultivated or noncultivated expanse, the rather rare Hebrew word for bush apparently means shrubs or plants that grow in the wild.[23] In contrast, "grains of the field" in line b represents field crops, plants that are grown for consumption by people and domesticated animals, plants that were the essence of life for agrarians.

The next two lines correspond to the first two: the conditions of line c allowing for the situation in line a to be reversed, and the cumulative conditions of lines c and d allowing for the cultivation of life-sustaining crops to take place. With rainfall, general vegetation will appear; and with both humans and rain doing their part, grains will sprout up from the earth. Note also the way in which "land" and "earth" are used. The former (*ereṣ* in Hebrew) is a much broader term than the latter, *'adamah*. Although the word for "land" can mean earth or ground in certain instances, it can also be used in a more cosmic sense, to represent the antithesis of heaven (as in Gen 1:1; 2:1, 4). Even where it does mean ground, it is more inclusive; it can refer to unproductive, barren regions as well as arable places.[24] But "earth," as we have already explained, specifies arable soil.

But wait! God does not proceed to put the newly formed human out into the fields to work at growing grain. The reality of human existence in the highlands, as described in Chapter 3, does not yet materialize. Instead it is God and not the human who plants a garden, with fruit-bearing trees. Caught up in the cycle of labor-intensive activity needed to produce grains in the hill country or to build terraces for hillside vineyards and orchards, what better situation could a highland farmer ask for? It is God who brings fruit-bearing trees to the stage of productivity, at which point the human guardians can tend them and collect the edible fruits. The humans have been spared the back-breaking labor of field agriculture and of establishing orchards and vineyards. Furthermore, a steady water supply assures the fertility of the plants.

The human is created in the middle of these two situations: one without rain or workers and hence without food as expressed in verse 5, and the other with availability of food temporarily established by God in verses 8–9. Because the creation of humanity occurs centrally to this arrangement, this passage is telling us that human existence is inextricably caught up with concern for sustenance. The Israelite highlanders, confronted with the daily reality of intensive labor, were drawn to the idea that life might be otherwise. Hence the narrative unfolds; it holds up the ephemeral state of Eden for a brief glimpse and then brings the humans at last into the real world. Why must this be so? Why must humans experience harsh reality? The narrative provides an etiological response to the precariousness of Israelite life, and Yahweh's speeches in Genesis 3 to the female and male give sanction to the apparently inevitable life-style of the Israelite highlanders (see below, pp. 92–94 and Chapter 5).

Let us return now to our lone human standing in the midst of a garden that provides sustenance and beauty, because both are apparently central to human life. While sustenance alone would be sufficient for animals, recognition of an intrinsic human need for more than mere survival is present in the phrase "pleasing to the eyes" (2:9). Differentiation of humans from lower life forms is already anticipated.

Animal life first appears in 2:19–20, but it does not constitute the completion of human existence. God does not intend for the unity of human life, the "one flesh" of 2:24, to consist of a single individual. Hence God casts the human into a comatose state, a state far closer to original nonexistence than is "sleep." The Hebrew of Genesis uses a word that is translated as "deep sleep" in many versions and is different from the word for ordinary sleep. It was a special term for the unconscious state necessary for the the cosmic surgery that will finally bring about sexually differentiated human life.

Gendered life is introduced, and the language describing it establishes the connection between female and male. The relationship between the first two beings, the Woman and the Man (i.e., between any conjugal pair), is set forth in the phrase "suitable counterpart." The traditional English translation, "help meet for him" (King James Version), has given rise to "helpmate." Close analysis of this phrase is thus essential, and the results are revealing. It consists of a noun, based on the verb "to help" and meaning "one who helps," and a prepositional phrase. The function of the latter becomes clear only by noting the ambiguity present in the former. That is, how does "one who helps" or "helper" stand in relationship to the one receiving help?

Traditional interpretations of this story would have us believe that a helper is an assistant or subordinate, who renders aid to a master or superior. Yet, in the Hebrew Bible the noun "helper" can refer to just the opposite, namely, to a superior, notably God, to whom one turns for help in time of distress. Think of the familiar words of Psalm 121:1–2: "From whence does my help come? My help will come from the LORD." Or, consider the etymology of the name Ezra, which is a shortened form of a theophoric name (containing the divine name) meaning "[God is] helper." Or look at Azariah, which means "Yahweh has helped" (one of the most popular names in the Bible, it is used for more than two dozen different individuals).

The noun "helper" can thus indicate either a superior or a subordinate. How can one resolve this ambiguity in any given case? The prepositional phrase in Genesis 2:18 and 20 provides the answer by telling us which kind of helper is meant. In fact, the answer is neither of the possibilities suggested above: the helper stands neither higher nor lower than the one being helped. The prepositional phrase establishes a nonhierarchical relationship between the two; it means "opposite," or "corresponding to," or "parallel with," or "on a par with."

In Genesis 2 the ring, or cyclic, structure of creation[25] is completed by the differentiation of human life into complementary female and male beings. Only now do specifically gendered words appear in the narrative, and only now are the creative acts of Yahweh complete. The creation of humanity in its sexually nuanced form brings to an end the sequence of creation begun when God took up a formless clod of earth and formed a human being. Subsequently God created plant and then animal life. Then the creative sequence is ended when the second human—the suitable counterpart—is formed. Unlike the linear arrangement of Genesis 1, where the creation of humanity constitutes the final, climatic creative act, the Genesis 2 structure has the creation of humanity enveloping the rest of creation, or at least that part of creation over which human beings can exercise control.[26]

Feminists have long looked to Genesis 1 for affirmation of sexual equality. The verses describing God's final creative act (1:26–27) apparently place male and female on a par with each other:

And God said, "Let us make humanity [*ha'adam*] in our image, according to our likeness. . . . Then God created humanity in his image; in the image of God he created it; male and female he created them [translation mine].

Already in the nineteenth century, *The Woman's Bible* found in these verses a "plain declaration of the existence of the feminine element in the Godhead, equal in power and glory with the masculine. . . . Scripture, as well as science and philosophy, declare the eternity and equality of sex. . . . [with the] masculine and feminine elements, exactly equal and balancing each other."[27] Other feminists have followed Elizabeth Cady Stanton's lead. However, in their enthusiasm to find sexual equality in Scripture, they have not properly appreciated the largely biological orientation of these verses in the opening chapter of the Bible. In fact, the parity of male and female in Genesis 1 probably was not meant for anything beyond the pairing of male and female for procreative purposes.[28] The structure and purpose of Genesis 1 simply does not address the social world of humans.

But Genesis 2 does concern social relations. And if *The Woman's Bible* and other subsequent critics misconstrued the language of Genesis 1 as indicating social relations, they have also failed to appreciate that the structure and language of the second creation story presents humans as social beings. In the ideal world of Eden, male and female complement each other. In Genesis 2, before Eve is named—that is, before her symbolic identity as the "Mother of All the Living" is proclaimed (3:20)—a relationship aspect of the first couple's existence brings chapter 2 to a close.[29] Verse 24 declares, in a world not yet witness to childbirth or parenthood, that a couple's union supersedes the parent–child relationship. The conjugal bond rather than the parental bond is given priority. Only in marriage are male and female complementary parts of the whole, for the parent–child relationship is an intrinsically hierarchical one in a way that the wife–husband one is not.

Emergence to Reality: Genesis 3 Reconsidered

The traditional interpretations of Genesis 3 are, if anything, more firmly entrenched than those of Genesis 2. Postbiblical interpretations interfere with our appreciation of the meaning and function of the story, and we must seek first to dismantle some of those obstacles. The introduction to this chapter suggests that the focus on Eve as the source of sin is not rooted in an intrinsic component of the Eden tale. It is time now to look more closely at the textual basis for our assertion that the focus on sin and punishment in the traditional exegesis of Genesis 3 is a distortion. Disobedience and its consequences clearly figure in the story of the first human pair; this is the characteristic way for a creation story to suggest that the assertion of independence from any authority is a feature of first (= all) human life. But to allow the theme of disobedience to be of paramount importance to our interpretive eyes is to oversimplify a rich and powerful narrative. Even worse, letting the idea of disobedience dominate our conceptual field means obliterating other features of the story that were equally important, and perhaps even more significant, for the ancient Israelites.

Why then should we seek to put aside the readings that have prevailed for over two millennia? Perhaps the paramount reason is that there is no explicit reference to sin[30] in the narrative purported by tradition and theology to be in essence about the beginning of sin in the world. None of the words that are part of the Hebrew vocabulary for sin and transgression are present in the story. Even when God utters the fateful words leading to the banishment of the primeval couple from their idyllic life in the well-watered garden, only the specific act—the eating of the fruit of a tree that was forbidden—is cited. Interpreters may label this act as disobedient; exegetes may consider it sinful. But *God* does not provide such a judgment within either the narration or the discourse of Genesis 3. Nor, as we have pointed out, does the Hebrew Bible ever associate any of the many sins later perpetrated individually or collectively by the children of Israel with the behavior of the woman and the man in Eden.

Not until Cain and Abel, the first naturally born humans, are involved in the act of murder does sin make its strange and fateful appearance, as a demon external to the infamous brothers. Sin then comes knocking—literally "couching"—at the door (Gen 4:7), ready to tempt people in any of their contacts with others. It may be an argument from silence to make much of the absence of sin from the vocabulary of the Eden narrative; but it is an argument that speaks audibly because not even the horrendous deed of the offspring of Eve and Adam is linked with a parental model of sinful disobedience. Even the prophets, whose writings are filled with harangues against the sinful behavior of the Israelites and other nations, never mention Eve or Adam. In their concern for judgment, punishment, and banishment, the prophets could cogently cite the Eden story. Yet they do not.

The absence in the Hebrew Bible of an intrinsic identification between the acts in Eden with human proclivity for sin thus makes it difficult to look at Genesis 2–3 as a narrative dealing primarily with sin. Similarly, the etiological flavor of the story calls into question the traditional interpretations that focus on the supposed cause-and-effect relationship between the "sin" and the punishment. The very fact that the serpent is held accountable along with the woman and the man diminishes the truly human theme of disobedience to God's word. The participation of the serpent as a creature equally responsible for obeying God's word (which had not been directed toward it) and equally capable of transgression brings the etiological dimension to the fore. Here we have a sample of how people coped with their abhorrence or fear of a certain order of mysterious, apparently self-regenerating, and sometimes dangerous reptiles. No animal could "naturally" be so awesome and awful; it must have "done" something to end up that way. Similarly, humans should not naturally have such difficult life conditions as they did in ancient Palestine, where the tale originated. The etiological workings of the human mind suggest that something must have happened to have produced such a state. The act in question, the eating of a forbidden food, is appropriate for a folk explanation but hardly has the same force as does murder, in the Cain story, as a paradigm for human sinfulness.

If sin is to be removed from consideration as the basic thematic element of the Eden tale, what might take its place? The matter of vocabulary is surely important. We have already pointed out that the absence of certain words is significant and intentional. Similarly, the language that does dominate the narrative conveys meaning. The repetition of words and phrases is a characteristic way in which Hebrew literature provides emphasis for ideas or objects that the writers wish to convey to their audience. The Eden narrative is replete with such repetitions; yet they tend to be overlooked. The failure to take repetitions into account is a shortcoming of traditional interpretation and scholarship that only recently has come to light. The noted literary critic Robert Alter has pointed out that the Hebraic device of repeating words or phrases or even longer units is among the most difficult for western readers to appreciate:

> One of the most imposing barriers that stands between the modern reader and the imaginative subtlety of biblical narrative is the extraordinary prominence of verbatim repetition. Accustomed as we are to modes of

narration in which elements of repetition are made to seem far less obtrusive, this habit of constantly restating material is bound to give us trouble, especially in a narrative that otherwise adheres so evidently to the strictest economy of means.[31]

One of the most common types of repetition, as scholars and commentators have long noted, is the reiteration of individual words. The repetition of key words (*Leitwörter*) as a sign of a motif of an episode nonetheless is not always visible to the reader of the Bible in translation. Most English translations carefully vary vocabulary, consistent with English stylistic norms, rather than repeat the selfsame English word each time the Hebrew word recurs. The failure of English translations to capture the reiterative force of the original is compounded by the fact that a single root can recur in Hebrew in verbal and nominal form. Both forms would clearly signify the same root and constitute part of a repetitive pattern, but this distinction is not always true in English. The passage under scrutiny here contains a prime example. In Hebrew, the verb "eat" and the noun "food" are developed from the same root, and the use of both noun and verb in a passage constitutes repetition. In English, "eat" and "food" do not constitute repetition.

Perhaps the most prominent theme word in the Eden tale is precisely the word just mentioned: the root '*kl*, "to eat." This root recurs in one form or another more frequently than any other word of these two chapters except "human/man/Adam" ('*adam*). It also figures prominently as a structural element in the story: its appearance in certain places in the narrative sets up correspondences and draws attention to pivotal features of the actions.[32] This striking repetition and placement carries its own message; it tells us that the beginning of human existence coincides with a concern for food.

The narrator lives in a world in which he sees the Israelite struggle for sustenance as a dominating concern of daily life. Consequently, the first human (= all humanity) is presented as being concerned with food. The very first words that a living being hears in Genesis 2:16—"And the LORD God commanded the human, saying, 'You may eat freely of every tree of the garden' " [translation mine]—concern the existence of a food supply. The storyteller is acutely aware that the existence of human life goes hand in hand with the availability of growing plants for sustenance. The negative equation set up in 2:5, in which no person plus no plants equal no creation (see above, p. 83), is restated in 2:16 in positive terms. A living being now exists and is shown the food supply that can sustain its life.

Original human consciousness, as set forth in the Eden story, thus consists of two vital aspects: the human's ability to hear and comprehend God's instructions and the human's need to know about the source of sustenance. These two features of human life are portrayed as inextricably linked. Eating in this scheme is not simply or primarily a vehicle for introducing the concept of disobedience. It is a central issue in itself. One can sense the profound anxiety about life, and about the food necessary to sustain life, in the pivotal use and frequent repetition of the root for "eat" and "food." The daily, central, interminable concern of the farmer in the highlands of Palestine has shaped the movement, focus, and vocabulary of the Eden narrative.

The classic statement of Martin Buber concerning the way a key word functions in a text is worth repeating, for it expresses clearly the powerful effect of repetition on the reader or listener. Buber, who worked with Franz Rosenzweig on a German translation of the Bible, took great pains to preserve in German the repeated Hebrew words and roots, for he recognized the dynamic quality of recurring terms:

> I call it "dynamic" because between combinations of sounds related to one another in this manner a kind of movement takes place: if one imagines the entire text deployed before him, one can sense waves moving back and forth between the words. The measured repetition that matches the inner rhythm of the text, or rather, that wells up from it, is one of the most powerful means for conveying meaning without expressing it.[33]

The concentrated repetition of a word both establishes a mood and expresses a theme. The mood in this case is the gnawing concern about the availability of sustenance. And the theme is the integral relationship between sustenance as essential to human life and the need to accept the difficulties of securing sustenance in the Israelite world. The difficult reality is recognized in the speeches to the woman and man in 3:16–19, where the inevitability of that cycle of birth, toil, and death is given the sanction of divine will.

This brings us back to the issue of genre. Along with creation "myth" and etiology, Genesis 3 constitutes another sort of literary piece. It belongs to the genre of Israelite literature—wisdom—that addresses the realities of life, the particular difficulties involved in daily life, and the acceptance of those circumstances. The Hebraic wisdom tradition is characterized in part as a literature meant to help the individual cope with life. Biblical wisdom is most apparent in the sayings and aphorisms that are found in Proverbs. The tragic story of Job and the bold skepticism of the Preacher (Ecclesiastes) are the other major examples of

Hebraic wisdom, broadly conceived. But those books do not exhaust the instances of wisdom literature in the Hebrew Bible. Embedded in historical, prophetic, and legendary materials are less conspicuous fragments of what can aptly be called wisdom.[34]

Genesis 3 is just such a fragment. In terms of the structure, literary techniques employed (vocabulary and use of puns and *double entendres*), setting, characterizations, and even its "plot," Genesis 3 follows the form of a parable.[35] It might be even more accurate to call it a "wisdom tale," because it does concern the function of a wise agent (the "cunning" serpent) and the conferring of wisdom (3:6). Indeed, many scholars now recognize the background of wisdom in the Eden tale in terms of both its literary form and its existential concerns.[36] Unlike the pragmatic, instructional wisdom of a book like Proverbs, the third chapter of Genesis—like Job, Ecclesiastes, and certain Psalms—belongs to the speculative type of wisdom that deals with the meaning of the paradoxes and harsh facts of life.

Now, finally, genre brings us to the matter of gender. The prominent role of the female rather than the male in the wisdom aspects of the Eden tale is a little-noticed feature of the narrative. It is the woman, and not the man, who perceives the desirability of procuring wisdom. The woman, again not the man, is the articulate member of the first pair who engages in dialogue even before the benefits of the wisdom tree have been procured. This association between the female and the qualities of wisdom may have a mythic background, with the features of a Semitic wisdom goddess underlying the intellectual prominence of the woman of Eden.[37] Be that as it may, the close connection between woman and wisdom in the Bible is surely present in the creation narrative, although it is hardly limited to the beginning of Genesis. This relationship actually reaches its climax in the personification of Wisdom as a woman in Proverbs.[38] It relates probably also to the female gender of the Hebraic word for wisdom, *ḥokma*.

The Genesis text serves as preparation for what is to come in the portrayal of Woman Wisdom, of various wise women,[39] and of women acting wisely. We shall return in Chapter 7 to explore the dynamics of Everywoman Eve's role as wisdom figure. For now, it is important to note that the Eden tale sets forth a primal relationship between woman and the acquisition of whatever it is that the tree of knowledge provides. It portrays the female rather than the male as the first human being to utter language, which is the utterly quintessential mark of human life. And it has the female respond to the overtures of an animal described as the "shrewdest of all the wild animals that Yahweh God had made"

(3:1). The serpent at this point is not a cursed creature. Hence the woman's dialogue with the prudent reptile should be considered not a blot on her character but rather a comment on her intellect.

The poetic form of the oracles (3:14–19) that provide the climax of the Eden story is another feature that relates this tale to speculative wisdom literature. In the next chapter the poetic nature of the oracles will be examined as part of the literary analysis of God's oracle to the woman in 3:16. For now, the poetic structure of the oracles figures in a consideration of the time frame of the whole tale. We have not yet considered the date of the Genesis 2–3 story and have no desire to enter into a prolonged discussion of the chronology of this or any piece of biblical writing. Most biblical literature is notoriously difficult to assign to a chronological scheme, because most parts of the Bible are the result of a process that took place over the course of generations, if not centuries. Materials from varying ages were thus inextricably merged into a finished product.

Nonetheless, it is worth noting that the Genesis 2–3 creation story is generally considered to be part of the oldest narrative tradition of the entire Hebrew Bible. Scholars treat it as part of the J (for "Jehovah" or Yahwist) tradition, with "J" being a rubric for the anonymous and gifted author or compiler of many of the most memorable narratives in the Pentateuch. The J source is normally dated to the tenth century,[40] at the very beginning of the Israelite monarchy. Within the J materials, the poetic oracles of the Genesis 3 narrative have been identified as a special and individual type of document, a truly unique literary unit.[41] Because the fragments of poetic material embedded in the narrative tend to be among the most archaic pieces of Pentateuchal literature, it is possible that the oracles preserve parts of an even earlier form of the Eden story, for which the prose portions are reworked tenth-century versions. In short, on formal or literary grounds, it is entirely conceivable that these poetic oracles of Genesis 3 predate the tenth century and thus belong to the formative period of Israel's existence.

The content of those oracles provides further clues to the life setting. As we have already suggested, all three of the oracles share at least an etiological character. Yet all three need not be lumped together if for no other reason than the address to the serpent includes a curse, but God does *not* curse either the woman or the man. In the latter case, however, the ground itself is cursed in the context of God's words to the man. The earth is seen as not being the naturally productive substance that it potentially could be. Therefore, to cast aside another common misinterpretation of the story, human existence itself is not cursed; but it comes closer to being cursed in God's address to the man than in the address to the woman.

Analysis of the divine address to the woman is central to our task, but a few remarks about the man's situation will help set the contextual scene that is crucial to our whole approach. The oracle to the man sets forth the material basis for human life in the highlands of Palestine. In Genesis 2:15, the human is placed in the wonderful garden "to work *it* and to keep *it*" [emphasis mine]. The antecedent of the pronouns (*it* and *it*) is "garden of Eden." But now, in reality, it is not a garden (the tending of which is not viewed as arduous), but rather the accursed ground itself that the man must face. The fruits of tree and vine may be part of the highland economy, but once planted they do not require the unremitting labor that is prescribed in 3:17. Only the growing of field crops—of cereals—requires an annual cycle of labor-intentive tasks: plowing, sowing, weeding, harvesting.

The human meant "to work the earth" and so to bring forth the "grains of the field" (2:5 and 3:18) for bread (3:19) has at last entered the environment where such tasks constitute the core of the agrarian routine. But the earth resists; without significant human intervention only the tough and inedible "thorns and thistles" (3:18) sprout forth. The famous phrase, "by the sweat of your brow" (3:19), has captured for all time the intense labor required to grow cereals in that environment. This graphic phrase accompanies the more abstract word "toil" (3:17). Together they depict the difficult nature of humanity's intrinsic connection to the ground in the Palestinian highlands. The language about sweat and work is not in essence metaphoric, although it certainly has subsequently been applied to a wide variety of situations in which hard work of any sort is involved. Rather, it is realistic language, describing a life that appears perhaps too difficult to the highlanders of Palestine, who know that to the east in Mesopotamia (if not also to the southwest in Egypt), the riverine environments and the flat stretches of arable land provide ecosystems that are somewhat less taxing of human energies.

The content of God's address to the man thus indicates a sensitivity to the exigencies of the real world. The purpose of such a wisdom parable or *mašal* was to help the audience to which it was directed accept an aspect of reality that could not effectively be conveyed by more direct means.[42] Understanding the contextual reality of the Israelites is thus central to interpreting the original message and function of Genesis 3 as a wisdom tale. The tale, and in particular the oracles, must not be lifted from their social and literary context. They must be seen primarily as helping highland settlers cope with life's demands, difficult as they may be. If that be the case for God's words to the first man, Everyman, with respect to the laborious character of his daily life, so also is it the case for the first woman, Everywoman. We turn now to see what a close reading of the oracle to the woman in Genesis 3:16 can reveal about the lives of Israelite women and the demands placed on them.

5

The Genesis Paradigms for Female Roles, Part II: Genesis 3:16

Perhaps no single verse of scripture is more troublesome, from a feminist perspective, than is the divine oracle to the woman in Genesis 3:16. Ever since the earliest translations of the Bible, which are contemporary with the oldest extant extrabiblical sources connecting Eve and Eden with sin and suffering,[1] the verse has been rendered in a way that communicates two persistent beliefs about female existence: first, women are associated with severe pain in childbirth; second, they are portrayed in a relationship subordinate to men.

Virtually every translation, from the most ancient to the most recent, provides a reading that conveys both those understandings of God's charge to the woman. The oldest translation, known as the Septuagint, was completed in Egypt in the first century BCE. For Genesis 3:16 it reads:

> I will greatly multiply thy pains and thy moanings;
> in pain shall you bring forth children.
> And thy submission shall be to your husband,
> and he shall have authority over you.

The Vulgate (Latin) translation of the fourth century CE renders the first line rather differently, and it makes the third line even stronger, with respect to suggesting male dominance. St. Jerome gives us:

> I will multiply your toils and your conceptions; in grief you will bear children, and you will be under the power of your husband, and he will rule over you.[2]

Similarly, the most recent English versions might vary the vocabulary; but they do not significantly alter the interpretation of the Hebrew established by the ancient versions. The new Jewish Publication Society translation of Genesis, completed in 1962, provides the following:

95

> I will make most severe
> Your pangs in childbearing;
> In pain shall you bear children.
> Yet your urge shall be for your husband
> And he shall rule over you.

The Jerusalem Bible, originally produced in French, was first published in English in the 1960s, rendering 3:16 with a particularly harsh twist to the last line:

> I will multiply your pain in childbearing,
> You shall give birth to your children in pain.
> Your yearning shall be for your husband,
> yet he *will lord it* over you [emphasis mine].

Yet another recent translation, the popular New International Version, which was completed in 1978, reads:

> I will greatly increase your pains in childbearing;
>   with pain you will give birth to children.
> Your desire will be for your husband,
>   and he will rule over you.

Most of us, however, are familiar with either the classic English translation, the King James Version (KJV), or the widely used Revised Standard Version (RSV). The former, a product of seventeenth-century England, has a very interesting rendering of the first line. It perhaps has retained the Hebrew syntax better than any other translation, as we shall see below. The King James or Authorized Version (1611) gives us these lines set in prose rather than as poetry:

> I will greatly multiply thy sorrow and thy conception; in sorrow thou shalt bring forth children; and thy desire *shall be* to thy husband and he shall rule over thee.

Finally, the best-selling Revised Standard Version, published in 1952 and currently itself being revised, reads:

> I will greatly multiply your pain in childbearing;
>   in pain you shall bring forth children,
> yet your desire shall be for your husband,
>   and he shall rule over you.

While vocabulary and syntax in each of these renderings vary somewhat, none of them alters in any significant way the meanings of this pivotal text set forth already in antiquity by the translators of the Septuagint and by Jerome in his influential Vulgate. Can we let it go at that? Can we assume that two millennia of experience in the difficult process of translating Hebrew Scriptures has provided an accurate and acceptable translation? The plethora of new translations that have appeared in the last few decades provides a clue that there is no such thing as a final, complete, exact, and fully accurate translation.

The current "rage to translate—really to retranslate—the Bible"[3] is the result of our acute awareness of two things. First, language and style change, so that what was current and comprehensible in 1611 (KJV) may be obsolete and incomprehensible—albeit elegant and pleasantly archaic—in the 1980s. Second, archaeology and philology are continually providing new information that sheds light on certain biblical phrases, words, or whole passages for which a scientifically accurate reading has long remained elusive. The frequent appearance of new translations and the burgeoning of information about the biblical world should signal to the reader of the Bible in English, or any translation for that matter, that what he or she sees in translation may fail to communicate accurately the meaning of the text in its original language. In short, despite its great familiarity to many people and its apparent accessibility to all, the linguistic as well as the chronological and spatial distance that separates modern readers from the ancient text means that the Bible is not the open and available document we think it is. To use a metaphor from modern technology, much of the Bible is not user-friendly, a fact which religious leaders tend to ignore or gloss over.[4]

The process of translating the Bible has a peculiar self-perpetuating quality to it. That is, meanings provided in the earliest translations, even if arrived at by error whether unwitting or intentional, tend to be replicated in subsequent translations. Previous translations have subtle influence on subsequent ones. Translators invariably consult the products of their predecessors' efforts; or, for many well-known passages, existing translations are already familiar. Consequently, one finds a tendency for certain renderings to be retained or repeated. This accompanies or offsets a countertendency, whereby the translators feel compelled to provide a "new" or "fresh" reading. For Genesis 3:16, as for many biblical texts, the earliest versions seem to have consistently influenced the later ones, as the examples quoted above indicate.

The ancient translations, we must remember, did not necessarily purport to be verbatim or faithful word-for-word renderings. In some places it is clear that literal translations were attempted, but in other passages or in whole sections, or even whole books, the translators provided rather free renditions. To be sure, the concept of translation as a word-for-word enterprise is most consistent with the notion held by all ancient scholars that the biblical text is the revealed word of God and hence should not be subject to alteration. Yet the process of translation is by its very nature an act of interpretation in every instance—of which there are many—in which there exists no simple lexical or syntactical correspondence between the original Hebrew and the language of translation. Consequently, it is incumbent on each generation to reexamine the original source, particularly for texts that provide controversial doctrinal materials.

Genesis 3:16 deserves just such a reconsideration. A careful, word-by-word analysis of God's words to the woman in that verse is the proper way to evaluate the accuracy of the traditional translations. It must not be assumed, simply by reading it in translation, that the meaning is self-evident.

While the lines of 3:16 are poetic, the grammar is rather straightforward and there are no particular problems with the Hebrew text itself. However, two aspects of the language in this verse, as in many cases, require judgment on the part of the translator and hence create a situation in which inappropriate choices may have been made: one is syntax, whereby the arrangement of the elements in a sentence has implications for the relationship of those elements; the other is the matter of lexical nuance, in which a given word can offer various shades of meaning, not all of which are relevant to a particular passage. Both of these aspects need to be reexamined for Genesis 3:16. The syntactic options can be explored with respect to word choice, and lexical nuances can be identified by an analysis of the Hebrew word, in which its usage elsewhere in the Bible is examined so as to determine its range of meanings and to identify analogous contexts where the nuance is clear.

Verse 16 begins with a narrative introduction identifying the audience, the woman, to whom the oracle given by God is addressed. The oracle itself contains four lines. Although scholars have used various systems and nomenclature for dividing and subdividing them, for our purposes it is best simply to number them from one to four, corresponding to the four lines that appear in the English translations that arrange 3:16 as poetry.

The assignment of four line numbers, however, should not obscure the way in which the lines stand in relationship to each other. These four separate pieces really constitute two units, each with two parts. The essence of Hebrew poetry is its parallelistic structure, whereby the parts of each of the poetic units stand in close relationship with one another. One line of Hebrew poetry relates to the next one or more lines in several ways: there is usually parallelism of meaning and of syntax, and often parallelism in stress; sometimes there is also an inverted (chiastic) relationship between one or more pairs of elements.[5] Of course, while some typical examples contain all these features, most poetic sections are not so regular, hence the proliferation of works on biblical poetry trying to identify some overarching system of parallelism that is always operative.

The lesson to be learned from much of the discussion of parallelism is that two successive lines (or, two parts to one line) have an intrinsic interconnection of form and meaning. Although their elements may constitute formal equivalents, the meanings of the paired elements are not to be construed as equivalents. One line is not simply a mirror of the previous one. A noun in one line followed by a parallel noun in the next is not simply adding a synonym but rather is qualifying or elaborating the first noun. Most characteristically, such a device intensifies[6] and in so doing heightens the emotional or dramatic impact of the poetic mode.

The implication of this understanding of parallelism for our passage is that the first two lines constitute a pair. Together they develop an idea that the shaper of the oracle wishes to convey. The second two lines go on to another concept that is related to the first in that it is part of the overall poetic unit, yet contains its own message.

A Close Reading of God's Oracle to the Woman: Lines 1 and 2

The first line begins with a complex verbal structure. The regular verbal idea, "I will make great" or "I will increase," is accompanied in the Hebrew by an infinitive absolute, another form of the same verbal root (*rbh,* "to become much, many"). The use of the infinitive absolute before the verb serves to emphasize or strengthen the action represented by the verb. The absolute certainty of the action is expressed. In English, which has no syntactic equivalent to this doubling of the verb, that sort of intensification can be best represented by the addition of an adverb to put greater stress on the verb. "Greatly increase" is preferable to "multiply," because the former at least indicates that Hebrew uses two words to express the verbal idea.

The verb *rbh* is a fairly common word in Hebrew. Its range of usages nearly always involves a concept of numerical increase. A quantity of something—beasts, people, money, things, sins—is indicated. Even in the rare and somewhat more abstract usages, such as when a person is said to have become great, the implication is that a person's status has increased because he or she has more of something—money, retainers, or land—than do others. This particular construction, verb plus infinitive absolute, is found twice again in Genesis. Both of those other passages are part of the same narrative tradition as Genesis 2–3, and in both places the idea of population increase is expressed by this verbal arrangement. The growth of the two peoples, the Ishmaelites and the Israelites, in the lineage of Abraham is promised: "I will so greatly multiply your descendents" that they cannot any longer be counted (Gen 16:10) or so that they are as uncountable as the stars in the heavens or the sands by the shore (Gen 22:17).

Because of the way the root *rbh* ("to become many") tends to be used for commodities or persons that can be counted, its usage with "pain" as the direct object is surprising and would be an unusual, if not impossible, occurrence. Pain defies quantification. Modern medicine struggles to find methods of measuring pain, because the experience of physical or psychological distress is so individual and subjective. It is difficult to imagine the ancients conceiving of pain in quantitative terms. Thus a verbal phrase that suggests quantification should make us suspicious of the traditional renderings of its object or objects.

This brings us to the other two words of the first line, which in Hebrew has only four words. Hebrew is a highly inflected language, so that the pronominal objects or subjects as well as some connectors are often part of or attached to the verbal form; furthermore, pronominal possessives, as is the case in this line, are part of the noun form. The first matter to explore with respect to the object(s) of the verb in this line is whether we are dealing with one subject or two. This question arises because of another characteristic of Hebrew, namely, its relative paucity of adjectives. One way that Hebrew deals with this is through hendiadys (the use of two coordinate terms, such as two nouns, joined by a conjunction to express what in English would be expressed by a noun and an adjective). A classic example appears in Genesis 1:2, where "unformed-and-void" means "a formless void."

In this line of Genesis 3:16, the noun usually translated "pain" and the one often rendered "childbirth" are frequently considered a hendiadys. In the Anchor Bible commentary on Genesis, Speiser calls these two nouns "a parade example of hendiadys."[7] Strictly speaking, if the order of the pair is to be heeded, "pain" comes first. Therefore, in the form of "painful," it should qualify "childbirth" or "childbearing." But that would provide a reading, "I will greatly increase your painful childbirths," that translators unanimously have rejected. However, it is not certain that the first term in a hendiadys compound must modify the second. Consequently, those translators working under the assumption that the two words constitute a hendiadys usually retain "pain" as the object and make "childbirth" part of a prepositional phrase modifying it. The translations with which we are most familiar hence read: "pain(s) in childbirth" or "pangs in childbearing" or some such variation.

Having said all this about the possible presence of hendiadys, we must now consider whether in fact it is legitimate to recognize the use of that device in this passage. The Septuagint, cited at the beginning of this chapter, did not see hendiadys. Instead, it provided a compound direct object ("thy pains and thy moanings") of the verb. The King James Version probably followed the lead of the Greek in likewise giving us two objects ("thy sorrow and thy conception") of the verb. Grammatically, hendiadys is possible but not necessary. Thus we must ask if there is any way to determine the correct relationship between the two nouns at the end of the first line of 3:16. Should they be rendered as hendiadys or not? And does it matter?

This passage has been so powerful in setting and sustaining gender-related dogma in the past two millennia that we must a priori assume that it could well matter a great deal to establish the proper relationship among the units of this verse. All questions of the suitability of understanding hendiadys may not be easily resolved, but in this case lexical study comes to the rescue. The two object nouns have rarely been subjected to the scrutiny that they deserve, and looking at the meanings of the Hebrew words rendered "childbirth" and "pains" produces some surprises.

Looking at the vocabulary of this and the next line means dealing with the language of human procreation. This passage is frequently cited as the classical location for the biblical view of pregnancy and the pain [*sic*] of childbirth.[8] For example, Fabry, who thus draws attention to the powerful role of Genesis 3:16 in western attitudes toward the birth process, also claims that human birth and pain, two discrete entities, have been closely associated ever since the "Fall." It is surprising that he could make such claims in a theological dictionary concerned with establishing lexical nuances, because he does not attend to the vocabulary of Genesis 3:16 but only to one word (*ḥbl*), which denotes the final stages of pregnancy as culminating in birth and in itself does not contain any emphasis on pain.[9] The birth process and pain are not inevitably linked, despite his assertions to the contrary in the same entry.

The fact is—and this must be kept in mind as we look at the vocabulary of this and the next line—that Hebrew contains a semantic field of birth language that is quite well developed. Not only are there discrete terms for the various phases of the process of conception, pregnancy, and childbirth; there are also semantically similar but less common synonyms for the words that constitute the core of the childbirth vocabulary. Each of the apparently synonymous terms brings a new shade of meaning to the language describing this aspect of human experience. Indeed, so fundamental and at the same time so wondrous and mysterious is the reproductive process that it would be surprising to discover that a language had few terms expressing its various stages.

Let us begin with the second of the two nouns of line 1, the word often translated "childbirth" when hendiadys is assumed. The Hebrew term *heron* in fact does not mean childbirth. In the developed biblical vocabulary of human reproduction, it refers to the period of pregnancy and not to the process of childbirth, which terminates pregnancy. Perhaps the best passage to cite as example that this word for pregnancy does not include birth is Jeremiah 20:14–18. It is here that the prophet rues the day of his birth. So miserable is he with the excruciating mission he feels compelled to carry out that he, like Job (3:10), curses the very bearer of what was normally glad tidings, that a "son is born to you" (Jer 20:15). Jeremiah wishes that he had died in the womb, with his mother serving as his grave. He puts it most graphically with the wish that "her womb would always be pregnant" (*harath olam*; Jer 20:17). Obviously a term that included childbirth could not possibly have the impact the prophet desires to make in his anguish.

Clearly *heron* does not mean childbirth but rather indicates pregnancy. In general, it might refer equally to any or all of the nine months of human gestation. However, the word shows a tendency to be more associated with the initiation of pregnancy rather than with its duration or conclusion. In its verbal form, the word regularly means "to become pregnant," that is, "to conceive," rather than "to be pregnant." Used in close association with words for intercourse,[10] it does not refer to the sexual act itself but indicates the physiological condition that was the desired result of intercourse in Israelite society. The proximity of the state of pregnancy to the sexual act in Hebrew narrative is exemplified in the repeated accounts throughout Genesis of patriarchal intercourse followed by matriarchal pregnancy. Take the experience of Hagar, for example (as reported in Gen 16:4): Abraham "went in to Hagar, and she conceived" (= became pregnant). In short, the word *heron* can be translated "conception" as well as "pregnancy" because of its close association with the sexual act.

One other consideration leads us again to reject the common translation of "childbirth" for *heron*. In the following and parallel line, a word that does represent the birth process is used. In accordance with what we know about parallelism in biblical poetry, parallel terms are normally not meant to be exact synonyms. Rather they enlarge or develop an idea. Called complementary parallelism by some,[11] the parallel but unequal terms are part of the subtle process by which Hebrew poetry exhibits narrative movement.[12] Consequently, the appearance of a term for childbirth in the second, parallel line would preclude the existence of a word meaning precisely the same thing in the preceding line.

Returning to the hendiadys problem, we are faced with a situation whereby pain and pregnancy would be linked if hendiadys is assumed. But such a linkage is highly improbable. Pain is a suitable concomitant of the language of childbirth, but it is neither an accurate nor a suitable part of the description of pregnancy. In biblical narratives, becoming pregnant is highly desirable. None of the texts in Genesis, for example, that deal with the themes of barrenness and pregnancy associate conception with pain. Nor, for that matter, do they associate childbirth with pain. Furthermore, considering the close association in ancient Hebrew parlance between the sex act and conception, the possibility that pain is a normal part of that aspect of human procreation becomes all the more remote. If we reflect again on the renderings of the verbal idea in line 1, the intensification of whatever the object is, we see that a prior state of that condition already exists. Something cannot be multiplied unless it is already there. God's charge serves to increase a natural state, and there is no reason to think that pain in pregnancy or conception was a primeval aspect of the female reproductive experience.

To summarize this part of the discussion, the first line of the oracle to the woman has God greatly increasing a female's conceptions, or pregnancies. A close look at the language involved indicates the presence of a word specifically meaning conception or pregnancy and *not* childbirth. St. Jerome recognized this long ago in producing his Latin translation, which we quoted above. But clearly it has been the Septuagint, with its language of pain, that has influenced most English translations.

The appearance of a word for pain as an inextricable part of the increased pregnancies as described in line 1 thus becomes inappropriate if not absurd. The task ahead, then, is to examine the word nearly always translated as "pain." Do we have another traditional yet erroneous translation? Or does the poet exhibit woeful ignorance of the language, physiology, and affect that surround the birth process? The latter is unlikely, and a focus on the lexical range of the word rendered "pain" or "pangs" or "sorrow" is the way to proceed.

The Hebrew word in question, the one usually represented in English as "pain," is *'iṣṣabon,* a noun apparently formed from the verbal root *'ṣb,* which means "to upset, to grieve." However, of the fifteen places in which that verb is used, all but one refer explicitly to psychological or emotional discomfort, not to physical pain. Even in that one late instance (Eccles 10:9), in which a physical state is indicated, the verb seems to refer to an injury rather than the accompanying pain of that injury.[13] The mental anguish expressed by the verb is most explicit in Isaiah 34:6, where someone forsaken is said to be "grieved in spirit."

With only three usages in the Hebrew Bible, it is difficult to understand the development of the noun *'iṣṣabon* from such a verbal root. Looking at the passages in which the verb is used indicates that the idea of physical pain is to be ruled out. The nuance of *'iṣṣabon* in this one passage is in question, but its meaning in the other two places is much clearer. The other usages are in related texts and hence convey the meaning of *'iṣṣabon* in Genesis 3:16.

In the very next verse, God informs the male that the earth he will know and work will not be the same as that which he experienced in Eden. Food will not be there for the taking. Instead, the earth will sprout naturally only thorns and thistles (3:18). Grains for bread will be the result of human initiative and effort, and that effort will have to be great. In verse 19 God tells the man that agricultural labor is to be done "by the sweat of your brow." And in verse 17 he is told that, because of the cursed[14] or condemned state of the earth, he will eat of it only through "toil," *'iṣṣabon.* That physical labor and not simply "difficulty" (or some other abstract reference to agrarian tasks) is intended becomes clear if we look at the third place in which this noun is found (Gen 5:29).

The genealogy of Genesis 5 offers an interesting etymology for Noah's name. It suggests that his name means "comfort," or "rest," a situation constituting relief from the predicament set forth at the expulsion from Eden. Verse 29 refers obliquely to the Genesis 3 story: people need comfort or rest "because of the ground which Yahweh condemned." The task of making the ground productive involves "our work and the toil [*'iṣṣabon*] of our hands." Here the word "toil" breaks up a stereotyped phrase, "work of the hands," which refers to human labor (as opposed to divine deeds). The word for work sometimes explicitly designates—alone or with "hands"—agrarian labor (e.g., Judg 19:16; Exod 23:16; Hag 2:17), and it certainly does so in this passage. The doubling here, with *two* words signifying labor, serves to demonstrate how hard the work is. This intensification makes the "rest" dimension of Noah's name all the more meaningful.

In short, the most appropriate interpretation of the use of *'iṣṣabon* in

Genesis 3:16 is as physical labor rather than an abstract condition of distress—but not ordinary physical labor. The Hebrew Bible has a nuanced vocabulary designating work and labor. The biblical view of labor, by which is meant the efforts to procure food and satisfy human needs, is generally positive.[15] In this case, however, labor is not so positively regarded. The difficulty or distress of agricultural work in an unfriendly environment is indicated. Not only does "toil" (not "pain") fit the lexical data for the use of *'issabon* as a noun; it also suits the verbal idea of difficult work.

Remember that "toil" is the object of the verbal phrase "greatly increase." This phrase, we have already seen, implies a quantifiable commodity rather than a subjective, nonmaterial one. In addition, to say that the amount of work the woman must do is being increased is consistent with a view of productive labor itself as not a punishment but something already extant in Eden. The first human was placed in the garden "to work it" (Gen 2:15). Indeed, the very existence of an inhabitable cosmos is equated in Genesis 2:5 (cf. above, pp. 82–84) with the presence of rain and of human life "to work" the earth. God's oracle to the woman does not assign her a new aspect of existence but rather intensifies what was seen as an intrinsic part of existence, namely, human labor.[16]

In light of this detailed discussion we propose the following translation of line 1:

I will greatly increase your toil and your pregnancies.[17]

The two objects of the complex verbal form are independent concepts. On the one hand, the passage sets forth the woman's enlarged role in the productive, agrarian tasks of society; on the other, it mandates an increased procreative role. The female contribution to society is thus intensified by virtue of a quantitative expansion of these two aspects of female existence. Until we have examined the next three lines of the Genesis 3:16 oracle, we shall refrain from relating the first line to the wisdom purposes of the passage as a whole. Yet we mention that the demands of the life situation of early Israel, as described in Chapter 3, bear a striking congruency with the opening line of this charge to the archetypal woman.

Because the second line of Genesis 3:16 stands in parallelism with the first, the general subject matter and intent of the first line prepares us for what is to come in the second. The narrative movement of Hebrew poetry is evident in the use in the second line of a word meaning having children. The woman, assigned multiple conceptions ("pregnancies") in line 1, will eventually produce offspring. The verb used for childbirth (*yld*) belongs to the biblical vocabulary of pregnancy and birth, and refers to the childbirth process itself, not to the preceding stages of intercourse, conception, and gestation. However, unlike some of the specific terms describing the travail and pangs of labor and birth, the verb *yld,* often translated "to bear children," can also be a general term for having children, applied to either or both parents. For example, the familiar "begats" of biblical genealogy (as in Gen 5 and 10, or 1 Chron 1) use *yld* and have the (male) ancestral figures "bearing" the succeeding generations. Obviously, they do not give birth in the literal sense. Rather, they become parents, a status related to the object (the names of children) of this transitively used verb in the genealogies.

When the biblical writers employ *yld* to refer to the birth process itself rather than to the related, but not gender-specific, notion of having offspring, they tend to use the verb intransitively. For example, Genesis 30:3, which is one of the few passages that gives any information about ancient practices related to the actual birth process, describes Rachel asking Bilhah "to bear" (i.e., to give birth) on her knees. Exodus 1:19 gives the impression that Israelite women, unlike Egyptian women, had easy deliveries and that they "gave birth" before the midwives could get to them. In contrast, the idea of having offspring involves the verb followed by an accusative, namely, a noun denoting "children" or else the actual name of the child. In short, when the verb *yld* is intransitive, it normally denotes the birth process; but when it is used transitively, it refers to the status of parenthood.

Line 2 of this verse has the latter construction. The verb "to bear, beget" is followed by the noun "children." The emphasis is consequently not on labor and parturition but rather on the more abstract notion of becoming a parent, of having children. The personal, physical process is not specified, but the social condition of contributing to family growth is prescribed. This understanding of line 2 finds support in the absence, as in line 1, of any of the words belonging to the vocabulary that describes the labor and birth process and that indicates physical distress. We thus translate *yld* here as "beget," an English word used more frequently with the male parent. Precisely for that reason it is useful here, because it does *not* connote physical childbirth.

There is one more word to consider in line 2. This word relates to the verb and noun combination just examined but carries a rich array of meanings of its own. The first word of this second line, in Hebrew, is *beʿeṣeb.* The initial syllable (*be*) is a preposition, but the noun itself—as even the English reader will notice—is related to the word "toil" (*ʿiṣṣabon*) of the previous line and of the succeeding verse. If nothing else, *'eṣeb* also evokes the sense of "toil." In this way, if understood as "labor" or "work," it preserves the parallelism of meaning of the two halves (lines 1 and 2) of the whole poetic line. It does so in the absence of syntactic parallelism.[18] That is, the structure of line 2 does not repeat that of line 1, which has a verbal complex followed by two object nouns. Line 2 instead shifts to a verb and its object preceded by a prepositional phrase. The verb and object in line 2 ("you shall beget children") expand or complete the idea of multiple conceptions expressed in line 1 ("I will increase . . . your pregnancies"). The prepositional phrase in line 2, then—in keeping with the pattern of parallelism—must amplify the concept of "toil."

How does *'eṣeb* develop the idea of physical work or "toil" introduced in the previous line? That it might simply be a synonymous term, chosen for its near identity with *'iṣṣabon,* would be contrary to the dynamics of Hebrew poetry. Only by examining other biblical usages of the word can its semantic range be elucidated. Found in fewer than ten other passages, *'eṣeb* is most at home in biblical wisdom literature. It appears in four different places in Proverbs, in two Psalms with wisdom affinities, and in a prophetic passage also related to wisdom.

In five of its usages, which might not always be apparent in English translations, our word clearly refers to productive physical labor. For example, Proverbs 14:23 contrasts the value of work ("in all labor [*'eṣeb*] there is profit") with the folly of words alone ("but speech of the lips leads only to want").[19] In a sixth passage (Isa 14:3), *'eṣeb* might mean either physical labor or mental anguish—or both. Another passage (1 Chron 4:9) is clearly based on an interpretation of the present verse and therefore cannot be used to interpret it.[20] But in two more instances, the word is undoubtedly derived from the normal usage of the verbal root (see above) meaning "to upset, grieve." Proverbs 15:1, for example, proclaims that "A soft answer turns away wrath, but an upsetting [*'eṣeb*] word arouses anger."

This is not the place to examine the problem of whether the apparently disparate meanings of physical toil or labor, and of emotional turmoil or grief, are inherently related and indeed are derived from the same verbal root. At various places in the Bible and especially within closely related wisdom contexts, *'eṣeb* is capable of meaning either. In this passage, the meaning of the physical phenomenon of work is clear on the basis of its parallelism with *'iṣṣabon,* "toil." But it would be a mistake to let it go at that; it is more than a synonym. Surely the meaning of emotional distress is also present, and there is no reason to suppose that both nuances are not present as they are in Isaiah 14:3, where the prophet looks forward to the day when God will provide "rest" from three things: "hard work," "turmoil," and 'eṣeb, which has aspects of both the previous two.

In short, 'eṣeb works effectively in two directions. It continues the parallelism with the previous line by signifying the productive labor that accompanies the maternal role for the archetypal woman and hence for all (Israelite) women. At the same time, it suggests that a life of hard work and multiple childbirths will not be without its times of distress. Just as "having children" rather than "giving birth" is a social rather than a physical statement, a word denoting the stressful aspects of hard work indicates the psychological toll of the physical condition. It does not take much imagination to supply the possibilities of what such mental discomfort might entail: the anguish of parenthood, and the angst of difficult labor not always bringing the desired and necessary measure of productive returns.

While the Hebrew effectively brings together both physical and mental aspects of 'eṣeb, the translator finds no satisfactory English equivalent. Consequently, we choose here "travail," a word that means "very hard work" and so preserves the parallelism with "toil." It also provides a hint that the Hebrew word for "toil" and "travail" are related. Also, we avoid the word "labor," which is used frequently in English translations at this point but can also signify the process leading up to the moment of birth, a process not within the lexical range of the Hebrew word. Of course, "travail" can also refer to difficulty in childbirth, but the difficulty here seems to be the stresses of parenting rather than the strains of parturition.

The preposition or particle that introduces "travail" is normally rendered "with" or "in." In this case the former, indicating that one thing accompanies or goes together with another thing,[21] is more appropriate than the latter, which has an instrumental flavor. Together, then, the parts of line 2 read:

(Along) with travail shall you beget children.

It is important to add to this analysis the way in which "travail" in line 2 heightens the meaning of "toil" in line 1. The repetition of nearly the same Hebrew word is not a mechanical reproduction of a term but a purposeful reiteration. It produces a more complex idea: the seeming repetition of a root signifies the intensity of the concept being expressed.[22] The audience of the oracle is not simply being reminded that women work and have children. Rather, they are learning that the work is unremitting and is not mitigated by the procreative demands placed on female existence. Moreover, they are learning via the different shadings of meaning expressed by the second term that the fulfillment of God's charge does not automatically entitle one to bliss and joy, that anguish is inevitably an accompaniment to the carrying out of life's tasks.

Close Reading of God's Oracle to the Woman: Lines 3 and 4

The detailed discussion just completed has attempted to correct long-standing but misleading traditions of translation. The third and fourth lines require less detailed lexical analyses, because (at least for line 3) the usual renderings in English are not so egregiously disruptive of the original meaning. Instead, our expository attention will be directed toward the relationship between the first unit (lines 1 and 2) and the second unit (lines 3 and 4) of Genesis 3:16.

To begin with, we note that lines 3 and 4 are syntactically connected. Both are introduced by a conjunction (*waw*), most frequently rendered as "and," but also capable of meaning—depending on context—"but," "for," and "yet." Indeed, a considerable variety in the choice of particles by which this connector is rendered can be found in the English translations of this verse, those cited at the beginning of this chapter and others. Leaving aside for the moment the issue of how the conjunction might best be represented here, it is important to note that the very presence of this particle in poetic language, which is characteristically spare in its use of particles, is significant. Its presence tells us that the content of lines 3 and 4 is meant to be related to that of the first two lines of Genesis 3:16, and it also indicates that lines 3 and 4 are meant to stand as a pair.

Line 3 opens with the prepositional phrase "to your man." The word for man is *'iš*, a gender-specific word, rather than the general "human" that dominates the beginning of the Genesis 2–3 account (see above, pp. 81–82). With the subject matter of the oracle including conception and having children, a word explicitly denoting the person's sexual identity is entirely in order. Although this word for man can signify the human species (as perhaps in Judg 9:49), it usually means "man" as a gender term ("male") or as a designation for "husband."[23]

It is difficult to know whether in the present instance one or the other of the two latter possibilities is intended. My hunch is that they are both present. Obviously the meaning of man as male is dictated by the context, because the succeeding word has sexual connotations. But so is the meaning of man as husband, as the male with whom a woman carries out the imperative of this oracle: having children and also engaging in productive labor. We would retain the translation of "man," however, because "husband" conjures up the image of marriage, which does not fit the archetypal literary setting of the Eden story.

But note that "man" has attached to it a possessive pronoun, "your," which certainly does suggest a close relationship between the woman and this male. It would not, however, indicate any legal or personal possession—and instances in which "woman" or "wife" appear with the pronoun "his" similarly do not express ownership of female by male. Rather, the "one flesh" notion of the male–female, pair-bonding relationship presented in 2:24 is implied by the possessive with either husband/man or wife/woman.

The word "man" is preceded by a preposition meaning "to" or "for," which in Hebrew is the first word (preceded by the attached particle "and") of this line. The line must end, therefore, by informing us what it is that the woman is directing to or for her man. But the clause lacks a verb and therefore expresses a stative, existing condition. The "desire" that the woman has for her companion is an attraction that already exists and is not part of the divine prescription of the oracle.

The strong and earthy meaning of the word *tešuqa,* translated as "desire," is clear, although its verbal root happens to be dubious. The noun is found in only two other places in the Hebrew Bible. In the Song of Songs, where the reciprocal nature of human love is the keynote, a short love song beginning in 7:11 has the woman telling of the man's "desire" for her. The ultimate consequence of the love attraction is sexual activity (7:12,13). What is fascinating about this love song is that intervening between the expression of the man's yearning and the statement that the woman will give him her love is a depiction of what the couple will do together in the interim (i.e., between the declaration and its sexual fulfillment). The mutual attraction of the couple is not simply a sexual meeting, because their physical union apparently follows a day's work. The man and woman rise early, first to make their way through fields, vineyards, and orchards, and then to make love.

The use of "desire" in the love lyrics of the Song of Songs is thus associated with a rather leisured and altogether pleasurable venture into the agrarian milieu of the couple. If the Song of Songs is indeed a midrash, or exposition, of the Eden story,[24] the presence of sexual desire along with a sharing of agricultural tasks is a striking echo of Genesis 2–3 motifs. The idyllic world of Canticles (Song of Songs) recaptures the nonarduous labor of Eden. It also indicates the same interrelationship of sexuality and productivity that Genesis 3:16 emphasizes. Only the Song of Songs returns us to Eden, where the pleasure of sexuality stands out apart from the tribulations of its procreative aspect, and where the tending of a beautiful and productive garden does not entail great effort and anguish.

Despite the broader aspects of "desire" in Song of Songs, one might be tempted to assign an exclusively sexual meaning to this word. Indeed, at least one scholar would translate it "desire for intercourse."[25] Yet in its other (third) biblical usage the word lacks sexual connotations. Immediately following the Eden story, the Cain and Abel narrative uses "desire" to refer to the attraction that the demon sin[26] holds for Cain, and consequently for all people, according to the symbolic role of Cain. As the first naturally born human, Cain is representative of human life and the problem of sinfulness. The concept common to this usage and to the sexual nuances of the Canticles and Genesis 3 instances is that of a strong urge of one being for another. "Desire" is an emotional and/or physical attraction that transcends thought and rationality. Consequently, it is an entirely suitable designation for the sexual nature of the mutual attraction of a female and a male.

The strength of the woman's feelings for her mate is thus indicated in this line of Genesis 3:16 by "desire," which includes but is broader than sexual attraction alone. But how does the statement of the female's attraction to her male partner follow up the meaning of the first two lines? If the content of the second part of the oracle is related to the first part, how does the thematic connection between them operate? To answer this let us look back for a moment at the content of lines 1 and 2. They depict an intensification of two main aspects of female existence: an increase of work load and of procreative responsibilities. This mandate is presented in the form of a divine oracle, an address from God Yahweh to the archetypal woman. Such a form constitutes a way to sanction, or gain acceptance for, a stance or program that is not independently or naturally present. In other words, within the rather negative atmosphere of the punitive expulsion from Eden, we might deduce from this emphatic presentation that women would just as soon not be expected to work so hard or to have so many children. Such reluctance is elliptically yet powerfully present in the oracle.

It does not take much imagination to understand that there is present among workers everywhere some reluctance to face unending days of toil. Our own search for leisure is indicative of a need momentarily to put aside the weight of daily life. And in ancient Israel the establishment of a Sabbath, regardless of any other cultic or symbolic value it may have had, can be seen as an enlightened legal response to a social condition in which the majority of the populace endured a daily existence of sunup to sundown drudgery, accompanied by the stress of living in a risky agrarian environment.

A reluctance to have many children might be viewed in terms of the additional work and responsibility that a large family involved. However, this attitude projects too much of a contemporary perspective on a peasant life-style, in which large families were advantageous to parental labor. Instead, female hesitation to beget many offspring can more accurately be set against the information available to us about life expectancies in the ancient world.

Archaeology in Palestine was once not particularly assiduous in its treatment of skeletal remains; far too few of the bones recovered in the excavation of tombs or burials have been subjected to osteological analysis. With much of biblical Israel subjected to antiquities laws prohibiting even the excavation of burial groups, contemporary archaeology does not offer much possibility for rectifying past deficiencies. The few existing reports of tomb excavations tend to focus on typologies of grave goods or of the tomb chambers themselves. Yet some investigations did include studies of the bones. Limited as they are, the results of such studies can be considered as valid evidence for general demographic conditions in ancient Palestine, because the results of those studies correspond exceedingly well to the results of similar studies on all premodern populations.[27]

The first notable fact to be retrieved from the study of ancient Palestinian burials, as at Jericho, Lachish, and Meiron,[28] is that the death rate was highest among the preadult population. In one tomb group, 35 percent of the individuals died before the age of 5, attesting to a high infant mortality rate. And childhood and adolescence were likewise fraught with risk: nearly half of the individuals did not survive to the age of 18. Paleopathologists have established that the cause of death in at least half, if not more, of all deaths—of both children and adults—was endemic disease (see Chapter 3, pp. 64–66). It just so happens that young children and old people are most susceptible to such infections and are most likely to have succumbed. In ancient Israel, as in most premodern societies, the begetting of many children was a response to the complex situation of economic needs and expected losses. To put it succinctly, in normal times (i.e., when unusual outbreaks of plague did not decimate the population), families would have had to produce nearly twice the number of children desired in order to achieve optimal family size.

The mortality rate for females in the childbearing years greatly exceeded that of males.[29] In a population in which the life expectancy for men hovered around 40, women would have had a life expectancy closer to 30. The physical risks related to childbearing constituted a gender-specific life threat. The matriarch Rachel is probably a representative case insofar as she died as she gave birth to her second son (Gen 35:16–18). In the modern western world, we are accustomed to thinking of women as living longer than men. However, in the premodern world, at least in agrarian populations tending toward large families, life expectancies for women were significantly lower than for men. It is no wonder that ancient biologists, Aristotle among them, proclaimed that the males of all species live longer than the females. It is a relatively modern phenomenon that the converse is true for humans.

It is against this background of the mortal risks involved in childbearing that the oracle of Genesis 3:16 must be seen. How does a woman overcome an understandable reluctance to have many children? The natural sexual and emotional desire that she experiences toward her mate is the answer. And this is accompanied by the male's response to her, which the last line of the oracle proclaims.

The words of line 4 are perhaps the most problematic in all the Hebrew Bible from a feminist perspective. They seem to establish an absolute and hierarchical dominance of males over females. The simple words have had a profound and persistent influence on sexual politics for millennia. Even modern biblical scholars who take pains to deal with the lexical subtleties and contextual aspects of many other vexing passages succumb to the canon of tradition when it comes to the final words of God's oracle to the woman in Eden. The subservience of women and the mastery of men are the double message of the oracle's conclusion, according to both early postbiblical exegetes and contemporary critics with access to methodological developments unavailable to the ancients.

One influential German commentary, for example, fails to analyze the language and syntax of Genesis 3:16, although it gives a fairly close reading to the oracle directed toward the man. The author of this classic treatment of Genesis discovers in 3:17–19 the background of the difficult life of a Palestinian peasant and sees the passage as an etiological response to hardship. But for the words addressed to the woman he does not even consider the contextual aspect. Rather, he points to "severe afflictions and terrible contradictions," and he summarizes the woman's lot as one of "humiliating domination."[30] Surely the use of such language on the part of a scholarly treatment signals a subjective judgment and a lapse of attention to critical exegetical procedures.

Even studies of Genesis 3 that do undertake to ascertain the grammatical and lexical nuances of verse 16 still suffer from the influence of traditional conceptualizations of the Eden story as an account of human sin and the fall from grace.[31] Thus, modern exegetes along with the ancient expositors have understood the last line of the oracle as divine approval of the social conditions of patriarchal control. In the words of one recent commentary, the narrator of Genesis 3 acknowledged and cheerfully [sic!] acquiesced to the social order of his people which accorded to women an inferior status and declared her, in theory at least, the chattel of her husband.[32]

Although postbiblical exegesis, both ancient and modern, has been nearly unanimous in reading line 4 of this poem as a mandate for the social dominance of male over female, there is one significant group of commentators that did not fail to notice the connection of the fourth line to the previous line, with its sexual connotations. The medieval Jewish commentators clearly understood that the words "he shall rule over you" lie within the context of the female's "desire" for the male. As such, those words do not constitute a general assertion of male dominion.

Only one modern scholar, to my knowledge, takes into account the observations of the medieval sages. In a fascinating survey of biblical passages dealing with human sexuality, a British scholar conversant with the medieval commentators rejects Genesis 3:16 as an expression of general male superiority or dominance:

> No such expression of "male chauvinism" is, however, called for in the present context which deals exclusively with woman's sexual predicament. The passage has thus been consistently misunderstood as an assertion of woman's general subservience to man, whereas in reality the two parts [lines 3 and 4] of the second hemistich hang closely together. . . . Medieval Jewish commentators had no doubt about the correct interpretation of the verse.[33]

Neither the medieval commentators nor the author of the above statement were social historians. Yet they have astutely recognized the relationship of the oracle in Genesis 3:16 to the issue of human sexuality. However, they do not comment on the place of that sexuality in the world of ancient Israel. It remains for social historians or anthropologists to point out that premodern societies inevitably created reproductive strategies congruent with their needs. It is this social phenomenon which helps us comprehend the oracular sanctions of Genesis 3:16. We shall explore the matter further below, after our exposition of line 4.

The theme of the female's sexual desire is extended in line 4, which begins with a pronoun subject, "he." Hebrew syntax does not require a separate pronominal subject, because such a subject is normally subsumed in the verbal form. Thus, the presence of a separate pronoun can serve to create a fuller clause than would the verbal form alone. Such a consideration is relevant in a poetic passage like this one. The addition of the pronoun can also provide emphasis for the subject. In this case, the independent "he" would give weight to the subject, the man, who is the object of the desire in the previous line. Neither syntactic possibility can be ruled out, and perhaps both are admissible.

The real crux of the final line lies in the verb, "to rule." The Hebrew root is *mšl*. Although the translation "rule" is appropriate in nearly all of the more than eighty instances in which this verb is found in the Hebrew Bible, it would be a mistake to think that in each passage it indicates precisely the same thing about the kind of rule or control involved. The author of the entry on *mšl* in a recent theological dictionary, while failing to recognize the context of the verb in this Genesis passage, nonetheless is well aware of the difficulty in providing a single definition or translation of the word for "rule": "The precise nature of the rule is as various as the real situations in which the action or state so designated occur. It seems to be the situation in all languages and cultures that words for oversight, rule, government must be defined in relation to the situation out of which the function arises."[34]

In the Bible the range of the subjects of the verb "to rule" and of the objects (i.e., those things or persons being dominated) is enormous. At the macrolevel is the concept of divine dominion, in which God rules over not only Israel but also all the nations as well as the natural world (e.g., Ps 22:28; 59:13; and 89:9). On the microlevel, in wisdom literature, "rule" can refer to the individual's self-control (Prov 16:32). In between is a variety of other usages, many of which have an explicitly political meaning, as when the author of Judges refers to a time when the Philistines were ascendant in Israel (Judg 14:4; 15:11).

It is intriguing to note that, except for the imperial dominion of David and Solomon or the eschatological hope for a similar extent of Judean control, the Israelite kings are never said to "rule" over their people. The verb *mšl*, in its political contexts, seems to refer to an extension of Israelite dominion beyond its primary locus. Solomon rules, for example, beyond his own Israelite kingdom; he "has dominion" over all the kingdoms from the Euphrates to Egypt (1 Kgs 5:1). Or, Og controls a group of territories besides his own Bashan (Josh 12:5). An earlier attempt to comprehend the nuances of "rule" led to the idea that *mšl*, except when used of God, suggests a dominion that does not naturally or legally inhere in the person exerting it.[35] Such a possibility should not now be eliminated, but it is not at the core of what is important to know about *mšl* as "rule."

This word takes on a larger or smaller scope depending on its context, and in this context the reproductive sexuality of a couple is what is to be subjected to the control of the male. Because of the life situation to which this oracle is addressed, the domination of the male is not a statement that his passion or lust is more important than that of the female. Rather, in light of an understandable reluctance of women to enter into the risks of pregnancy and birth, and because of the social and economic necessity that she do so frequently, the male's will within the realm of sexuality is to be imposed on the will of the female. He can insist on having sexual relations, with the hope that conception will result. Yet, because she experiences desire and yearning for the man, such male control would not be experienced as oppressive. In any case, to assume as most have done that this line presents hierarchical control, pervading all aspects of female–male interaction, is to wrench a clause from the specificity of its position in the oracular portion of a wisdom tale.

An analogy from a more recent period of human history may help to underscore the point that this line of Genesis 3:16 is a sanction that will facilitate childbearing to meet social needs. As such it is a "nationalist" text, similar to one that will be described at the beginning of Chapter 8. Hence, an example of the relationship between depopulation and nationalism as it affected authoritative sanction provides a telling comparison. The falling birthrate in nineteenth-century France was perceived as a grave threat to the Third Republic's role as a world power.[36] Although their voices were not welcomed by most male political figures of the time, French feminists rightly saw depopulation as a female as well as a male problem. One of the most outspoken feminists, Maria Martin, urged legal sanctions to encourage marriage and also childbirth, with or without marriage.[37] She claimed that young women needed to be encouraged to have many children and that there needed to be official incentives for that: many young women did not want children because they had seen their mothers suffer.

The solution to the depopulation problem in France, advocated by both feminists and patriarchists, was legislation that would promote natality. Ironically in light of recent feminist attitudes, motherhood became the claim to citizenship. The solution to the need for an increased birthrate in early Israel took the form of a divine ruling that gave men the power to overcome female reluctance. Motherhood likewise was to be encouraged as being in the national interest.

The typical translation of Genesis 3:16 that provides "he shall rule over you" is thus lexically correct, so long as its context is kept in mind. However, the difficulty in divorcing this translation from its millennia-long attachment to the concept of generalized male dominance and female subservience suggests that a different translation is warranted. Clearly it is time to put aside forever the unwarranted chauvinism of such translations as the Septuagint's "he will have authority over you" or the Jerusalem Bible's "he will lord it over you." It is also compelling, in light of the foregoing discussion, to dispel the patriarchal notion of divinely sanctioned male supremacy that "he shall rule" conjures up. Consequently, a translation that diverges from the usual ones even at the cost of some awkwardness in English is in order. The temptation is simply to switch English word order: "he will overrule her," to wit, in the matter of whether or not to satisfy desire, an act which hopefully would have implications for procreation. Alternatively, we suggest "he shall predominate over you," which preserves the concept of rule (dominion) yet allows for the less than absolute imposition of male will. Instead of projecting the idea of legal control, as does "rule," "predominate" at the least can avoid the connotation of authority and take into account the specific context of these poetic lines.

To summarize, lines 3 and 4 together should be understood as responses to the situation established by lines 1 and 2. Women have to work hard and have many children, as lines 1 and 2 proclaim; their reluctance to conform, which is not explicitly stated but can be reconstructed by looking at the biological and socioeconomic realities of ancient Palestine, had to be overcome. Lines 3 and 4 tell us how: female reluctance is overcome by the passion they feel toward their men, and that allows them to accede to the males' sexual advances even though they realize that undesired pregnancies (with the accompanying risks) might be the consequence.

The Eden Oracle in Context

Our investigation of the words and syntax of Genesis 3:16 has been extensive, chiefly because that passage is so fraught with implications for an understanding of women in the biblical period as well as for a sense of how postbiblical exegesis has used, or misused, canonical materials. These pages of close scrutiny are the least we can offer in the face of two millennia of tradition that saw in God's oracle to the woman something fundamentally different from what this examination has revealed. In each word or phrase, lexical and poetic considerations have led us to a translation that departs considerably from those with which most of us are familiar. Let us now put together our line-by-line rendering, as just worked out, as a prelude to a discussion of the societal conditions to which it speaks:

> I will greatly increase your toil and your pregnancies;
> (Along) with travail shall you beget children.
> For to your man is your desire,
> And he shall predominate over you.

If there can be any doubts as to the conditions to which such an oracle is addressed, the oracle to the man that follows should help put them aside. Genesis 3:17–19 depicts a life in which enormous effort is required to secure the essentials—"bread," the staff of life. Bread both symbolizes all sustenance and alludes to the field crops that hill country farmers had to work so hard to produce. The information gleaned from archaeology, historical geography, and the study of ancient agriculture (see Chapter 3) has shown that in the isolated hill country of premonarchic Palestine, life would have been more difficult and existence more fragile than in most other areas of the ancient Near East. The soil is inhospitable and suitable only for thorns and thistles. To those who seek to make the land life-sustaining, it is indeed "cursed."

The man's lot is to labor unceasingly. But for the female, a twofold responsibility is laid forth in response to the demographic as well as the environmental conditions. Her role will be to have more children than she might otherwise desire and to contribute more extensively to productive tasks than was expected of peasant women of the late second millennium. Just how much more, or what the patterns of female agrarian labor were, will be considered in Chapter 7.

Genesis 3, as a wisdom tale, addresses the conditions to which the highland settlers had to adapt. It deals with elementary questions about life and its hardships, about the endless and unremitting efforts it requires. The gnawing questions are addressed as to why life is so difficult and why there is so much labor for simple survival. This question is of the same order as, but perhaps even more fundamental than, the existential predicaments underlying the eloquent discourses of Job and Ecclesiastes.

Genesis 2–3 responds to the human anguish about the crushing realities and uncertainties of life with a parable or tale, in much the way that mythographic expression constitutes a response to the human predicament in other ancient literatures.[38] The nature of the response is comparable in the Bible and in pagan literature: the human condition is ordained by God and must be accepted as such. Further, although the Genesis 3 tale itself does not deal directly with this, biblical wisdom in general does not leave us with an entirely gloomy picture. For example, two wisdom psalms (127 and 128) that are thematically related to Genesis 3 in their concern with labor and procreation take the assumptions about hard work and large families a step further: acknowledging God's sovereignty, along with accepting one's lot in life, brings its own rewards of happiness and fulfillment.

Because the Genesis 3:16–19 description of the human condition does not include the positive potential involved in accepting God's imperative, it has repeatedly been seen as having an inherent connection with the disobedience of the primeval couple in the first part of the chapter. Yet, as we have already suggested, the poetic portion (3:14–19)—on literary criteria alone—may stand apart from the surrounding prose narrative of Genesis 2–3, which contains its own punishment: the expulsion from Eden. Even critics adhering to traditional sin–punishment readings of the text recognize the discrete character of the oracles.[39] The oracles have an independent etiological force. Hence, the prescriptions in them become penalties only in their canonical position within the prose framework. God's poetic pronouncements, involving a curse for both the serpent and the soil and the establishment of complementary life roles for the archetypal couple, function on their own as divine sanctions for societal conditions. God ordains certain patterns of behavior for the people who have acknowledged his sovereignty and who need the support of divine prescription in order to sustain their pioneer efforts.

The divine call for increased female procreation in particular must be seen in relation to the social situation. As explained in Chapter 1 (p. 22), religious sanctions in premodern societies operate, often quite unconsciously, in some ways to allow for optimum human adaptations to the environments on which they depend. Viewed anthropologically, population growth is a "human possibility which is *encouraged* by certain institutions, as well as technological or environmental circumstances, but equally may be discouraged by other circumstances."[40] If this be so, then a situation in which population growth was advantageous would call for an increase in conceptions and also in cultural values encouraging such increase, which is just what Genesis 3:16 provides. That it does so becomes evident when it is compared with a mythographic response to the opposite demographic situations.

Situations of overpopulation also evoked adaptive sanctions; in such cases, a decrease in human fertility naturally would be encouraged. A fascinating text from Mesopotamia contains a mythic description of the desirability of miscarriages, of infant (and adult) mortality, and of vocations for women that preclude marriage and childbearing. The gods ordain such measures in response to the "great noise of mankind," in other words, the multiplication of people and the ensuing tumult and unrest.[41] Such a text apparently arose from, and helped society adjust to, recurring eras of overpopulation that strained the resources of the land between the rivers.[42]

In sum, the societal conditions—the context—which best suit the thrust of the poetic oracles to the female and male in Genesis 3:16–19 seem to be those of the Israelite highlanders in the earliest period of their corporate existence and of their self-consciousness as Yahweh's people. That was the period which called for an outpouring of labor and a growth of population that would have exceeded preceding or succeeding eras. The early Iron Age stands out as the period in which the historical and environmental features provide the most suitable background for the blunt imperatives concerning the use of human energy in these oracles. The survival of a nation of pioneer farmers called for extraordinary efforts during this period of settlement. Never again would the need for so powerful a mandate for increased toil and family size be so acute.

The evidence that Genesis 3:16 is addressed to Israelite women in the premonarchic period would be precariously circumstantial were it not for some additional chronological data. Genesis 3, in terms of thematic content and also (though to a lesser extent) in terms of actual language, is related to several poetic passages that belong to an early stage of Israelite literature. The two wisdom psalms (127 and 128) mentioned above have an archaic quality that suggests that they are at the beginning of the tradition of Israelite psalmody. Similarly, the Song of Hannah (1 Sam 2:1–10) deals thematically with the issues treated in Genesis 3. God provides unexpected assistance in the three basic areas of human activity: the battle is won, the barren conceive many, the impoverished receive bread. While Hannah's song itself dates from the early monarchy, at exactly the point (verses 4–5) where it is most relevant to the Eden oracle it depends on the language of Psalm 113, which can in fact be dated to the premonarchic period.[43]

The message to the first woman as Everywoman arose in a context which demanded an intensification of female labor and fecundity. Precisely because of Eve's archetypal role, the Eden passage seems to mandate such a pattern for all who follow in the Yahwist tradition. The first woman stands for all, and all therefore must increase their productivity and procreativity. Or must they? In a way, the silence of the rest of the Hebrew Bible about Eve and Adam provides a mute comment on the ongoing validity of the female job description. One might test the universal applicability of God's address to the woman by asking if the parallel imperative to the man means that males must forever plow a thorny field? As the context determines the prescriptive validity of the proclamation to the archetypal male, so must it also be the crucial factor in the words to Everywoman.

6

Eve's World: The Family Household

Everywoman Eve, in the formative centuries of Israelite existence, lived in small villages in the highlands of central Palestine. Archaeological surveys and excavations in the highlands have revealed a virtual explosion of small, unwalled settlements coinciding with the origins of ancient Israel. Cataloguing of the number and density of hill country sites has been accompanied by studies of the economic basis for the survival of the new settlements in previously unsettled places. This analysis of the village ecology and technology provides crucial information about the demands and constraints communities placed on their inhabitants. The demographic and subsistence challenge confronting the pioneers in the hill country has emerged from the mists of a history undocumented in conventional sources. Against such a backdrop, the mandate for significant female contribution to societal tasks and to demographic growth appears functionally essential.

To this point, we have considered mainly the largest societal setting— all Israel—and the symbolic individual component, the woman or Eve. For a closer look at the life of Everywoman, we must examine her immediate and determinative social context. As in all preindustrial societies, the dominant social world for virtually all members of society was the household, or domestic living group. There were larger social units, which we shall describe briefly; still, it was the household unit that shaped and sustained daily existence for nearly everyone. All women, children, and nearly all men occupied in everyday life social niches determined by the structure of the unit of people with whom they worked and lived. That structure, in both a physical and social sense, provided the direct, constant, and most significant context for the lives of all the individuals. If we wish to focus on the lives of Israelite women, we must try to see their immediate living environment. In short, the nature of the Israelite household is the salient factor in reconstructing Eve's life.

It is not easy to sketch the Israelite household. Superficially, it would seem that the researcher could go to the biblical text, identify the vocabulary that deals with houses and their residents, and then analyze the various passages in which the language of domestic arrangements is utilized. Would that such a process were possible. As it happens, the biblical vocabulary for the smallest social unit greater than the individual is not uniform in what it depicts and hence confounds attempts at analysis of terminology.

Before dealing with the household level of social organization, it will be helpful to look at the overall structure of Israelite society. Note that the individual is not considered to be a discrete unit of society in this analysis. The reasons for not treating the individual are complex and probably justifiable. While the individual may universally be the smallest unit of society, the relational definition of social patterns precludes description of the individual alone as a social unit.

Furthermore, the ancient Hebraic (and Semitic) concept of the individual was not developed in the ways in which it is today. We are accustomed to thinking about people as autonomous beings. In so doing, we tend to abstract ourselves and our own personalities from our familial and social contexts far more than did our biblical forebears. For them identity was relational, whereas for us personal identity tends to involve individuation and separation. These divergent perspectives are not necessarily diametric opposites. Nonetheless, to focus on the individual in Israelite society would be to give undue weight to a member of a group for which corporate existence was the fundamental grounding of life.

Awareness of this communal orientation of ancient life is essential to any consideration of the matter of exploitation of individuals. This issue cannot be pursued in the same way for ancient Israel as for post-archaic societies. When the meaning of individual existence is so fully subsumed into the characteristics and exigencies of the groups on which the individual is dependent for survival, the possibility of dehumanizing or abusive behavior toward categories of individuals may in fact be nonexistent. Thus the feminist perspective that condemns ancient Israel for putative sexism and gender inequality by and large fails to recognize the thorough integration of personal identity with social context in Hebraic thought. Such distortion is particularly true in feminist suspicion of biblical texts urging human fertility. The nationalistic basis (see Chapter 8, pp. 165–166) for such texts is virtually ignored.

In 1926, the Danish biblical scholar Johannes Pedersen set forth a classic delineation of the "soul," the individual as a totality and not as the sum of physical and mental or spiritual parts, in biblical thought.[1] His exploration of the individual and of his or her identity led him to conclude that individual existence is inextricably linked to its biological and social matrix and that an individual removed from or cut off from his or her social context is in pain and danger:

> Life is not something individual, to be shaped according to the needs of each individual. Man [= person] is only what he is as a link in the family. . . . When we look at the soul, we always see a community rising behind it. What it is, it is by virtue of others. It has sprung up from a family which has filled it with its contents, and from which it can never grow away. The family forms the narrowest community in which it lives. But wherever it works, it must live in community, because it is its nature to communicate itself to others, to share blessing with them.[2]

More recent treatments[3] differ at points with Pedersen's analysis, but none would deny the bonds integrating individual with community.

In short, although as human beings we have much in common with our fellow humans throughout history, and all over the world, we must recognize that fundamental differences among world views exist among various cultures. For our own biblical heritage, it is especially difficult to conceive of the otherness of the ancient Israelite world. Western religion holds the products of that world—the biblical canon—as sacred and authoritative. Such a stand makes the canon part of the modern world, brings the biblical past into some kind of equivalency with the present. Yet, for all the continuity, there are radical differences. The contemporary focus of western life on the individual, on autonomous development and self-fulfillment, is one crucial area of distinction between the biblical mind set and our own. Hence, we must take care to examine the context that defined individual female existence. We must also resist the temptation to judge the role and status of women in antiquity with the same criteria applicable to women today.

The Larger Contexts: Tribe and Clan

During its premonarchic period, ancient Israel is understood to have had three levels of social organization constituting the unified people "Israel": tribe, clan or family, and household. These levels defy exact delineation; but examining them means beginning with the terminology used in the Hebrew Bible itself, although that is not an easy task. The Bible is hardly a monolithic document and is certainly not a sociological treatise. It does, however, reflect social patterns that were established and then changed over the course of the millennia during which the canon took shape. Biblical scholarship has therefore long used sociological and anthropological categories to help make sense of the biblical data. In consideration of ancient Israel as a national entity, political analogies have also played a useful role.

For the all-inclusive national existence that subsumes the three levels of social organization, no single technical term exists in the Hebrew Bible. Israel speaks of itself as a whole by a variety of loosely applied nouns, such as "people," "nation," "assembly," "covenanted people," "congregation," "league." More often than not, Israelite national identity is expressed through the use of proper names designating a sociopolitical unity. The name "Israel," of course, stands out as the preferred one, with the expanded term "Israelites" being an allied designation.[4] It should be noted that the latter term, "Israelites," is literally "sons/children of Israel" in Hebrew. As such it is an expansion of a family term. Its usage as a term for all Israel indicates the conceptual importance of biological relationship as a meaningful indicator of common destiny. Although the political and ethnic nuances of the Israelite self-conception are neither uniform in a limited epoch nor consistent over time, the expression of national identity through the language of family bonds persists. Family context is a powerful and tenacious expression of identity at all levels. It indicates in the realm of language and conceptualization a prominence of family life equal to that revealed in our examination of economic, social, and political factors.

As regards the three levels of social organization that constitute the nation Israel, similar problems of imprecise biblical terminology and difficulty of sociological identification beset the researcher. The tribe, which was the primary unit of social organization in premonarchic Israel, perhaps comes closest to having a reliable and consistent designation within the biblical text. The term "tribe" in English Bibles is a translation of two different Hebrew words, but in most cases the words appear to be virtually synonymous in that they refer to the same groupings of component (tribal) units. Each tribal unit has its own name, derived from the name of its eponymous ancestor, one of the sons of the patriarch Jacob.[5] The tribes, though typically grouped as parallel units, were hardly uniform in their demographic or geographic size, nor did they have identical individual histories of formation and of appropriation of territory.

In the absence of extensive or uniform biblical descriptions and histories of all the tribes, the nature of individual tribes and their relationship to each other as a national unity has been the topic of considerable scholarly speculation and debate. This scholarly interest is far from subsiding, even in the wake of Gottwald's encyclopedic treatment of the subject in *Tribes of Yahweh*. Nonetheless, the skepticism about whether a national unity of tribes ever existed before the monarchic period has probably been dealt a mortal blow by the systematic social scientific analysis of Israel as a tribal society. My own work on tribal function indicates that the tribes, at least in Galilee, must have had political and supratribal orientation dating to their origins in the settlement period.[6]

The second subdivision of Israelite society—clan or family—is more difficult to locate, and its functional characteristics are more problematic to describe. The terminology is deceptively simple insofar as only two Hebrew words are involved. One (*mišpaḥah*) is preponderant and is usually translated "family"; with its strong connotations of nuclear family in English, however, this translation is unsatisfactory. The other (*'eleph*) is rarer and is a distinctively military term that suffers from a variety of inaccurate translations, including "thousands."[7] In sociological terminology, this level of organization is called a clan by some, or a phratry ("brotherhood," or groups of kindred who are related—in the case of ancient Israel—patrilineally) by others. Tribes were composed of these units, with the number of the "family" or clan units per tribe varying considerably. An average of fifty "family" groups—clans, or associated families—can be established for each tribe for the premonarchic period on the basis of the census lists in the Bible (Num 1 and 26; see Exod 6:16–19 and Num 3:14–20), although the lists of actually named groups gives the unrealistic impression that there were fewer of these subtribal units than was actually the case.[8]

These "family" groups themselves varied in size and strength. Note, for example, Gideon's protest about his ability to lead his people in a crisis situation. If social resources are the criteria of leadership ability, Gideon doubts his ability to rise to the challenge: "Pray, Lord, how can I deliver Israel? Behold, my clan is the weakest in Manasseh [tribe]" (Judg 6:15). Fortunately, Yahweh assures him that divine help will more than compensate for the deficiencies in his resources, and Gideon rises to the occasion. From our perspective, the implicit variation in clan size is what is relevant in that episode. A large "family" grouping or clan could itself occupy a whole village; alternately, many smaller associated "families" or clans could constitute the population of a village, or a large collection of "families" or clans might occupy several small settlements. That is, the social composition of a village was related, but not equivalent, to the territorial distribution of these "family" or clan units. However, it is probably better to reckon the size of villages (which was probably a reflection to a large extent of topography and resources) by the smaller social units that comprise these "families," as described in the next section.

The use of quotation marks with the term family is to suggest a difference from our culturally bound concept of the term. Family means to us either the nuclear family of parents and children occupying a common domicile, or the larger extended family, the network of grandparents, aunts and uncles, and cousins that gathers for cultural or religious events (holidays) or for landmarks in the lives of its members (e.g., births, birthdays, marriages, deaths). Because of its inherent ambiguity in English, this term is woefully inadequate to represent the lineage level of tribal organization.

To confuse matters further, the Hebrew word for the "family" or clan as the intermediate level of social organization is not always representative of biologically connected units. Like "children of Israel," it can be used metaphorically to describe closely related groups. Israel conceived of itself genealogically, via a family tree. The Bible links diverse geographic or ethnic components through the symbolic language of kinship relationships.[9] Consequently, while real biological connections may often have been present, they are subsumed to nonbiological ones in a pseudogenealogical scheme emphasizing connection and unity. Again, such an arrangement indicates the power of family imagery and thus of family structures as key social units in ancient Israel.

The third, or smallest, level of social organization in ancient Israel is sometimes referred to as the "family," but the term is no more appropriate to denote this tertiary level of Israelite society than it is for the secondary level. Consequently, we refer to the coresidential unit as the "household," a word that also has limitations. This smallest social unit of ancient Israelite society, though perhaps the most elusive, is probably the most significant in terms of how it defined the daily patterns of existence for the individuals who were included within it.

The household is usually considered the fundamental unit of society by social scientists.[10] The tribe, with its artificial basis, was probably the least significant social dimension for the men and women of ancient Israel. The intermediate social unit of "family" or clan was probably the basic determinant of land apportionment and of geographic identity and was next in importance. It was also the level at which problems involving the component social units of the clan were negotiated. And it provided material aid, protection, and marriage possibilities for its members. Yet, the inner workings of the household, constituting the "family," created the general frame of reference of daily life, making the smallest social unit the primary and most important part of premonarchic Israel. The household determined an individual's roles and responsibilities as members of society. As such, it was not functionally subordinate to the clan and tribe but rather was a quasi-independent and effective unit within the larger levels of social organization.[11]

One might view the individual in early Israel as standing inside three concentric circles, representing the three levels of social organization. The immediate or smallest circle was fully and directly visible to the individual positioned in the center; the other two impinged less directly and less frequently on one's consciousness but still were an inextricable part of the individual's world.

Examining the Household Unit

Unlike the situation in the modern world, effective membership in ancient Israelite society for nearly everyone would have been possible only through membership in a family household.[12] Again, the biblical vocabulary provides the starting point for examining the character of this basic unit of society. As for the other levels of social organization, the biblical terminology is deceptively simple. Only one phrase comes close to designating this innermost circle of Israelite life: *bet 'ab* which literally means "house of the father." The first word of this phrase can designate the physical structure in which people live. But it can also, as it clearly does in this phrase, indicate a living group and as such is difficult to identify on the basis of biblical texts.

The problems of delineating what is meant by "house of the father," which we will call "family household," derive from several quarters. First, the phrase is used in the Bible in several contexts in which it clearly refers to tribes and not to the smallest, family-based unit. This usage may be metaphoric for the pseudo-kinship structure the biblical writers have imposed on their understanding of the people Israel, but that fact does not mitigate the confusion of terminology it introduces. Similarly, the phrase sometimes refers to the clan level of organization, indicating the importance of the kinship conceptualization. The idea of "family household" was so powerful that it was used in reference to all levels of kinship.[13]

The appearance of the phrase representing the smallest unit of society as a designation for larger units complicates efforts to clarify the identity of the household. And even where the phrase does designate the household unit, there is considerable variability in what it means. This imprecision in the terminology may be the result of a certain fluidity introduced by the developing course of social organization over the long period of time (nearly a millennium) reflected in the various biblical references to the *bet 'ab,* the "family household." However, it is more useful to examine the imprecision in terms of variations that existed at any given point in Israelite history rather than as a mark of changing configurations over time.

Households were variable. They were flexible units of coresidency that adapted to divergent and shifting political and economic strictures. For most of Israel's existence, there were manifold family residential settings—hamlets, villages, farmsteads, regional urban centers, imperial or national capitals—and consequently there were probably a variety of residential patterns. That variety would in turn be compounded by the economic influences at work in shaping the size and makeup of a household. Classical scholars have a similar difficulty with terminology for family groups in the literature of ancient Greece and Rome. The classical world, like the world of the Israelites, was too disparate to permit a simple designation of a family group.

David Herlihy, a social historian who has studied the classical roots of the medieval household, has noted the irregular vocabulary for family and household in classical literature. He sees in this an indication that families varied widely across society and that there were fundamental differences among various configurations of domestic life.[14] In addition to inconsistent terminology, one of the signs of household diversity for Herlihy was that the Romans did not use the household as a unit for the census. The biblical material is comparable in this respect. The Bible records a number of censuses, for military or taxation purposes. In each case the assessment is made on the basis of the individuals (potential soldiers or taxpayers) rather than households. With respect to the vagueness of the language for households, the analogy between the classical and the biblical worlds is apt. Herlihy's conclusion about this imprecision is probably applicable to the Hebraic sources: "they lacked a concept of family or household that could be applied across all social levels."[15] His observation of the one exception to this is also noteworthy with respect to Israelite society. He identified the households associated with family-based peasant agriculture under Roman colonial expansion as having consistent patterns.[16]

In light of the specific conditions of agrarian development characterizing the formative period of ancient Israel, as described in Chapter 3, it is reasonable to assume the existence of commensurate household units across most of Israelite society during that noncentralized, nonurban period. The variety of households that emerged as Israel's economic and political life became more complex in later centuries would not yet have existed in the premonarchic period. Consequently, delineating households for tribal Israel would mean understanding the domestic groups in which most of the population of that time lived. This understanding of the domestic groups also suggests patterns that held for a significant portion of the population that continued to occupy relatively isolated agricultural villages even after the formation of the Israelite state.

Let us look more closely at the translation "family household" (for Hebrew *bet 'ab*). As a phrase in English, it is composed of two words that are congruent to some extent but are logically and empirically different.[17] In combination, the two words have important implications. Strictly speaking, "family" is a kinship term, whereas "household" is a somewhat more flexible term connoting both residency and social function. The latter is more inclusive; household can, notably in an agrarian setting, include a set of related people and also residential quarters, outbuildings, granaries, wells, tools and equipment, livestock, fields, and orchards.[18] It can also include people not related by kinship, such as captives, servants, and temporary residents or "sojourners."

Descriptive and analytical materials from the social sciences augment the material in the Bible about the household unit, as well as the tribe and clan levels of society. Rich as such a source of information might be, use of it is hampered somewhat by the lack of historical perspective that has characterized much of the work on family groups or households. The interest in family groups is greater than ever, but research on such groups in past history is remarkably sparse. A comprehensive bibliography of studies in this field lists only about 2 percent of the titles as dealing with historical themes.[19] The lack of interest in past domestic arrangements obviously is related to the difficulty in obtaining accurate, ample, and balanced information. It is challenging enough to investigate the structures directly visible to the observer in today's world. To examine social units of a past world seems understandably almost impossible to most social scientists. As a result, information about family households in premodern times has come more from historians with a vested interest in particular epochs than from social scientists.

The paucity of data from ancient periods has not been the only obstacle to the description and assessment of domestic groups in antiquity. The intellectual barrier imposed by nineteenth-century evolutionary models of domestic households has yet to be fully dismantled. Although modern anthropology and sociology are in great measure the result of a rejection of the Darwinist schemes of such Victorian theorists as Bachofen and Morgan, the residual assumptions of a linear development of domestic structures, from large and complex to small and simple, have not been fully expunged.[20] Victorian perceptions of family life still interfere in subtle ways (see below) with attempts to reconstruct households of previous times.

The last statement concerns the matter of household function as much as of structure. These are two distinct and important features of the household, and they should not be confused or interchanged.[21] That is, identifying the familial structure and sometimes the nonfamilial supplements (servants, slaves, sojourners) to a household group does not provide automatic entree into what takes place within the household unit. The composition of the domestic unit is not a simple determinant of the interaction of its members or of the range of individual and social needs that the household provides. The Victorian explorers, fascinated with foreign societies around the globe, were obsessed with the descriptive task. They carefully recorded family structures as they saw them during relatively brief periods of observation, and they noted obvious domestic activities. But they were not yet conceptually or methodologically prepared to delve into the less visible functional dimensions of domestic life.

Such Victorian patterns of anthropological research have been unfortunately persistent. Ironically, perhaps this is because twentieth-century anthropologists have often been influenced by Marxist theories, which include the theories of family structure put forth by Victorian scholars. Engels' classic work, *The Origin of the Family, Private Property, and the State* (1884), has perpetuated evolutionary views in a surprisingly tenacious way until quite recently.[22] Therefore, those who might be most critical of a stereotyped view of family groups were nonetheless party to descriptive and classificatory modes of research that did little to demonstrate the dynamic and multidimensional aspects of households.

However, contemporary anthropological and historical data have challenged the validity of stereotypes and questioned the existence of universal schemes.[23] The research on contemporary households clearly realizes the need to analyze function as well as form, context as well as configuration. This realization has occurred in part because of feminist interest in delineating female roles and eliminating damaging stereotypes. For antiquity, too, we must recognize that the investigation of the structure of a household can tell only part of the story of women's position in society. Identifying the particular social and economic functions of the household as well as the relationship of those functions to the larger social context is fundamental to an understanding of the roles of women in any society. The domestic unit is a social one, not a "natural" one. In each setting, the domestic unit interacts with its specific environment and with the larger social units of which it is a part to produce a unique and dynamic structure. To deal with any historical example of domestic life, we must "deconstruct the family as a natural unit, and reconstruct it as a social one."[24]

Our task, then, is first to delineate as accurately as possible the structure of Israelite family households—particularly for the premonarchic period—and after that to explore the function of those households. In this way the immediate household context of female lives in ancient Israel can come to light, and the role of women in the domestic realm and hence in society as a whole will become more visible than traditional readings of the sources have ever allowed.

Household Structure in Early Israel

Our ability to retrieve the smallest unit of social organization from the darkness of a world several millennia removed is facilitated by the kind of synthetic approach described in Chapter 1. Archaeological materials, biblical passages, and analogies from social science combine to provide a reasonably accurate picture of the family household in the premonarchic period. Investigating the morphology, or shape, of the Israelite household is one kind of research dealing with the Bible and its world that is the beneficiary of recent developments in all components of the interdisciplinary approach.

Archaeological discoveries in ancient village as well as urban sites in Palestine has produced an interesting body of evidence that is relevant to an examination of the family household. The family household, at least for our purposes in examining Israelite forms, is a residential group.[25] Consequently, the size, shape, location, and interrelationship of domestic buildings provides basic information about households.

A number of field projects have produced data that bear directly on the investigation of the Israelite household. One project has excavated two village sites in the Judean hills north of Jerusalem. These sites, 'Ai (et-Tell) and Raddana, were excavated by Callaway and by Callaway and Cooley, respectively, in the late 1960s and early 1970s.[26] Another project has focused on the northern Negev, south of Jerusalem, where the village of Masos (Khirbet el-Meshash) was excavated in the 1970s by Kempinski and Fritz.[27] Both of these projects have uncovered remains of Iron I domestic groups, and the evidence from these three sites as well as from others has been collected and astutely analyzed in an article entitled "The Archaeology of the Family in Ancient Israel."[28]

Prevailing opinions, based on the excavation of more developed (i.e., urban) or later sites, supposed that the typical Israelite domestic building housed a coresident group that should be identified as a simple or nuclear family. This elementary family form would have been composed of a conjugal pair or a widowed person with unmarried offspring.[29] However, at these three Iron I village sites excavated in the past two decades, small dwellings that can be identified as those of conjugal units are linked together into residential compounds. Two or three individual units sharing a common courtyard and certain domestic installations and technological features are architecturally connected. Together, these units form a multiple-family dwelling. Not only are units architecturally joined, but also their spatial arrangement implies the economic and social integration of the subunits that occupied the individual components of these domestic compounds. A range of activities was carried out within the compound, and these activities served all the members of the living group and therefore linked them into a single household. The description of those activities relates to the function of the household and will be discussed separately in Chapter 7.

These compound dwellings were not isolated structures amidst a village of single-family homes; they were the rule, not the exception. Extensive excavation in large areas of the tiny Iron Age villages have shown repeated examples of domestic compounds. Together, these structures provide evidence that the family unit occupying the basic household of early Israel was larger than just the elementary couple with offspring. What may have been the family composition of such residential compounds? There is no single or simple response to this question, but a consideration of the theoretical possibilities in conjunction with some biblical texts provides a reasonable answer.

The family group that occupied these compound dwellings may have been what is called an "extended family household," a group composed of a conjugal pair and one or more relatives other than offspring. There might be one or more siblings or cousins of a member of the pair; one or more uncles, aunts, or parents of a member of the pair; or nieces, nephews, or grandchildren. In other words, the elementary unit can be extended laterally (siblings, cousins), upward (parents, aunts, uncle), and/or downward (nieces, nephews, grandchildren). It is not possible to determine which of these extended-family patterns would have prevailed. Probably no single pattern was more common than any other.

Rather, the extension of the family would have depended on the particular circumstances of any individual family. The survival of parents into old age, the death of spouses or of a sibling or a cousin, the orphaning of children of near kin—such events would have lent distinctive character to individual extended-family households.

Another possible living configuration for the occupants of these dwelling clusters would be what is called a "multiple-family household." In such a situation, two or more conjugal pairs with or without offspring would have been the inhabitants of the units of the domestic compound. The typical, laterally formed case would be of two or more brothers, with their families. This sort of arrangement, also known as a "joint family," might be augmented by other family members. If parents, uncles or aunts, or more distant single relatives were also present, the pure joint family begins to look more like the extended family.

In one of the few examples that can be gleaned from a biblical text, Judges 17–18 tells the story of Micah, the head of a household in the hill country of Ephraim. The narrative reveals a man living with his widowed mother (whose wealth is used for the enrichment of the family's cultic life), his sons and probably their wives, and a young priest whom he hires to serve household needs. The key verse in the account is Judges 18:22, which describes the men of Micah's household in pursuit of some Danites who had made off with Micah's cultic objects and his newly hired priest. The raiding Danites were pursued and apprehended by the "men who were in the houses comprising the household of Micah."[30]

This text is a remarkably apt description of a multiple-family household compound of the period of the Judges.[31] Like the clusters of dwellings found by archaeologists in the highlands, Micah's household involved multiple living units. Furthermore, several functional roles of such a family collective are revealed in the Micah narrative. At the least, economic, social, religious, and military characteristics of a household from the premonarchic period are present in Micah's household.

The physical shape of the compound dwellings of early Israel is clear in the archaeological record. But the structure of the kinship group occupying the compound cannot be rigidly identified. It would surely have been in flux, as generational shifts—the death of parents or grandparents, the marriage of children, the birth of children or grandchildren—proceeded. Evidence from ethnography supports the notion that no single pattern of family organization can characterize all the compounds at a given time nor any single compound over time.[32] The important fact to deduce from the archaeological and ethnographic evidence is that early Israelite households were consistently larger than the nuclear family but that various configurations of the extended- and/or multiple-family units would have existed simultaneously.

Biblical passages, such as the Judges narrative just cited, relate well to the archaeological and anthropological evidence for the existence of households larger than the simple conjugal unit. Other kinds of information contained in biblical materials likewise support this view of complex family structures, at least in isolated highland villages during Israel's formative period. Some two decades ago a British group concerned with "Social and Economic Administration" sponsored the publication of a carefully researched monograph, entitled *The Extended Family in the Old Testament*,[33] on family organization and kinship groups in biblical times. Although the adherence to the term "extended family" is unfortunate, the author's analysis of the kinship groups represented by two passages in Leviticus is compelling.

The passages under discussion, Leviticus 18 and 20, are the so-called incest taboos of ancient Israel. It is difficult to tell whether the prohibitions should be understood as regulating whom a man might marry or with which close family members a woman should not have sexual relations.[34] Porter rejects both of these explanations. At least for Leviticus 18, the regulations

> are not concerned with marriage, nor primarily with close blood kinship, nor are they to be explained as that of 'psychic community'. . . . they are not attempting to set out a general concept of chastity on a biological basis, as they have been commonly understood, but . . . they reflect the conditions of a particular period in the development of Israel's social organization, the situation of the 'extended family' living together as a unit.[35]

Porter asserts that a kinship group wider than our western nuclear family played a critical role in ancient Israelite society. The Levitical regulations (cast in Leviticus 18 in the absolute, apodictic "Thou shall not" form of unconditional premises) deal with the most fundamental of social concerns: the harmony of the basic household unit. According to the British scholar, A. D. H. Mayes, the laws of Leviticus 18:6–18 define marriage negatively by specifying those family members with whom marriage is prohibited. Marriage is forbidden within relationships that are defined as family (and not clan) and that presuppose a complex or extended-family unit. Mayes also notes that the concept of collective responsibility to the third and fourth generation, as proclaimed in the Decalogue (Exod 20:5), is meaningful only in families extending across three or four generations.[36]

That incest taboos governing complex family units stem from the earliest period of Israel is a conviction held by many scholars in addition to Porter and Mayes. The Pentateuchal sources in which family law is found are of disputed date; but regardless of how late family law took canonical form, many of the sources can go back to early stages of Israelite life. Incest taboos apparently governed the extended- or multiple-family households that existed in earliest Israel and that no doubt persisted later in certain settings throughout Israelite history.

Incest regulations governing living groups larger than the conjugal unit should be viewed as a means of coping with the tensions and temptations of close kin living under conditions of relative intimacy.[37] That is, incest taboos are related to the size as much as to the configuration of the domestic group. With incest taboos, two important questions arise. First, if family size affected the need for incest taboos, just how large were the multiple or extended peasant families? Second, if these regulations are coping strategies for complex households, why would large living groups form if they create difficulties of jealousy and problems with authority?

Let us first consider family size. Some archaeologists have estimated that eight people lived in a conjugal unit, an estimation that would suggest, correspondingly, twenty persons in a complex household.[38] But these estimates seem too large[39] in the light of anthropological studies of fertility and life expectancies. With a life expectancy of about 40 years and a reproductive rate resulting in four offspring per conjugal pair, such studies suggest that extended families could therefore only reach the size of twelve to fourteen persons.[40]

Household size is clearly dependent on a multitude of variables[41] that are not all determinable for a past society. Nonetheless, the suggestion of a compound dwelling unit housing up to a dozen individuals seems reasonable, particularly in light of the capacity of the cisterns in the hill country villages.[42] The circumstantial possibilities for sexual liaisons in the cycles of an extended or multiple family would be numerous, and the attempt to maintain a harmonious family life would have been well served by explicit taboos. The repetition of the taboos in the Pentateuch (in Leviticus 20 in conditional form and with severe punishments, and as part of a litany of curses in Deuteronomy 27) indicates their importance and points indirectly to the regulation of complex families occupying domestic compounds in early Israel. The tensions arising from the dynamics of complex families necessitated the authoritative control of divine law.

The incest laws relate only to kin-based family attachments; therefore, except for the priest of Micah, our discussion of household structure and size has omitted mention of household members who were not kin. The term "household" is preferable to "family" for the occupants of the domestic compound, because it avoids vagueness of definition and also allows for the possibility that individuals unrelated to the core family group might reside with the household, participate in its functions, and affect its size. With its attention to servants or slaves acquired for economic or military reasons, biblical law surely allows for the augmentation of the family group by outsiders. Law and narrative also attest to "sojourners," that is, persons who are temporarily (or permanently) removed from their own families and take up residence in a village distant from their own.

The frequency of such arrangements is difficult to determine, especially for the premonarchic period. As was the case for polygamous marriages (which were probably far less frequent than the familiar biblical tales of the patriarchs or the royal family would suggest), the formation of households involving unrelated individuals was probably not normative or frequent. The regulations dealing with servants, slaves, and sojourners are probably concerned with economic developments during the monarchy when large landholders emerged. Like the royal family, the families owning extensive estates would have included retainers and servitors who became attached to wealthy landlords for a variety of reasons. Despite the emergence of such compound households, the majority of the population in agrarian settings probably continued to form households composed largely of kin alone. Households, as coresidential social organizations, were primarily, though not exclusively, family arrangements.

The impetus for forming extended or multiple families in ancient Israel must now be addressed. Along with the data provided by biblical and archaeological sources, the analysis of contemporary complex families can provide insight into the reasons for the formation of large household compounds in ancient Israel. The notion that such households were an evolutionary stage in human social organization that eventually gave way to nuclear or conjugal units alone has been discarded, as we have already noted. Moreover, complex households seem to involve intensification of normal family tensions. Why then have expanded households existed at various times and places? The formation of households larger than the conjugal pair represents a social and economic response to a combination of ecological and historical influences.

Labor needs are determining influences in the formation of extended families and are clearly applicable to earliest Israel.[43] Agrarian environments in general tend to produce large families, and the specific conditions of early Israel (see Chapter 3) certainly mandated a large family size. Yet infant mortality and short life spans were countervailing forces, working to limit the size of individual conjugal units. Also, for a significant period of the time that children would have remained within their nuclear family, they would have been too young and small to have been a substantial resource for the exceptional tasks of the pioneering period. The conjugal unit by itself would have been too small to meet the labor demands.

The crop selection suitable to the hill country environment did not allow for an even commitment of labor throughout the months of an annual cycle. At certain times relatively few tasks had to be performed; however, periodically, diverse tasks required concurrent attention. Such situations demanding greater labor would have required large families. And when the conjugal unit alone is unable to meet the labor needs, then the development of more complex family structures provides the solution.

We can treat household morphology separately from its function; ultimately, however, these two dimensions converge at least in the productive or economic sphere. The shape and size of a household is intrinsically defined by its functional dynamics. The wider question of what it is that the household does for its members and for the larger circles of social organization must also be considered.

One can probably examine the configurations of Israelite households in much greater detail than does this discussion. The patriarchal–matriarchal narratives of Genesis, for example, might be a rich resource for analyzing family structure and dynamics. Those stories, however, are of dubious origin, both in terms of chronology and sociology. They are artfully crafted literary pieces. As such their function as instructional, sacred literature militates against their potential as repositories of sociological or historical data, rendering controversial their value for sociological analysis. Similar problems beset other potential scriptural sources of information about household structures. The few families that appear in other narratives are there precisely because they are exceptional or atypical, the royal family being the case in point. Consequently, the dynamics of the household and the role of women within it are now best understood by turning to the way the expanded family household functioned in the highland villages of early Israel.

7

Household Functions and Female Roles

If ever there were a situation in which the condescending phrase "only a wife and mother" should be expunged from descriptive language, the family household of early Israel should surely qualify. To use such words would be to impose an image of contemporary households, in which reproduction and homemaking characterize domestic life, on an ancient pattern of household activity that was far more extensive and also very different in character and form. In fact, the multifarious functions of the Israelite household in the premonarchic period virtually dominated all activity. Certain sporadic but essential needs of human existence may have been met at the wider two levels of organization, the clan-family and the tribe. Yet the early centuries of Israelite existence were marked by decentralization in all the vital areas of daily existence. Villages were relatively isolated and small, and their component households were de facto nearly self-sufficient arenas for human activities.

The descriptive phrase "tribal society" and the chronological designation "tribal period" are both misleading if they tend to focus our attention on the tribe as the determining feature in the lives of the Israelites in the early Iron Age. Tribalism pertains to Israelite origins as radically distinct from the city-state society that prevailed in Palestine at the time of Israel's emergence, in that authority was not imposed from above by a single ruler and bureaucracy. However, the most significant unit of society was not the tribe but the family household. The true distinctiveness of premonarchic Israel was the way in which economic and social power was exerted from the bottom and not from the top[1] (see discussion below of the economic function of the household). Thus, in the evolving fortunes of tribal Israel, the household remained the central institution for most economic, social, political, and cultural aspects of human existence. The village households verged on true self-sufficiency.

The central role of the household has been identified in social scientific theories of tribal society. The biblical record itself provides scant

139

clues as to the autonomy of highland village households. But the archaeological record is quite helpful in this regard. For one thing, extensive excavation of early Iron Age settlements has uncovered only one kind of architectural structure: domestic buildings. No public buildings have been located—no granaries, temples, stables, markets, or water systems. Furthermore, at least for the earliest phases of the Iron Age, circumference walls or any other sign of military defenses have rarely been recovered. An Iron I fortification wall has been discovered at Giloh, a site thought to be Israelite. But the excavator concedes that fortifications are rarely found in this period.[2]

The absence of public works in earliest Israel (unlike for the later biblical periods or for the earlier or contemporary Canaanite cities) agrees with the narratives in Judges at least in terms of political organization. Early Israel lacked a centralized political system, and the appearance of public works in the archaeological record has long been recognized as a sign of the emergence of more complex social and political systems, such as chiefdoms or nation states.[3] In such systems, public works represent activities serving the community as a whole and involve labor that takes place beyond the household group.

The absence of political or religious hierarchy is suggested by the absence of public works and is an important feature of early Israel. This absence of community facilities or structures also suggests something about the spheres of activity. With no labor committed to community-wide projects, the household constituted virtually the only locus of human activity. The absence of public works supports the idea that the full range of productive, cultural, and regulatory functions that served the highland settlers was carried out largely within the household unit.

In order to examine those household functions we need some system of categorization, but finding an appropriate scheme is not a simple matter. Social scientists have analyzed household activities in various ways in their attempts to identify features of household life that can be recognized cross-culturally. The prominent British anthropologist Jack Goody, for example, asserts that the household in agricultural societies serves a threefold purpose: as a dwelling unit, a reproductive unit, and an economic unit.[4]

But this classification seems too schematic for our purposes. Our archaeological description of Israelite family compounds has already dealt with the major physical aspects of the domestic setting. Also, considering the mortality rates in Late Bronze–Iron I Palestine, the labor needs of a new agricultural society in the Palestinian highlands, and the Genesis 2 and 3 narratives, we have amply demonstrated the importance of the Israelite household as a reproductive unit. Reproduction in this context means much more than having children; it also involves transgenerational relationships and the transmission of property (i.e., inheritance). But these dimensions of reproduction are best treated apart from the biological aspects (see below, p. 183).

Goody's third unit, the economic one, covers "the persons jointly engaged in the process of production and consumption."[5] Certainly this is a crucial household function that, in agricultural societies, may well be the keystone of household activity. But to limit the discussion of household functions to the economic sphere would be to ignore that wider range of cultural activities that occur in the domestic setting. For households that are relatively self-sufficient in more than just economic matters, the other activities taking place in the residential unit are also worthy of consideration.

A listing of activity categories by Wilk and Netting[6] is informative but, like Goody's list, not inclusive of the particular kinds of activities we wish to examine for early Israel. The Wilk–Netting set of five categories is little more than an expansion of Goody's list. Wilk and Netting describe households in terms of their reproduction and transmission activities. They list the production and distribution of goods as separate items, although these are both aspects of economic activity. Their separate listing of coresidence seems to relate it to economic function, thereby detracting from the centrality of the economic role. Again, we prefer to deal with coresidence as an aspect of the morphology, or form, of the living group (as described in Chapter 6) rather than as part of the dynamics of household life.

The discussions of household function in the social scientific literature have augmented our understanding of household dynamics but have not provided a suitable set of categories. Therefore, in looking at the family household in Israel, we will examine features that are part of Israel's unique social and cultural development, even though they do not exactly parallel any categories that anthropologists would recognize as being meaningful cross-culturally. The economic role of the household is fundamental for ancient Israel as for any premodern agricultural group and will be the focus of our discussion; but other aspects of life within the household unit of ancient Israel will also be examined.

Perhaps our difficulty in finding a useful set of functions in the social scientific literature arises from our conceptualization of household function. Some social scientists are uncomfortable with the term function when used in reference to the household. Wilk and Netting, for example, call it a troublesome term, carrying a "heavy burden of causative and teleological connotations." They would prefer to speak about what people do, not how groups function: "We do not in fact see people or groups function: we see them act."[7] Ideally they may be right. It would be far better to observe the ongoing activities of a family household in order to discern the place of the household unit in society and in order to describe and evaluate the participation of any one of a household's members, the latter being our ultimate goal.

For an ancient society such as Israel, such close observation is hardly possible. This separation in time and space from our own world makes distant observation a precarious project at best. We can see artifacts clearly, but we can see only dimly and sometimes not at all the people who used them. We can read the texts, but they rarely provide the data we seek in this enterprise. Hence we are left with the need to deal in part with abstractions and extrapolations based on hints and fragments. Because of this, only occasionally can the specific activities of individual household members be discerned. Yet, because we are interested in what women did, we must scrutinize the functions of Israelite households. That is, the reconstruction of the activities and roles of women can best be attempted on the basis of knowledge, somewhat more easily retrieved, about household function.

Women at Work: The Economic Function

Anthropologists appear to be unanimous in their assessment of the individual household as the basic economic unit in traditional, agricultural societies.[8] More than that, the economic activities of a household are at the very heart of its functional identity as a unit of social organization. Other aspects of the family household may vary, but the centrality of its productive activities is a constant feature. This is especially true for societies, such as early Israel, in which the tribe is the primary level of social organization. Marshall Sahlins, an anthropologist who has contributed significantly to the discussion and analysis of the tribe, asserts that tribal economies are based on what he calls the "familial mode of production."[9] In our terms, that would be the household mode of production.

The Hebrew word *bayit,* meaning "household," can in this respect be compared to the Greek term *oikos.* The ancient Greeks used that word, meaning "household," in their discussions of social organization. For some ancient Greek writers, it signified the material basis of household life. Others, including Aristotle, took it to refer to the group of people, kinfolk and servants or slaves, who comprised it.[10] In either case the Greeks, like the Sumerians and Babylonians, as well as the Hebrews, recognized the economic function of the basic coresidential group. It is no accident that the word *oikonomia* (economy) is derived from the term for household. The Greeks had no equivalent for the modern word "family"; but they wrote extensively about "economics," by which they meant "the art and science of household management."[11]

The archaeological evidence clearly supports this idea of the economic self-sufficiency of household units in early Israel. Each unit provided its own subsistence and was apparently responsible for the production of nearly every commodity essential for existence. There is very little sign of any craft or technological specialization in the formative period, with the exception of metal work. At Raddana, for example, an area set apart from the domestic compounds served as an open-air workshop for metallurgy.[12] But no other areas with installations for specialized processes have been located. Each household apparently provided for its own needs. The households of the highland villages subsisted on a mixed farming and herding economy. Domestic architecture and the assortment of artifacts recovered in the mountain villages attest to this assessment.

The buildings that formed household compounds have been subjected to intense analytical scrutiny. They were small rectangular structures, with two to four rooms on the ground floor, the largest featuring pillars or piers that supported a ceiling and probably a second story. There is a strong consensus among archaeologists[13] that the ground floor was the "barn," with the livestock owned by each unit being stabled in the small side rooms. This arrangement may seem odious to our standards of hygiene and foreign to our concept of the barn or stables as separate outbuildings; still, the evidence of certain biblical passages as well as of contemporary practice in isolated Palestinian villages supports this interpretation of the architectural remains. The medium at Endor, for example, prepared a meal for Saul by slaughtering a fatted calf that she had "in the house" (1 Sam 28:24). Early twentieth-century observers[14] also reported many examples of village houses with the ground floor used to stable a variety of domesticated animals—sheep, goats, cows, donkeys, and even camels.

Stager's summary of the architectural development of village dwellings indicates the range of activities. The typical pillared house, he says,

> was first and foremost a successful adaptation to farm life: the ground floor had space allocated for food processing, small craft production, stabling, and storage; the second floor (*'aliyyah*) was suitable for dining,

sleeping, and other activities. . . . The pillared house continued to be a popular form of domestic dwelling throughout the Iron Age and into much later times. Its longevity attests to its continuing suitability not only to the environment, especially where timber was available [for roof beams], but also for the socioeconomic unit housed in it—for the most part, rural families who farmed and raised livestock.[15]

The materials found within domestic compounds in the highland villages further attest to the household unit as the setting for the nearly complete range of activities essential for subsistence. The scattering of animal bones throughout the domestic areas indicates the role of animals in the household economy. The artifactual materials point to the household as the unit responsible for the production and processing of foodstuffs. Fragments of sickle blades used for harvesting grains have been recovered in most living areas. In nearly all the compounds excavators have found the querns and mortars used for grinding grains into flour. Ovens for baking bread and cooking other foodstuffs have been located in the common courtyards of the domestic compounds. Also, most of the pottery excavated in these highland village compounds falls under the category of common domestic wares: vessels for the storage, cooking, and serving of foodstuffs.

The nearly complete range of activities essential for subsistence in the highland villages was thus to be found within each household unit. Archaeological evidence provides two additional justifications for assuming self-sufficiency in the household economy. First, Palestine was at the crossroads of the Asia–Africa–Europe trading routes of the ancient world. For most periods of antiquity, the ruined cities show clear signs of a role in international commerce. Previous Bronze Age levels and subsequent Iron II period levels all contain fragments of ceramic vessels made elsewhere—in Egypt, Syria, Mesopotamia, the Aegean—and brought into Palestine either as containers for imported merchandise or as objects of exchange themselves. For Iron I, the initial period of Israel, these signs of commercial and political exchange with neighboring cultures virtually cease. The Israelites depended on no outside markets for any of their essentials; and the relative coarseness of their own wares and the modesty in the size of their buildings further suggest a no-frills subsistence economy.

This absence of imported materials is a kind of negative evidence—something missing in the Iron I period but present at all other stages. The second indication of Israel's self-sufficiency is positive—something present in the Iron I and far less frequently found for earlier and later periods. The early Iron Age settlements at some sites are characterized by pits. For example, the level at Hazor that the excavator, Yigael Yadin, called the First Israelite Settlement featured an unusually large number of these stone-lined installations. Yadin has identified them as silos and storage places.[16] Food supplies amassed at harvest time were stored in these pits, which dotted domestic areas. The presence of so many pits, and the absence of village granaries or storehouses, indicates that each household retained the products of its agrarian labors. The villagers neither marketed what they produced nor did they have access to the products of others.

This picture of the economically autonomous Israelite household— whether it was so by choice or by necessity being a moot point—allows us to deal with the question of gender roles. The specific tasks performed by men and women cannot be identified in the archaeological record, but it is almost beside the point to quibble over whether males or females made the pots, pruned the trees, or baked the bread. The essential point is that in a household responsible for producing and processing nearly everything it needed for survival, the range of tasks was maximal and could not have been accomplished without the active involvement of all household members. Our discussion in Chapter 2 about the labor requirements points to this, and our analysis of the Eden story in Chapter 4 bears that out.

The actual tasks performed by women also tend to be nearly invisible in written records. The Bible hardly provides us with the job description of an Israelite village woman (but see our discussion of Proverbs 31 in Chapter 8). Even for more recent historic periods, researchers have posited enormous female contributions for the subsistence economy while finding that "these functions are not traceable in official chronicles or codified laws."[17] However, ethnographic evidence specifically indicates the vital and active role that females play in societies in which the household is the basic unit of production and consumption. Thus it can be asserted that in tribal Israel, for which the household was the self-sufficient and fundamental level of social organization, women were involved in all aspects of the economic life: producing materials, allocating them, and transforming them into consumables.[18]

The last of the aspects of household activity just mentioned should not be underestimated. The conversion of raw materials into edible food was an enormously time-consuming and physically demanding task, and it usually was the responsibility of the adult women.[19] It is thus legitimate to assume that in ancient Israel, as in virtually all comparable agrarian societies, work classified in the category of cooking—that is, food preparation activities occurring within the residential compound—

was done predominantly by women. The results of Whyte's analysis, which we mentioned in Chapter 2, supports the common generalization that women are the chief preparers of cooked food (as opposed to raw foodstuffs) throughout the world.[20] Whyte, by the way, classifies such contributions as part of the economic function of the cultures he studied.

In biblical traditions about the opposition of the prophet and judge Samuel to the inauguration of a kingship in Israel, we find preserved some validation for our assumption that females and food preparation can be linked for early Israel. Samuel's speech in 1 Samuel 8:11–13, which is placed in a narrative dealing with the end of the premonarchic period of Israelite history, dramatically points out the liabilities of monarchic rule:

> These will be the ways of the king who will reign over you: he will take your sons and appoint them to his chariots and to be his horsemen, and to run before his chariots . . . , and some to plow his ground and to reap his harvest, and to make his implements of war and the equipment of his chariots. He will take your daughters to be perfumers and cooks and bakers.

In this scheme, males provide labor for military, metallurgical, and agricultural (field agriculture) purposes, whereas females are a labor source for food processing and the technologically allied process of perfumery.

The Samuel passage thus tells us that women produced cooked food and also suggests that women were probably not involved in field or plow agriculture, although their seasonal participation at labor-intensive periods cannot be ruled out, as anthropological studies of groups practicing plow agriculture indicate. Yet, although they did not primarily work in growing field crops, women in early Israel probably did contribute substantially to the hoeing and weeding, and the planting and picking, that vegetable gardens, orchards, and vineyards required. As suggested in Chapter 3, the extraordinary demands of the pioneer period would have mandated increased female participation in the production dimension of household subsistence, the first of the three aspects of the household economy listed earlier.

But let us return to the matter of food preparation, which deserves more attention than researchers normally accord it. For one thing, female responsibility for cooking meant that women would have also been involved in the second of the economic activities of the household, the allocation of resources. This task is an important consequence of the preparation of food for consumption.[21] Whoever spends the time, energy, and knowledge to convert raw foodstuffs into edible form—no small order in a self-sufficient preindustrial household—has a lot to say about how, when, and how much food is consumed. Whyte's research supports this contention: people tend to control the disposal and use of the fruits of their labor, with each gender tending to monopolize control over the products of the work they alone have done.[22]

In short, the control of food preparation and the allocation of the resources in agrarian settings entailed the control of a large and significant part of the economic life of the household. That is, the female involvement in cooking probably held a significance far greater than it has in contemporary life, where, at least until the recent women's movement, the largely female contribution to domestic food preparation had been held in some disdain. In an ancient or preindustrial setting, female control of food consumption would have contributed substantially to her domestic power and status.

Another important feature of the relationship between cooking and gender is that female responsibility for food processing puts women in charge of the technology of food preparation. The tasks involved were not only time-consuming and energy demanding; they were also, as Goody points out, quite complex even in the simplest of societies. In one group that Goody studied, the women who make soap, brew beer, process grain, dry vegetables, and transform raw produce into cooked foods are said to have a special knowledge called "working their wonders."[23] The aspect of food preparation men are most likely to take on— the cooking of meat—is perhaps the least technologically complex, especially with respect to roasting or cooking over an open fire. From time immemorial, men have put the steaks on the grill and women have concocted the stews: men have taken the easier way along the path of culinary domesticity.

This analysis identifies female and male activities but it is hardly comprehensive; subsistence crafts such as making clothing, pottery, and tools were also important.

Archaeology reveals the almost ubiquitous use of needles, spindle whorls, and other clothing-related tools in domestic contexts. But archaeology does not, of course, identify the gender of those who used these artifacts. Nonetheless, the fact that in nearby Egypt and Mesopotamia, spinning and weaving were largely done by women is significant. Similarly, the passage in Exodus about the contribution of women to the amassing of materials for the national shrine in the wilderness points to the association of women with cloth production: "All women who had ability spun with their hands, and brought what they had spun in blue and purple and scarlet stuff and fine twined linen; all the

women whose hearts were moved with ability spun the goats hair"
(Exod 35:25–26).

Other crafts are notoriously difficult to relate to gender in the absence
of textual references. Ethnographers suggest that women are responsible for producing domestic ceramic vessels almost 99 percent of the
time.[24] But some biblical texts seem to point to male potters. Jeremiah
talks about going to a (male) potter's house; and 1 Chronicles 4:23
mentions a guild of potters. However, such sources refer to the specialized ceramic workshops and mass production that existed in developed
urban conditions. They tell us nothing about the gender of those who
produced the simple utilitarian vessels that have been part of the essential inventory of every household's equipment in the Near East since the
Neolithic period.

The above reconstruction of household economic activities gives
some visibility to the division of labor in tribal Israel, which we can
now summarize. Food preparation was associated largely with women.
Plow agriculture—along with the pioneer tasks of cistern digging, land
clearing, and terrace building described in Chapter 3—was probably a
male domain. Other areas of production, including horticulture and
animal husbandry, were probably less identified with one gender;
males and females, adults and children, all performed horticultural and
pastoral tasks. Crafts, however, which are less dependent on specific
time constraints and conditions, and which require an acquisition of
technical knowledge, were likely to have been performed nearly always
exclusively by either males or females. Metallurgy was almost certainly
a male craft, but it was probably not a household task. Rather, it was
one of the few, if not the only, areas of specialization in the highland
villages. Weaving was surely a female craft, and pottery may have
been.

This division of labor represents a complementary pattern in two
ways. First, certain sets of essential tasks were the responsibility of one
gender or the other. (These were also probably age-specific tasks.) Because these tasks were essential for survival, the viability of the household unit rested on the specific contributions of its members according to
gender, creating a situation of interdependence. Second, the flexibility
of gender identification with other sets of subsistence tasks would have
created another kind of complementarity, with various household members contributing according to their availability. To the extent that this
scheme represents Israelite households, it indicates a balanced arrangement in which women and men each control certain portions of the
household's economic life. This complementarity in economic functions

has great significance for analyzing gender relationships and relative female and male power and status in ancient Israel. Much of the next chapter will provide such analysis.

Other Household Functions and Female Roles

The economic life of early Israel, as an agrarian society in the preindustrial world, was clearly grounded in the household unit. But economic activities did not constitute the totality of household function for ancient Israel. Nearly every aspect of human behavior was mediated through or contained in the range of functions that this basic level of social organization provided. Socialization, education, and even religious observance and jural (judicial-legal) action were part of the ongoing dynamics of the household. Not all of these activities are present in all preindustrial contexts,[25] but for early Israel, a good case can be made for at least minimal involvement in each one.

Socialization and Education

Even in modern societies in which the range of household functions is minimal, family life is critical for the socialization of the young. It is within the context of a child's living group that he or she learns the things necessary for becoming an effective member of society. The lessons of household life were manifold for early Israel, especially in that the household was an independent unit encompassing nearly all aspects of human activity and interaction. These lessons would have included the technical skills needed by the upcoming generation to participate in and eventually take over the productive and processing tasks of the family household. They would have included the social skills each generation must absorb from its elders in order to get along in the world, as well as the cultural values and norms that guided the behavior and constituted the beliefs of the larger community of which the household was the central institution.

There can be no doubt that women play a unique and critical role in the socializing process, broadly conceived. They not only bear the children who represent the future of the household and society, but are also the primary caretakers of the young and as such introduce them, especially in a household-centered society, to a sizeable proportion of the tasks, modes of behavior, cultural forms, and norms and values of their society.

In the Hebrew Bible, the concept of "wisdom" applies to most of what has just been described as the socializing process. Wisdom is one of those biblical words (*hokma* in Hebrew) for which a simple definition cannot be established. It can stand for many things that the English word does not usually include. For example, it can refer to technical expertise, to pragmatic skills for coping with the exigencies of daily life, to personal cleverness, and to the pursuit of an ethical life-style.[26] All of these aspects of wisdom can easily be related to the educative aspect of family life, and they are perhaps best represented in most of the Book of Proverbs, which is one of the three major pieces of wisdom literature in the Hebrew Bible (the other two being Job and Ecclesiastes). Other aspects of wisdom— skill in government, or legal sagacity—should be relegated to a more public function of wisdom, which would have developed in Israel only with the rise of public institutions during the monarchy.

But let us return to the family household and the wisdom—the technical and social skills, and values—of daily life. The dissemination of wisdom within the household would belong to the category of socialization and pragmatic education. Certainly both parents shared in this responsibility. The Book of Proverbs in its canonical form is hardly a consistent witness to the premonarchic period. Many scholars date it to the late sixth century; but they recognize that some parts of it derive from the early monarchy and that other parts are family or clan materials that can be even earlier, part of earliest Israelite traditions. Thus the use of evidence from Proverbs has some value in looking at the role of women as parents responsibile for the socialization process.

There is no biblical word for parents as such.[27] Thus, in Proverbs and elsewhere, the terms "mother" and "father" are used to denote parents, with the plural form of the latter sometimes representing ancestors, or former generations. The role of the mother in Proverbs is not as the biological bearer of children but rather as their nurturer and educator.[28] In a number of passages, which are typically formulated as advice to children, both mother and father are mentioned as those whose words and wisdom should be heeded. Consider, for example, Proverbs 1:8:

> Hear, my son [child], your father's instruction,
> and reject not your mother's teaching.

or Proverbs 6:20:

> My son, keep your father's commandment,
> and forsake not your mother's teaching.

The listing of each parent individually, rather than being an accommodation to the needs of parallelism in the poetic form of Proverbs, is probably an indication of the complementary contributions of each parent to the socialization of the young. Also, in the absence of a generic term for parent, it may have been the only way to express combined maternal and paternal responsibility.

The sharing of parental responsibilities implied by these references in Proverbs is echoed in legal texts indicating that mother and father shared parental authority. We shall examine those texts below. We mention them here only to underscore the fact that the maternal and paternal contributions to a child's education and socialization were complementary. The complementarity of parental roles in childrearing is clear, but does it involve equal roles for mother and father? We shall take this discussion one step further and suggest, on the basis of other materials in Proverbs, a greater magnitude for the mother's contribution. For several reasons, the mother's part in the educational function of the household may have had special prominence.

No doubt the care and nurturing of very young children was the female's domain,[29] albeit with assistance from the father, older siblings, and other household members as appropriate and necessary. In ancient Israel, as in most societies, the mother was the primary parent for the child's early years. At least until the age of weaning, probably around the age of three,[30] the care of small children was entrusted mainly to the mother. Psychologically as well as functionally, such maternal care and instruction mean that mothers play a dominant role in the development of children's lives, even when the mothers cease to be the primary caretakers.[31] In early Israel, with its extended- or multiple-family units, the proximity of children of both sexes to both parents continued into adulthood. Similarly, parental authority over children was also sustained into the adult years of the younger generation in the complex Israelite family household (see below, pp. 155–157). The influence and control of mothers thus hardly ended with the act of weaning.

For female children, the educative process involved those aspects of household labor that the mother carried out, whereas for the boys the father's tasks would be taught to the sons.[32] Children of both sexes were probably exposed to tasks that were part of the female's managerial contribution to the household, in terms of the female role in the transformation and distribution of food; but it is more difficult to conceive of the converse being true—that is, that children of both sexes were directly involved in the male's productive tasks. Although adults would have been helped by younger children of the same sex, in our reconstruction of the household division of labor, the mother probably had more direct and ongoing contact with all household members.

The very conceptualization of wisdom in the Hebrew Bible may be further indication of this broad role of women, perhaps more comprehensive than that of men, in the educative and socializing process. To be sure, the concept of "teacher" appears to be expressed by the term "father" (see Prov 4:1), and "father" can mean any authoritative figure who is not a person's biological parent. For example, in 1 Kings 20:35 and elsewhere, a prophet's disciples are called "sons"; and the prophet Elisha calls his mentor Elijah "my father" in 2 Kings 2:12. Yet the idea of wisdom itself, underlying the concept of teaching, is *not* associated with the masculine. The word for wisdom in Hebrew (*ḥokma*) is female in gender (compare Greek *sophia*). Wisdom, which attains the status of an independent quasi-divine entity operating as God's associate in the creation of the world, is personified as a woman. Proverbs 8 in particular is explicit in its depiction of woman Wisdom, who is linked with God as source of truth, righteousness, instruction, and knowledge.

How could such a role be relegated to a woman, in the patriarchal, male-dominated society we usually have held Israel to be? The appearance of a female as the personification of wisdom—a fact little discussed in the scholarship of biblical wisdom literature[33]—should be viewed as a cultural expression of the primary role of women in the educative process.

This view of the household's function in socialization and education and of the female's role in this aspect of household life can be augmented by a consideration of the more advanced kind of learning, what we would call "formal education," or learning under the guidance of professional educators at institutions called schools. As it happens, there is no conclusive evidence that schools, places to which young people came for instruction by a paid instructor, existed in ancient Israel before the Hellenistic period. The Hebrew Bible does not mention schools. A penetrating 1985 study by Crenshaw of "Education in Ancient Israel" suggests the obvious: schools are not mentioned because none existed.[34]

Yet literacy, the achievement of which is the basic *raison d'être* for schools, apparently did exist in ancient Israel. Scattered biblical references and a significant quantity of epigraphic remains recovered by archaeologists suggest that literacy was more common than we might have supposed. Indeed, Hebrew, as part of the Northwest Semitic language group, represented a monumental breakthrough in the path toward public literacy.

Sumerian, Akkadian, Egyptian, and perhaps Ugaritic—the languages that dominated the ancient world—were complex systems requiring specialized knowledge. Reading and writing for Egyptians or Babylonians meant the memorization of hundreds if not thousands of pictographic or cuneiform signs. For example, in ancient Sumer, which probably produced the first formal schools in human history, the original goals of formal education were to train scribes. The students were from elite families, for only the wealthy could afford the time and fees involved in becoming literate.[35] Hebrew, in striking contrast, is alphabetic, requiring the learning of only twenty-two letters. Hebrew thus allowed for the democratization of learning. The beginning of national existence for Israel coincided with the streamlining of an alphabetic script. Epigraphic remains in Palestine date from the Iron I period.

In the opinion of Professor Albright, this development led to widespread literacy. Albright was perhaps overenthusiastic in his estimation, but his remarks on the subject are nonetheless provocative:

> Since the forms of the letters are very simple, the 22-letter alphabet could be learned in a day or two by a bright student and in a week or two by the dullest; hence it could spread with great rapidity. I do not doubt for a moment that there were many urchins in various parts of Palestine who could read and write as early as the time of the Judges, although I do not believe that the script was used for formal literature until later.[36]

Albright may have pushed the notion of the widespread existence of literacy in Israel too early, but he was right in pointing to the existence of at least limited popular literacy during the formative period.[37] Judges 8:14, for example, shows that a young man apprehended by Gideon was able to write down, at Gideon's urging, some vital information that he needed in his war against the Midianites. This incident probably took place at some time in the Iron I period, in the twelfth or eleventh century.

The existence of literacy is one thing, that of schools another. Scholars have stressed the existence of well-established schools in Egypt and Mesopotamia and have extrapolated from that to suggest, despite biblical silence, that Israel too had schools. But such a contention does not take into account the vastly different, and vastly less complex, political and economic position of early Israel in comparison to that of its neighbors. Nor does it give ample play to the relative ease of learning Hebrew, or at least of learning enough to read a list, a name, some numbers. Such simple acts of reading are probably representative of the pragmatic dimensions of everyday Hebrew at that time.

Crenshaw would err on the side of caution. He prefers not to posit royal schools, let alone schools established in local centers at any period. Besides, even if some schools did exist despite the lack of conclusive evidence for them, that would not preclude the educative function of the family, including the more formal aspects of cultural transmission. "Parents," he asserts, "instructed children in their own homes"; and the repeated use of both "father" and "mother" in Proverbs means that the family setting for the teaching of technical skills involved both parents instructing both girls and boys for the attainment of rudimentary literacy.[38]

To summarize, the socialization and education of Israelite children took place within the household setting in early Israel and, probably for most of the population, throughout much if not all of Israelite history. As contributors to the household economy and as managers of specific aspects of household life directly affecting all household members, mothers played a critical role in the socialization process. Beyond their primary role as nurturers in their offspring's early years, they—along with others—instructed children by word and example in the technical skills and behavioral modes essential to household life. Furthermore, if formal education (such as it was) can also be associated with the domestic setting, then the household occupied an even more significant place than we are accustomed to attributing to it in the transmission of culture in early Israel. The parental role, and consequently the female's share of it, operated in ways more comprehensive than we can fathom easily, accustomed as we are to having specialists take on the lion's share of teaching our children beginning at ever-earlier ages. The instructional wisdom of woman in early Israel was an integral part of daily life.

Jural-Legal Aspects

The maintenance of order is a primary function of any community. Legal provisions are part of the cultural development of any society, whether formally expressed in authoritative bodies of law, or less formally stated but no less binding in customary traditions. The coercive power of a group to deal with actions considered wrong or disruptive finds expression in various forms of legal materials and at various levels of community organization.

Ancient Israel was no exception. On the contrary, legal tradition was a central part of its national character. Israel emerged in a world with highly developed legal systems, the law code of Hammurabi being the most famous example. Israel's core religious concept, a covenant between God and the people, was a legal formulation and gave all national

legal materials the force of religious law. The greater part of the Pentateuch, the first and perhaps most important section of the Hebrew Bible,
consists of legal materials. Religion, morality, and law were intertwined.[39]

As important as biblical law is, its character and function are not
always clear. Its stipulations do not fall neatly into the categories or
formulations that our western legal orientation finds familiar. Biblical
law is not a law code, if that term represents comprehensiveness and
systematization. Scholars have proposed various ways to organize or
categorize the often bewildering and unsystematic array of legal statements in the Hebrew Bible. One approach attempts to identify the types
of literary forms that legal statements take. Another approach seeks to
distinguish criminal law from civil law or torts. Yet another recognizes
the different social levels at which laws operate: nationally, personally,
cultically. These approaches are not mutually exclusive; all involve considerations applicable to all the legal materials.

Emerging from the voluminous scholarly investigations of biblical law
is the realization that many very ancient precepts are contained in the
Pentateuch and that some of those precepts might be termed family law,
which can be subsumed under the general category of customary law.
However, the designation "family law" does not automatically clarify
the domain of this kind of law. Does it refer to actions that involved
members of a household but that were of no consequence to the community at large? Such a definition would involve first and foremost the
regulation of marriage and divorce, the adoption of persons, and the
acquistion of servants.[40]

Marriage and divorce, while obviously matters of family behavior, are
not self-contained family issues. Marriage was a public not a private
matter; it involved interfamily, or perhaps even interclan or intertribal
relationships. Thus the development of the particular Israelite marriage
laws was more concerned with property transmission than with personal
or family dynamics. (We will discuss marriage in Chapter 8 in our examination of male authority.) The customary or legal treatment of marriage
and divorce, therefore, was not a matter of family or household function
and would not qualify as family law.

Perhaps, then, one should look at family law in terms of the internal
governance and authority structure of a household, if authority be the
legal right of persons to determine the behavior of others. Such a consideration underlies one recent and useful analysis of the Decalogue (ten
commandments), in which the centrality of the household in Israelite
national experience is recognized, and in which parts of the Decalogue

are viewed as measures to protect the household units (consisting of people and property).[41] According to this scheme, the eighth (stealing) and tenth (coveting) commandments seek "to protect the family *externally,* from the diminution or total loss of its property and thereby its economic viability and social standing."[42] The seventh (adultery) commandment, while dealing with the sexual conduct of family members, also involves parties external to the family group. Thus it is the fifth (parents) commandment, which relates to the family authority structure and so speaks most directly to the matter of internal family dynamics in juridical matters.

The fifth commandment clearly concerns parental authority and thus touches on the area of household adjudication. Perhaps the most striking aspect, at first glance, of the command to honor both father and mother (Exod 20:12; Deut 5:16; compare Lev 19:3) is that disregarding it has severe consequences. Opposition to parents apparently meant punishment by death (Exod 21:15, 17). Furthermore, there seems to have been no recourse to any extrafamilial judicial body (see Deut 21:15–18). Such treatment of disobedient children seems harsh, if we have in mind young children, a nuclear family, and a small household in which subsistence activities are not part of internal household functioning. By contrast in a large, complex family group, with its economic viability dependent on the labor of all of its members, the authority of senior members is critical. Children in these laws are not naughty toddlers but contributing adult household members.

Anthropologists, as we have noted in Chapter 6 (p. 136), have recognized the internal difficulties that arise in large households. The Victorian reconstruction of family history implied that extended or multiple families were quite large and also very common, but such was probably not the case. Complex families were probably smaller than usually assumed and also less common. Social scientists now realize that there is considerable difficulty in maintaining domestic order in large households with complex kinship structures. Few individuals would possess the administrative and social skill necessary to manage the personal and logistical dynamics of compound households.[43] The legal authority of the senior household members to make decisions about internal matters of resources and labor is thus essential for the stability of complex households. The Israelite legal materials about the behavior of children toward their parents thus makes most sense within the context of an extended- or multiple-family situation, such as existed in the premonarchic villages and perhaps also later. The great difficulty of maintaining order in a multigenerational household would explain the severity of the legal traditions governing parental authority.

It is of no little consequence that the stipulations about parental authority are not limited to male authority. There is no concept of a household chief quite equivalent to the *paterfamilias* known from classical sources.[44] The inclusion of both parents in these biblical family laws diverges from other Semitic bodies of law with which pentateuchal law is frequently and legitimately compared. Exodus 21:15, for example, deals with a child who "strikes his father or his mother." Hammurabi's code no. 195[45] deals only with a son who "has struck his father." The authority of both parents in Israelite families was supported in the oldest legal tradition in the Bible. The authority of family leaders in all aspects of household life was fundamental in earliest Israel and probably only gradually diminished in later times, as institutional court systems arose.[46]

The fundamental agrarian orientation of pre-state Israel should be underscored as a factor contributing to the significant authority of both parents. Among the major features of agrarian societies is the prominent value given to "filial piety" and lifelong loyalty and respect, including that of adult children. Obedience of offspring to parents is critical in the functioning of even simple farm households and especially in complex ones. It also assures that the surviving elderly, who are unable to contribute to the livelihood of the household, will be properly cared for.[47]

The jural-legal function of the family thus involved recognition of female authority over dependent or junior family members. The centrality of the household in the premonarchic economy, and the vital role of women in that situation, gave women considerable informal power and at least some legal authority. We do not wish to imply that this female jurisdiction was absolute or that it extended to all matters of household management and family decisions. The limits of female authority are in evidence, too; we shall return to this in Chapter 8.

Religions and Cult

In this area we must tread carefully. Archaeology and biblical scholarship have been consistently and enthusiastically concerned with the monumental and the official aspects of biblical religion. They have explored ad nauseam the literary descriptions of the temple in Jerusalem and the tabernacle in the wilderness, this writer being no exception.[48] They have turned their picks and trowels to the shrines and high places of Israelite cities. Yet little attention has been directed to private religion and its cultic expression, that is, to the ceremonies and rituals that allowed ordinary people to meet their human need to connect with the supernatural or transcendent power or powers in which they believed.

The paucity of information about popular piety is the result in part of what we described in the first chapter: archaeologists have until recently been drawn to the urban and the monumental. It is also a function of the prevailing interest of the biblical text itself in presenting official and institutional manifestations of national religious life and in downplaying and suppressing that which was not officially accepted.

Another and equally strong barrier to the recovery of popular or family religion has been the influence of modern orthodoxy, which works from preconceived ideas about Israelite monotheism and aniconography (the insistence that God cannot be represented in images). Orthodox views have pervaded even less stringent theological quarters. Consequently, there has been a reluctance to concede that Israel's monotheism was hardly pure and pervasive from the start or that Israelite worship was slow to do away with forms of worship involving images and symbols that had been part of Semitic religious tradition since time immemorial. In a recent critique of the archaeological investigation of Israelite cultic practices, the prominent archaeologist of Palestine, William Dever, adds this pointed assessment: "The conservative Protestant character of much American biblical scholarship (including "Biblical archaeology"), despite the appeal made to archaeology, tended to approach Israelite religion more in terms of theology than religious practice—almost as though cult were something of an embarrassment."[49]

Although these archaeological and theological barriers to the recovery of popular religion are breaking down, the material evidence for a private or family religion at any period in Israelite history has yet to be systematically collected and studied. However, even at this point there are several possible avenues for reconstructing the cultic life in Israelite households. Perhaps the chief of these is the theory that proto-Israelite religion was "personally and family oriented rather than institutionally conditioned."[50] This view take seriously the fact that, among the many epithets for the Israelite deity, the phrase "God of the fathers/ancestors," which appears over sixty times in the Hebrew Bible, is prominent and persistent.

Apart from this family orientation in a designation for God, most of the evidence for the family as the focal unit of the religious traditions that ultimately took on national and institutional shape is contained in the patriarchal narratives of Genesis. Individual figures who are not priests or cultic practitioners carry out various cultic functions: they erect altars, make sacrifices, and otherwise call upon their God. Those narratives, we have said, are problematic as historical witness.

But we do have the evidence of stories such as that of Micah's household (see Chapter 6, p. 134), which was postpatriarchal and premonarchic. Within his own household, "Micah had a shrine, and he made an ephod and teraphim, and installed one of his sons, who became his priest" (Judg 17:5). Micah later seeks the services of a professional (Levitical) priest. From this passage we learn that households had their own shrines; household shrines included cultic appurtenances, of which one—teraphim—implies divine images; a household member performed cultic functions. Micah had his teraphim, and he also had "a molten image and a graven image" (Judg 17:4) made for his shrine.

Consider, too, a fascinating episode in David's rise to power, recorded in 1 Samuel 19:13, in which Michal grabs a household image (teraphim), puts it in David's bed with its head on the pillow, and covers it with bedclothes in order to deceive those searching for David. The teraphim she uses appear "to be a usual piece of household furnishings, and were most probably tolerated by the Israelite religion of the time."[51] They are not condemned in any way by the narrator.

The absence of public temple buildings in Israelite villages[52] that was mentioned at the beginning of this chapter (p. 140) is a mark of noncentralized political and social life; it also indicates that ceremonial observances were largely family centered. Even if they involved groups of households, they could be performed without the special equipment and personnel that required economic investment or support by the villagers. The lack of monumental public cult structures along with the biblical passages cited above provide strong evidence for the existence of household shrines and images. Such shrines suggest general familial involvement: the sacrifice of foodstuffs, whether in the home or at a public sanctuary, involved a festal meal for all household members. But do they tell us anything about female involvement as such in the household cult? Certainly there is no direct evidence, but there is some indirect information worth examining.

To begin with, look at the way Micah's official priest is designated: "father and priest" (Judg 18:19). The title "father" seems to stem from the priest's function as a diviner, the provider for oracular advice, usually offered in "yes" or "no" form.[53] Household decisions in household shrines, performed by a household leader—the father—apparently gave rise to such a title. But it should not be overlooked that one prominent woman of this same premonarchic period—Deborah—is called "mother in Israel" (Judg 5:7). The designation "mother" does not refer to a biological maternal role (we actually know nothing about her family except for her husband's name) but rather to her divinatory leadership, her ability to provide answers to Israel's problems.[54] Like "father," "mother" sometimes was a title for someone bearing a particular kind of religious authority. Can we not construe this as testimony to a female divinatory role in household shrines? Note also that the northern Israelite city of Abel may be considered an oracular center[55]; it is called "a mother in Israel" (2 Sam 20:19) and is also the place where a "wise woman" resolves a crisis involving David's general Joab (2 Sam 14:1–24).

Such texts, along with several others such as the ones depicting women as attendants at the Tent of Meeting (Exod 38:8; 1 Sam 2:22), have long held the attention of those concerned with the place of women in the Israelite cultus. The discussion has tended to focus on the question of whether these instances of formal female cultic activity are exceptions or not: whether they are signs that women regularly participated in Israelite religious life, or whether they are individual cases overshadowed by the normative cultic institutions constituted and controlled by males. Although this analytical perspective is not in and of itself wrong, it is misleading in its failure to adequately grasp two important facts about the examples just cited.

Those examples are noteworthy first because they, and others like them, stem almost exclusively from the premonarchic period, the period of Israelite beginnings. The implications of this fact will be part of our concluding discussion of female power in Chapter 8. The second notable aspect is that they all concern female roles in official, or public, cultic activity. The discussion of women in religious roles almost never considers their nonpublic or domestic actions, except when such are heterodox and are singled out and judged negatively both in the biblical text and also in the scholarly literature. The women (and the men) worshipping the Queen of Heaven in the late monarchic period, for example, are condemned by the prophets (e.g., Jer 7:17–18; 44:15–19).

It should not surprise us that the known female roles in Israelite religious life are the public ones, because the canonical source is largely concerned with public and institutional matters. Nor, because the monarchic period shifted the focus of organized community life from the household to the public, male-dominated institutions of kingship, priesthood, and the bureaucracies associated with both, should we be surprised that women virtually disappear from public religious roles. The institutions of public life were male institutions, cultic life included.

However, if we focus on the apparent absence of women from the formal cultic arena throughout most of Israelite life, we ignore the role of popular religious practice. To be sure, most of the texts describing the general participation of the people in festivals or other cultic activities are addressed to males, but this may be abstract masculine-gender language that in fact was inclusive of the community as a whole. Furthermore, anthropological research shows that important aspects of religious activity take place in domestic settings. Such a context often constitutes the core of women's religious experience and also the major part of her participation in religious life.[56] This situation would certainly have been the rule in the monarchic period, when women were largely excluded from public religious leadership; moreover, it must also have been the case earlier, when the household was the predominant area of human organization.

The nature of domestic religious practice is virtually impossible to envision for a society such as ancient Israel, which barely mentions such practice in its texts and then only when it is to excoriate practice that runs counter to officially accepted modes. In addition, the possibility that at least some domestic religious activities, such as girls' puberty rites (Judg 11:39–40) or harvest dances (Judg 21:20–21) or childbirth rites (see Lev 12:6–8), seem to have been exclusively female may have been unknown to or largely ignored by the male shapers and transmitters of the canon.

As in other instances in our consideration of female roles in Israelite life, however, we can turn to evidence other than the written sources to aid in reconstructing women's participation in religious life. Archaeological remains provide another kind of evidence linking women with household worship. From sites of the monarchic period come hundreds of small figurines. Thus far they are scarce for the premonarchic period, but that may be because the premonarchic Israelite levels that have been excavated or identified are less extensive than the monarchic ones. These small terra-cotta statuettes are almost exclusively of naked females, and they come from household contexts. That much is well documented, but interpreting their function and significance is another matter.

Most scholars attribute them to popular worship of some kind, an attribution that makes good general sense and is part of the growing awareness that pure, widespread, Yahwism, without graven images, was a relatively late development in Israelite history.[57] Some have linked them with goddess worship, in which case they would have been used by both men and women because both are castigated in the Bible for such disloyalty to Yahweh. Yet both men and women are also denounced for worshiping pagan male deities, and virtually no examples of male terra-cotta figures have been recovered. Furthermore, these small figurines seem to depict human females rather than deific ones. Statues of gods or goddesses tend to be of precious metals or of stone, are usually found in public shrines as well as or instead of in household shrines, and normally exhibit some symbols of divine identity in headdress, garb, pose, or attached object.[58] One should be skeptical about identifying any of these terra-cotta statuettes, or related clay plaques, with goddesses at all, let alone with any specific goddess such as Ishtar, Anat, or Asherah.[59]

If these figurines of females indeed depict humans, or are "symbols of womankind in general" as Pritchard suggests,[60] they may well have been part of the domestic life of women in ancient Israel both religiously and socially. Such a possibility is based on the observation of the depiction of the female body. In an artistic sense, the terra-cottas are in the tradition of the "fertility figurines" well known from Canaanite sites of the Middle and Late Bronze Age, preceding Israel's emergence. Those Canaanite statuettes typically depict nudity and emphasize female reproductive features: breasts and/or pudenda.

The Iron Age examples differ from the Bronze Age ones in an important way. The statuettes discovered in the Israelite milieu are largely of the type known as "pillar figurines," in that from the waist down they are simply cylindrical in shape. Thus, the only sexual features rendered by the ancient artisan are the breasts, and they appear to have been modeled to signify maternal rather than sexual (i.e., heterosexual) activities.

It may be possible to conclude from this that the Israelite female figurines, like the Canaanite examples, were some sort of votive objects expressing the quest for human fertility. Israelite women were challenged to increase their reproductive role, as our analysis of the highland environment and economy in Chapter 3 and our reading of Genesis 3:16 in Chapter 5 indicate. The appearance of many examples of female pillar figurines thus may provide a witness to the hope of Israelite women that they would nurture many children. Unlike their Canaanite sisters, however, they used votive objects that did not include emphasis on the sexuality associated with the lower body. Perhaps this focus on the upper body was a way to obviate the emphasis on sexuality apparently involved in Canaanite fertility cults; perhaps it was simply a way to emphasize the maternal role, or maybe it was both.

The reason for the pillar shape of the Israelite figurines can only be speculative. Similarly conjectural is the question of whether the women who used them invoked the Israelite god, or an associated goddess,[61] or some other deity or deities. If the Canaanite figurines cannot be related to deities, neither can their Israelite counterparts. What we should not lose sight of, particularly in the absence of analogous male figures, is that the terra-cottas represent female religious expression. As votive objects, probably not idols as such, they are concrete expressions of particularly female religious life and of concern for the exclusive female role of motherhood.

Circumstantial as this kind of information about household cult and female involvement may be, it surely suggests a place for women in household religion. Furthermore, if any vestiges of goddess worship existed, women would probably have been directly involved with religious activity in domestic and perhaps also public shrines. But even without that possibility, and even excluding the specifically female focus on motherhood that the votary objects may have represented, household worship of any kind could hardly have taken place without female participation, whether normative or heterodox.

Cultic rituals typically involved food offerings and ritual meals. Thus, if only because in the household context the female controlled food preparation, women must have shared the informal practices that household observances entailed. To be sure, women did not function as priests with the establishment of official and formal public shrines; neither did most men. The priesthood was a select, hereditary group; as I have suggested elsewhere,[62] the omission of women from that group was likely not a sexist statement of female inferiority but rather a pragmatic measure in the face of competing Canaanite practices (sexuality in sanctuaries) and of Israelite demographic needs. A coterie of female professionals, diverted from pressing family needs, would not have been in the best interest of the community as a whole. Yet women were still worshipers, and no doubt they functioned as such in domestic contexts throughout Israelite history.

Much of what we have said throughout this study has pointed to the self-sufficiency of village households and to the virtual absence of public functions or functionaries. Metallurgists and priests were perhaps the only regular, full-time specialists whose livelihoods came from nonagrarian pursuits. Still, other suprahousehold leadership and service positions did exist on a nonregular basis. Councils of elders met sporadically to adjudicate interfamily or clan disputes and to deal with community-wide problems (see Judg 11:5). Young men answered periodic musters to form militia units (Judg 4:6; 6:34–35). Judges became leaders locally or even nationally (Judg 2:16) in times of crisis.

Women also sporadically held a place in the limited life outside the household of early Israel, and that place was mostly related to Israelite religious life. They played a special role in the early musical, literary, and theological life of Israel. They were the formers and performers, from the twelfth to tenth centuries BCE, of some of the oldest, and theologically most important, texts in the Hebrew Bible. A fascinating study of ancient musical tradition has revealed that a long-recognized genre of biblical poetry, the Victory Song (e.g., Exod 15:21 and Judg 5), must be attributed to female "traditioners."[63] Women composers–performers are described in the Bible (Judg 11:34; 1 Sam 18:6–7) in association with a certain instrument (*top,* or "hand drum") and with "dances" (*meholot*). These women stand apart from other musical traditions in ancient Israel, and their role is specifically connected to premonarchic songs of pivotal significance in the development of Israelite beliefs about Yahweh's power and plans for Israel.

Although these women singer–composers were professionals, they were not supported by the community as were priests and metallurgists. They performed erratically, as the occasion demanded. Composition and performance techniques were acquired skills, and a tradition of women holding such skills is well known for early Israel and also for other ancient Near Eastern people. If men were called out to battle, it would be these women awaiting their return who poured forth the victory songs. Judging from the few fragments preserved in the Bible, the content of these songs was theologically significant. Hence, the existence of a scattering of female musicians would stand with those few other public professions that existed in the premonarchic period. Their function was broadly cultural but was religious in content. As such, it can probably be loosely connected with female roles in the household cult. A society in which women sang officially to the Lord in public could not have restrained them from doing so in the dominant domestic setting.

8

Reconstructing Gender Relationships

It has become fashionable among educated western women to want to "have it all." Life is seen as consisting of three compartmentalized arenas: career, marriage, and motherhood. Many women struggle to combine all three, when only one alone might be construed as a full-time occupation for at least part of a woman's life. What a different reality existed for Everywoman Eve, whose life intrinsically encompassed all aspects (although one would hardly characterize her work load as a "career") and who might have willingly relinquished some of her broad responsibilities. Indeed, it seems almost absurd to think of work as a distinct category of behavior for rural women in ancient Israel, or in any preindustrial society for that matter.

The preceding chapters have reconstructed the family household and the variety of ways it functioned in the small highland villages of early Israel. The analysis of the household unit enables us to envision rather specifically the daily or ongoing responsibilities and roles of the senior female members of the domestic group. Although the process of socializing and educating young children was included among the spheres of activity that characterized household life and female experience, we chose not to include the reproductive function as such in our catalogue of household activities. Bearing children was clearly and critically related to the labor needs within a household unit, as we have shown in Chapters 3 and 5; however, the importance of having children transcended the family unit.

The female reproductive role in ancient Israel was important beyond household parameters on both the clan and the tribal or national levels. The normal biblical word for human (and animal) increase, "to be fruitful, to multiply" (*prh*), is often related to the ability of the people as a whole to possess and defend their land.[1] Exodus 23:30, for example, indicates that the Canaanites and others who dwelt in Palestine would not be displaced until the Israelites "are increased" and then can occupy territory.

Similarly, the frequent mandate in the Genesis narratives "to be fruitful and multiply" is directed neither to an individual woman's biological destiny nor to an individual man's need for heirs, as much as it is to a corporate need for demographic expansion. Consider the language used to describe patriarchal (*sic*) fertility, as in God's promise to Abraham: "I will make you exceedingly fruitful [*prh*] and I will make nations of you. . . . And I will give to you, and to your descendents after you, the land of your sojournings" (Gen 17:6–8). God's charge to Jacob has a similar agenda: "God Almighty bless you and make you fruitful [*prh*] and multiply you, that you may become a company of peoples . . . that you may take possession of the land of your sojournings" (Gen 28:3–4; see 35:11).

The concern for increasing numbers was also related to the issue of security, that is, of having the manpower necessary for defense of territory. In light of the continual military threats surrounding Israelite life during the premonarchic period, it is no wonder that the census lists in the Book of Numbers were explicitly directed toward military call-up. Probably stemming from the premonarchic era,[2] these lists preserve a reckoning of tribal quotas committed for military action. The people to be numbered are "all in Israel who are able to go forth to war" (Num 1:3; 26:2).

Such census data have long been recognized as military musters, similar to census lists well known in many ancient cultures. But what has not been generally recognized is that the concern for the numbers of fighting men in Numbers is directly related to the sense of population loss following the widespread epidemics of the times (see the section on "Survivors in the Land" in Chapter 3). In Numbers 26 the command to undertake a count of the males eligible for fighting units begins with the words "*After the plague* the LORD said to Moses and to Eleazar the son of Aaron, the priest, 'Take a census . . .' " (Num 26:1–2; emphasis mine).

Population increase thus had a tribal or nationalistic context. The canonical sanctions for human fertility reflect a situation in which the need to become numerous was part of the public or communal consciousness. Bearing children was also central to the dynamics of property transmission or inheritance. The latter was a crucial aspect of family and interfamily life, but it did not impinge in a regular way on the configurations of a woman's daily schedule.

This emphasis on the supra-household dimension of motherhood is not intended to obscure the fact that motherhood as such would have occupied an enormous part of a woman's time and energy. To the extent that families responded to the demographic challenge at both household and tribal–national levels, childbearing and rearing have been prominent among the activities of women.[3]

The way in which childbearing is singled out as a category of women's lives today should not be automatically transposed to groups living under radically different conditions. In short, as Tilly points out in her review of the study of women and the social sciences, we should not be "present-minded" in our analysis of the reproductive role for women in other, especially premodern, societies. She points out that the

> all-absorbing aspects of childbirth and child-rearing are more salient in modern economies in which women specialize in child-rearing and in which children themselves are valued for delayed, future returns rather than quick ones. In economies where differentiation and specialization are less complete, where fertility and mortality are high, childbirth and child-rearing may, paradoxically, be less central to women's lives and other economic activity greater. In such economies, women's vital, economically productive activity . . . may strongly countervail the centrality of childbearing in women's lives.[4]

The amount of a woman's life span involving the physical aspects of motherhood—pregnancy, breast-feeding, caring for young children—may have been one-third or higher in ancient Israel. With relatively few women surviving to menopause, and with marriage and childbirth beginning not long after the onset of puberty, as much as half of a woman's life span would have been taken up with maternity. One might say that motherhood and adulthood were practically coterminous. That situation contrasts radically with our own contemporary experiences: with small families and long life spans, women today devote only about one-seventh of a 75-year life to bearing children and caring for them in their early years.[5]

Despite the enormous proportion of a woman's life span involved with motherhood, woman's work probably suffered little interruption, because as for most preindustrial societies, household functions were relatively integrated with maternal functions. Or, as Bridenthal and Koonz succinctly put it, "production and reproduction meshed."[6] The notion that pregnancy, birth, and breast-feeding might limit or interfere with the productive capabilities of women is a modern postindustrial notion.

It is not our intention here to suggest that the reproductive function does not have a place in our discussion of gender relationships; however, its importance emerges more in consideration of matters of interfamily marital arrangements and transgenerational continuity than in an examination of the dynamics of daily household life. We shall return to such suprafamily aspects below, in the context of looking at male authority.

For the moment, we reiterate that in a household unit working its own land there was a high degree of integration of activities—for men as well as for women. The popular notion of the domestic realm as a female realm in such cases is a misconception; the household activities were the responsibilities of both females and males working together.[7] This integration of responsibilities did not preclude division of labor along gender lines. In reality, individual, gender-linked responsibilities would have been tightly woven together into the fabric of everyday life. Furthermore, not only the household activities were highly integrated, but so too were the accompanying values—the interests, attitudes, and policies—of the domestic unit.[8]

Clearly, the Israelite household was the central unit of an agricultural society during the centuries preceding the establishment of a centralized government at the beginning of the tenth century BCE. Reconstructing the nature of household organization, size, and function enables us now to turn to the dynamics of male and female interaction, and then to the position of women, within that unit of society. It allows us, finally, to deal directly with the assertions of patriarchal dominance to which we have earlier objected in theory. Did men in fact dominate and exploit the women in their domestic settings, as the traditional interpretations of biblical texts lead many to believe? Or, have we discovered a different reality for Eve, a reality antithetical to the traditional views of female subordination?

Male and Female: Household Complementarity

Recognizing the nature of premonarchic Israel as a peasant or folk society is critical for looking at relationships between males and females. The constituent household units, as we have seen, were typically self-sufficient and relatively isolated. Although technological developments were essential to Israelite survival in the hill country, the technology was not so advanced as to have required specialization, except perhaps with respect to metallurgy. All other essential tasks were performed within the family household. All household members, except for tiny children and the infirm aged (of whom there were probably few), were directly involved in subsistence tasks. Most of the time there would have been little food surplus and hence little opportunity for exchanging commodities or obtaining luxury goods.

These conditions characterize groups that social scientists have identified as being rather homogeneous and somewhat free of the kinds of hierarchical differentiation that appear in more complex societies. They lack a class system and have limited ways of differentially rewarding people along gender, age, or occupational lines. Early Israel might readily be termed an egalitarian society.[9] Gender equality is not necessarily a characteristic of all egalitarian societies, but the absence in early Israel of developed hierarchies in political and economic spheres created an atmosphere that would have allowed for nonhierarchical gender relationships.[10] It is essential that we not allow androcentric biblical texts to obscure this fact of gender equality, and not permit the hierarchical Victorian views of the family, which are still quite powerful in western thinking,[11] to interfere with an assessment of gender relationships in an egalitarian farm household.

Cross-cultural analogies suggest that both males and females worked very hard and contributed nearly equally to the demands of establishing arable plots of land and eking out a living from them in the rocky, seasonally arid hillsides of the Palestinian highlands. Anthropological studies of small agrarian communities living on marginally productive lands provide these analogies. Because most of these comparable communities are part of nation-states with bureaucracies, with public roles for some (largely men), and with access to commodities of goods produced outside the family household, the analogies are not perfect. Yet even so, within the household itself, the striking absence of hierarchical control of male over female is noteworthy. Although not readily apparent to an external observer, such village households are organized in a relatively balanced way with respect to gender.

A quantitative measure can be introduced into the discussion of the male–female balance in agrarian settings. Sanday's research has led her to suggest that the most balanced societies, those in which men and women share nearly equally in subsistence tasks, are societies in which females contribute a maximum of 40 percent of the productive labor.[12] Women fall short of exact parity because of the percentage, relatively small but nonetheless present, of their energies taken up by their reproductive role. Sanday also points out that the status of females seems to reach its highest level when a 40 : 60 ratio of female to male contributions to household productivity exists.[13] If female participation exceeds such proportions (as it does in some societies), there is often a negative effect, with the prestige accorded to women diminishing rather than increasing.

Leviticus 27 offers some support for the notion of balanced responsibilities in early Israel. This text does not provide an explicit statement about gender balance yet it does relate indirectly to the quantitative measure we have just described. As unlikely and irrelevant a source as it may seem, it contains quantitative data that may be considered a measure of the ratio of male–female contributions to the household economy of early Israel.

The last chapter of Leviticus (27) comes after the long section known as the Holiness Code (chapters 17–26) and stands as an appendix or supplement to the third book of the Pentateuch. This chapter's relationship to the rest of Leviticus is unclear, because there is little content connection and because it is a rather self-contained unit.[14] For these reasons, many scholars have attributed it to a late period in the formation of the Pentateuch.[15] If that were so, its reliability as a source for the premonarchic period would be legitimately called into question. However, certain features of its language and content are rooted in archaic and conservative cultic practices. The material in Leviticus 27 should be considered part of Israel's early cultic traditions and not a late addition to priestly materials.[16]

Why is this chapter of Leviticus a source for gender balance in early Israel? Leviticus 27 concerns the commutation of gifts—such as people, property, and animals—vowed to Yahweh. In Israel, as in other Semitic lands of the ancient Near East, persons or materials were on occasion given over to a sanctuary or its deity. The biblical narratives record several rather dramatic instances: for example, the case of Jephthah's daughter (Judg 11:30–35) and the dedication of Samuel to the sanctuary at Shiloh (1 Sam 1:1–36). Such vows, which were voluntary but binding, typically arose from a situation of distress, involved a petition or request of the deity, and were fulfilled contingent on the petition being answered.

The making and fulfillment of vows were surely part of Israelite religious practice from earliest times. It is not difficult to imagine a personal or familial crisis, during which women or men vowed materials or even the service of individuals to a local shrine (of which there were many until well into the period of the monarchy) in an attempt to seek relief. It is also not difficult to conjecture that sometimes the person making a vow would need to regain that which had been given as a vow. Let us say a child (such as Samuel) was dedicated to the deity, but then in a labor-intensive period the child's labor was sorely needed in the household. The parent could then reclaim the child by payment of a monetary sum set forth in a table of valuation or, if a person was too poor, by payment of whatever the cultic official deemed suitable (Lev 27:8).

Leviticus 27 presents just such a table of valuations to allow for redemption of property or persons. The valuations are expressed in monetary terms, the absolute values of which themselves may not be ancient; however, the principle of dedicating and of redeeming itself rests on ancient tradition. The scale of assessments of persons is arranged in a most interesting way: according to gender and age. This structure indicates exactly the way in which the vowed persons contributed to the shrine, that is, in terms of their labor.[17]

The age groups are four in number: 0–5, 5–20, 20–60, and 60+. For three of these four age groups, the female percentage of the combined value of a male and a female of the same age hovers at or near the 40 percent level. It is actually highest (at 40 percent) for the over-60 age group, probably signifying a decrease in gender differentiation for the most senior members of society.[18] The only departure from this pattern is with the 5- to 20-year-old group, in which twice the value is required to redeem males as opposed to females. One would expect such a divergence at this age group, when males were coming into their own as productive workers and females were beginning childbearing with its attendant demands and mortality risks.[19]

The Leviticus passage, viewed as a source for socioeconomic analysis of gender balance in early Israel, thus provides the remarkable information that women assumed close to 40 percent of the productive tasks. Social scientists have assessed this balance of male–female labor to be optimal for both gender relations and maximum prestige accorded to females. The position of females in any society is a reflection to a certain extent of their contributive role, in a quantitative sense, to essential societal tasks.

This juggling of numbers must be tempered with the realization that nearly equal contributions of males and females does not suggest they were doing the same tasks. All members of the household were part of the labor force, but (as our discussion in Chapter 7 of household functions suggested) there was division of labor, as in all societies.[20] This division of household tasks is most notable for the critical economic function. Some tasks could be performed by either male or female, and some probably were performed by both—especially at harvest or other labor-intensive periods. However, clearly defined and tradition-reinforced responsibilities, divided along gender (and age) lines, would have existed in ancient Israel, as in any society.

The division of labor has clear organizational advantages, at least for those household activities that involve certain levels of skill, experience, and technical expertise. The premonarchic society as a whole was nearly lacking in occupational specialists from outside the household unit, but the household itself had its specialists and the division of labor reflected the specializations.

This division of labor along gender lines has long been recognized and recorded by social scientists. The complementarity of this division, and the dynamics of the relationships between male and female that it entails, have been less noticed. In examining the division of labor, there has been a tendency to identify tasks (usually those taken on by males) in terms of higher accorded value, and there has been insufficient attention to the invaluable aspects of the labor supplied by both females and males and hence the intrinsic value attached to both.

The feminist perspective that the woman's movement has brought to social science has produced several studies that underscore the interdependence that is implicit in a division of productive tasks.[21] Our contemporary egalitarian ideal, in which men and women would share or equally divide time spent on the *same* tasks—each doing half the cooking, let us say, or taking half of the child care hours—should not blind us to the efficiency, and also the stability, inherent in a situation in which there are distinct labor patterns according to gender.

Gender differentiation, particularly in a society living at subsistence level, implies complementarity and hence interdependence. The concept of either men or women striving for personal independence is antithetical to the dynamics and demands of a premodern agricultural society. The role of women is pivotal in such societies. They bear children and perform many essential tasks of household management. In so doing, they exhibit a broad range of talents in managerial and economic roles. Even in societies with developed patterns of female subservience, at least as is visible to external observers, the internal dynamics reveal functional equality and male awareness of dependence on female talents and labor.

A case in point is provided by Datan's study of a contemporary highland village in Palestine, for which she uses the fictitious name Kafr Ibrahim. Village life there exhibits a cultural adaptation to the same harsh ecology that determined the life patterns of the earliest Israelite villages in the highlands. Datan was able to penetrate the external or cultural forms that signaled male dominance. She observed that, despite official hierarchical arrangements, the primacy of the women's contributions to subsistence secured their positions "more effectively than could any verbal affirmation of equal rights."[22] The husbands and sons depended on the women's expertise in many economic tasks, and the women accordingly were psychologically advantaged by their awareness of controlling and contributing to vital aspects of household and village survival.

Similar pictures appear in other parts of the world. The recent study, for example, of an Andean village perched precariously on marginal mountain land reveals a great deal of emphasis on gender complementarity. Household organization is markedly balanced with respect to male and female tasks, and there is little sense of the separation or categorization of family members according to gender.[23]

Such studies show internal household gender balance even in settings in which there are public structures or bureaucracies that favor males and that tend to lend more prestige and status to men. If we consider a society such as premonarchic Israel, in which such public forms of differentiation were not yet developed, the implication is that the position of females would be even stronger than in societies in which a private–public opposition does exist. When females as well as males serve as skilled managers in critical areas of economic life, as in household production systems, women as well as men are accorded prestige and experience self-esteem. Gender hierarchy in work roles is virtually nonexistent.[24]

Female Power

Feminist critiques of the concept of a private–public dichotomy are justified in the case of premonarchic Israel. The structural opposition between low status in the female-linked domestic sphere and high status in the male-linked public sphere may be appropriate in analyzing western industrial societies; however, as we have already indicated, it distorts an understanding of the nature of relationships between males and females if it is applied to small-scale or prestate societies. Rosaldo puts the issue forcefully in her assertion that the analytical consequences of contrasting the familial sphere with political-jural (public) systems is not only linked to modern western ideology but is also incompatible with the study of relationships and of their articulation.[25] In short, distinctions between domestic life and public life are inadequate to describe most social interaction in peasant societies, for which the dynamics of gender interaction in daily life are best understood through the realization that complementary household roles are determinative.

In prestate Israel, social organization outside the immediate household was relatively weak. Early Iron Age Israel exhibited fully those features which made the household the central unit of social organization and function. Schlegel outlines those features as follows[26]:

1. Production is for subsistence or for small-scale exchange.
2. Defense or expansion needs do not foster male-centered military organization.
3. Civil or religious bureaucracies are absent.

Our discussion (in Chapters 3, 6, and 7) of the highland economy in the period of earliest Israel has emphasized the subsistence level of village life and the virtual absence of trade or the exchange of goods. Localized and sporadic defense problems existed during this period, but they were met by a noncentralized, ad hoc militia system. That system eventually proved too ineffectual for the military problems that beset the highland settlers, and the rise of the monarchy is related to the need for a structure for organizing a standing army. Schlegel's second point agrees with the biblical accounts of Deborah and Yael (Judges 4 and 5): without the formalized structure of a standing army, women could and did contribute to the defense effort. Female participation in the military realm is in fact a typical feature of pioneer societies.[27]

Our examination of early Israel has pointed to a virtual absence of specialists or of bureaucratic structures, which agrees with Schlegel's third feature. Probably a male priestly hierarchy was already functioning; yet local and/or household religion operated independently of such a structure. Similarly, while legal-jural mechanisms operated as needed at a village or even tribal level, households still maintained important aspects of legal-jural function.

In light of such considerations, the centrality of the household in prestate Israel emerges as a critical factor in determining gender relations. When the household occupies the preeminent place in a society, women have a strong role in decision making and consequently exercise considerable power in the household. This is especially true for complex households, such as the extended or multiple-family units that made up a significant number of the domestic compounds in Israelite villages.

Many traditional arguments in social scientific literature maintain that the size and structure of complex families tend to create hierarchies—specifically, situations in which men dominate. However, this predicted relationship between large or extended families and female subordination is not borne out for prestate, simple societies. On the contrary, the power accruing to women by virtue of their technical contributions to family subsistence is augmented when there are more family members involved. Women, particularly in the older generation, gain authority—

the recognized right to control—by virtue of having more people with whom to interact and control.[28] Our examination of the legal and sapiential biblical texts affording filial respect and authority to both parents (Chapter 7, pp. 154–157) supports this supposition, which recent anthropological research has formulated.

When public society is not highly differentiated from the domestic realm, the role of women is significant. In the self-sufficient Israelite household, the woman's participation and expertise in crucial matters of domestic function gave her the ability and right to control key aspects of family life. Israelite women preformed manifold tasks every day, and these tasks involved decisions about economic resources. Furthermore, the technical skills of these women made them "wise women" and thus instructors to those less skilled. If any hierarchical arrangements existed in such households, they were probably based on age and expertise rather than gender.

Again, recent anthropological research provides a useful model. Friedl's work in Greece during the 1960s[29] anticipated the feminist perspectives that came later in the 1970s. In the farming village of Vasilika she found, as might be expected, that men and women contributed about equally to the farm and household labor needs. What she also observed was that women in this village exerted considerable power not only over household economic decisions but also over the economic and marital futures of the children. Women and men performed different tasks, and the expertise of women in certain areas gave them control and attendant power. Furthermore, men were aware of their dependence on women, even though the society as a whole is male-dominated and the external appearance is of a male-controlled household. The situation was very much like the tiny village in southern France studied by Rogers and described in Chapter 2: male dominance is a public attitude and not a functional reality, and female power is functionally active though culturally concealed.

Female power is considerable in this Greek village, despite public or cultural appearances to the contrary. Viewed pragmatically, because "the family is the most significant social unit, then the private, and not the public sector, is the sphere in which the relative attribution of power to males and females is of the greatest real importance."[30] If this be the case in a community such as this Greek farming village, which does have bureaucratic superstructures and the consequent public accordance of authority and prestige exclusively to males, then how would gender relationships appear in a community in which such public structures were nonexistent or only minimally present?

Because the premonarchic period in ancient Israel lacked significant public life, this question needs to be addressed. With households managed by women, the decisions made by them will have great social impact. In short, female power will be as significant as male power, and perhaps even greater. To put it another way, in a prestate society in which the household is the fundamental institution and the primary locus of power, females may even have a predominant role, at least within the broad parameters of household life. This hypothesis brings again to mind the Victorian theorists who proposed the existence of a primary matriarchy. They did not actually suggest a matriarchal structure like the patriarchies they observed, with females simply reversing positions with males. Furthermore, they did not postulate the existence of matriarchies on the basis of public rule by females. Rather, they perhaps correctly recognized that women had an important place wherever public life is not significantly differentiated from domestic life.[31] They erred in calling such situations matriarchies, but they astutely recognized the prominence for females in a world dominated by the very realms in which females most typically exert control.

Ideally, we should ferret out some sign of female eminence in domestic life in the Bible. However, this is difficult to do because the biblical source itself (as pointed out in Chapter 1) is largely a product of (male) public structures, of male-dominated civil and religious bureaucracies. Many scholars have nonetheless turned to such texts as the patriarchal—or matriarchal—narratives of Genesis for information about family dynamics in ancient Israel. We have resisted using the Genesis narratives as reliable sociological data for earliest Israel and will look instead at other texts.

However, the Genesis ancestor traditions combine two features relevant to our methodological perspective: first, they are oriented to the domestic or household world, with the interaction between the Hebrews and other peoples taking place through a single, eponymous "family" (Abraham, Isaac, and Jacob) over several telescoped generations; second, women play an especially prominent role in these narratives, with the outcome of critical family decisions determined by female activity and initiative. These observations imply that this literature reveals women exerting power in charting the course of family and, by extension, national well-being.[32]

Despite the intriguing possibilities of the matriarchal tales for recovering the social history of early Israel, the complexity of their literary formation and the highly crafted if not fictive nature of their final arrangement in the canon makes their relevance problematic. It would be useful to look at some other biblical depiction of the nonpublic world of ancient Israel. And there is one such source, namely, that most "unbiblical" of all biblical books, the Song of Songs (also known as [Canticle of] Canticles or the Song of Solomon).

As early as the mid-nineteenth century, the Song of Songs was noted for its special attention to women.[33] More recently, the author of one of the most detailed commentaries on the Song of Songs, Marvin Pope, calls the eloquent exposition by his nineteenth-century predecessor a "pioneer manifesto on the emancipation of women."[34] Though largely unaware of insights expressed over a century earlier, feminist biblical scholars have naturally turned to the Song of Songs as a source for affirmation of female worth. The mutuality of love in this book makes its representation of gender relationships stand apart from the impression of male dominance that permeates much of the Hebrew Bible.

The question, then, is whether the gender relationships portrayed in the Song of Songs can contribute to our discussion of gender balance and female power in early Israel. One would first look to the date and context of the Song of Songs in order to answer that question; however, as for several other biblical books to which we have turned (e.g., Proverbs), this poetic work confounds the usual attempts of biblical scholars to pinpoint its origins. Nonetheless, some scholars have recently cast aside long-held views of a late date (Persian period, sixth–fifth century, or later) and instead suggest a date in the early monarchic period.[35] Furthermore, even if the Song's final form is an achievement of the end of the Iron Age, it surely incorporates much older material and contains a significant number of archaic literary forms.[36] Consequently, its value for the understanding of the premonarchic and early monarchic period is considerable.

The Song of Songs is notable for its significant divergence from the urban public context of most other biblical writings. The poetry is uncommonly replete with natural imagery. Full of the language of human love (language so explicit that postbiblical Christian and Jewish commentators treated it as allegory rather than as reality) the activities of the lovers are set against a rural backdrop. Mountains and vales figure prominently. The metaphors and similes drawn from the natural world are not limited to pastoral or wild settings; cultivated orchards, fields, and vineyards receive playful and rich attention. Domesticated animals find their place alongside wild animals. Cities are not unknown to the poet or poets, but the countryside overwhelmingly provides the extravagant images that make the language of love so vivid. Indeed, the richness and variety of flora and fauna make the poem a kind of response or counterpoint to the Eden story of Genesis 2–3.[37] The garden setting itself and also some specific stylistic features create remarkable congruences between the Eden and Canticle gardens.

Even though there is a royal Solomonic presence at points in the Canticle, the relationships portrayed are entirely domestic and private. The language of close kinship is prominent: mother, daughters, sons, sisters, brothers—even though the love-struck couple is not explicitly identified as married. The love relationship is set apart from (and above!) the legalities of the contracted union that marriage was in the ancient world. The qualities of a relationship on its own terms operated apart from the words for husband (which as we shall see later may have hierarchical implications) and wife.

Within this rural, private world, the relationship between male and female is entirely consistent with the principles of gender balance. The mutuality of the lovers seeking each other is striking. There is no stereotyping of either sex; neither male dominance nor female subordination is present. The female is as aggressive in the pursuit of her loved one as he is in seeking her. If anything, the female dominates in her interaction with her lover.

The dominant role of the female is conveyed by various literary features.[38] The reported speech of the female, for example, occurs much more frequently than does that of the male. Of the verses that can clearly be identified as spoken by one or the other, fifty-six are spoken by the woman and only thirty-six by the man. The woman is far more verbal. She dominates the spoken interchanges and soliloquies; and it is her utterances that open the Song and close it. Note, too, that "father" does not appear in the list of the terms of family relationships that appear in the Song of Songs, whereas "mother" appears a perfect—in Semitic symbolism—seven times. Just as the structural emphasis on the woman's speech elevates the female position, so too does the repetition of "mother" to the exclusion of "father." In addition, the supporting characters in the Song of Songs are largely female. The "daughters of Jerusalem" figure prominently in the poetry, but there are no corresponding male figures.

There are two other fascinating uses of imagery with respect to gender. The first is the use of military metaphors. Although the language of gardens, hillsides, plants, and animals predominates, in a few instances military images and references to monumental architecture (towers and cities) are interspersed.[39] Such images are exclusively attached to the female. She is compared to a "mare of Pharaoh's chariots" (1:9); her neck is like "the tower of David, built for an arsenal, whereon hang a thousand bucklers, all of them shields of war" (4:4); she is akin to "an army with banners" (6:4,10); her neck again is the subject of comparison, "like an ivory tower" in 7:4, with her nose "like a tower of Lebanon"; and she is a wall with "battlements" (8:9,10), her breasts "like towers" (8:10). Apart from the question about whether or not the military imagery is flattering, its association with the female and not the male is striking.

The second unexpected use of metaphoric language comes in the way faunal imagery appears. In the large repertoire of animals in the Song of Songs, only the woman is linked with the powerful ones, the lion and the leopard (4:8).[40] Like the military images, the faunal images contain depictions of the female that are counter to stereotypical depictions.

The architectural and animal images convey might, strength, aggression, even danger. That is, conventional or stereotypical aspects of gender portrayal have been reversed. The language of the military and of the hunt is nearly always male language, and here it is used for a woman. These associations of the female with power should not be taken literally, as meaning that women were warriors or hunters. Rather, those images are metaphors for power and control, and they are used in the Song to suggest female attributes. As literary images, they can be compared to certain graphic images found in ancient art: the appearance of lions or weapons of war in the iconography of goddesses in the ancient Near East.[41] These visual symbols are not images derived from any projections of Amazonlike female behavior onto the world of the gods and goddesses. Rather, they convey the power attributed to the female deities.

The many unusual aspects of gender portrayal in the Song of Songs mandate consideration of its social context. Another rare image alerts us to the Song's inherently private social milieu: the poem twice mentions *bet 'em*, "mother's house" (3:4; 8:2). Nowhere in the Song is the masculine equivalent ("father's house") used. The appearance of "mother's house" is striking in view of the overriding importance of "father's house" (*bet 'ab*) as the biblical term for the family household, which was the innermost circle of Israelite life (see Chapters 5 and 7) and the major sphere of existence during the premonarchic period.

"Mother's house" is a rare term not only in the Song but also in the Hebrew Bible as a whole. It is found elsewhere only in the domestic scenarios of Genesis 24:28 and Ruth 1:8. In addition, the so-called Woman of Worth of Proverbs 31, a poem considered premonarchic by some,[42] repeatedly refers to "her house" (*betah*, in 31:21, 27). The industrious woman of that poem "not only runs the household but, in effect, defines it in a manner analogous to the more usual reference to the *bet 'ab*."[43] Interestingly enough, the strength of the woman of Proverbs 31 is portrayed mainly in terms of her economic functions.[44]

Because "father's house" is the normal term for the household unit, the use of "mother's house" demands close scrutiny. The term "father's house" is clearly male oriented and derives from lineage concerns, that is, from the way descent and property were reckoned along patrilineal lines. But here in the Song we encounter a situation devoid of such concerns. Rather, the situation is one of relationships, and the primary orientation lies with the female of the pair. Without the matter of lineage reckoning as part of the dynamics of the Song (or of Proverbs 31), the internal functional and relational aspect of household activity, in which females played a strong if not dominant role, is appropriately expressed by "mother's house" and not "father's house."

The Song of Songs, standing virtually alone among the biblical books apart from the stratifying consequences of institutional and public life, reveals a situation of gender mutuality. There is no trace of subordination of female to male, and there is a presence of power images for the female and not the male. As a uniquely "popular" work,[45] it reflects a setting in the family that predominated in the premonarchic period and that continued to exist, though perhaps in altered ways, thereafter (see Epilogue). The Song is a product of domestic life and not of the public world of kings and priests, bureaucrats and soldiers. It preserves a glimpse of the gender mutuality and female power that existed in family households.

For the most part, the active role of women in household-oriented societies is not visible in the public written record. Even in this century, the place of women in such societies lacks visibility.[46] Females in such settings do have real power. The cultural expression of female power in early Israel has miraculously survived in one small part of the official, canonical record of that society. Females and power images are prominently linked in the Song of Songs, the lyrics of love.

Female power in a complex household can imply a significant control by females over so-called public or extradomestic functions,[47] few as they may have been in a prestate society. Cross-cultural studies suggest that public roles for women, though neither formalized nor regularized, were not trivial. First, the very way in which reproduction was viewed in the context of public as well as domestic needs (see above, pp. 165–166) indicates a role for women in society at large. Second, the existence of female charismatics such as prophets, who were engaged in occasional public leadership activity, is a sign of the acceptance of females operating in areas affecting large segments of society. The few female prophets and wisdom figures visible in the Hebrew Bible are not questioned in their authoritative roles. Third, the elevation of the concept of wisdom and skill expressed as a female figure to semidivine status perhaps points subtly to the acceptance of female influence in public political and economic life. At the same time, however, since wisdom typically involves indirect influence rather than the exertion of formal control,[48] the association of females with wisdom would be a signal of informal social power rather than legally recognized authority to act.

Incipient gender hierarchies may have existed even in earliest Israel and were certainly present in the monarchic period. Yet, female power deriving from the various roles (economic and other) played by women in the complex peasant households enabled them to minimize or offset whatever formal authority was held by males. Assumptions of male dominance and female subservience in ancient Israel, derived from formal texts and from postbiblical traditions, may be part of the "myth" of male control masking a situation of male dependence. Gender relationships are the consequence of complex influences, involving specific social and economic arrangements; reconstructing the internal dynamics of a society thus is the only legitimate way to dispel the "myth" and to increase the visibility of Eve. Our examination of Israelite society allows us to see Eve as a figure no less powerful than her male counterpart.

Male Authority

It is perhaps lamentable but nonetheless inevitable that this exploration of gender relationships in early Israelite society should conclude with a consideration of male authority. Women may have not only had more power than the literary sources alone would lead us to believe; for a time—at least as long as the household was the major social institution—they may have even had a dominant role. But the strength with which male authority emerges in the written sources tells us that it would be naive and foolish to treat it as a feature emerging de novo at the transition from a decentralized village to a centralized monarchic society. In short, no matter how elevated a position we can posit for females in early Israel, the existence of certain areas of male dominance cannot be overlooked.

This is hardly the place to explore the source of the ways—limited though they may have been—in which men exerted authority over women. The search for origins and quest for explanations of gender asymmetry are matters best left to anthropologists.[49] The hierarchical control of males over females in ancient Israel is probably rooted in a patrilineal legacy of the Canaanite society that preceded Israel in Palestine. After all, the Israelites for the most part were Canaanites. Israel broke with Canaan in many significant political, social, and religious ways, but also retained and perpetuated some Canaanite cultural forms, especially those that had proved adaptable to the highland environment of the Israelite pioneers. Archaeologists see evidence of this adaptation in the material culture. For example, pottery forms associated with the Israelite villages in the early Iron Age are a continuation—albeit without the finer or luxury pieces—of Late Bronze Age Canaanite forms.[50]

Did the Israelites invent or select patriarchal, or patrilineal, patterns as a matter of policy? One would hardly say so. Yet, existing patterns[51] continued (and perhaps others were initiated) in the social organization because they met certain functional needs. Where gender differentiation appears discriminatory to women, the possibility that there are compelling functional origins must be entertained.[52] What is labeled exploitative or dysfunctional in the modern world may in fact have had a vital functional grounding in the Israelite highland villages.

It is to the marriage relationship in law and custom that the charges of biblical patriarchalism are most applicable. Thus, we need to examine Israelite marriage patterns in order to determine the functional values of hierarchical arrangements. Indeed, most of the few biblical legal statements concerning women alone depict the marriage relationship and the apparent legal rights of husband over wife. The very word for "husband" (*ba'al*) means "master" or "possessor" and has led many commentators to suppose that women were mere chattel, owned by their husbands. They cite such passages as the tenth commandment, in which woman seems to be listed as the husband's property: "You shall not covet your neighbor's wife, or his manservant, or his maidservant, or his ox, or his ass, or anything that is your neighbor's" (Exod 20:17; but see Deut 5:21).

However, the absolute sovereignty of one person over another is expressed not by *ba'al* but by another word, *'adon* ("lord"), as in the control of a conqueror over the vanquished or of a master over the slave. *Ba'al* as the term for husband is not so absolute, because it involves an intimate relationship, a limit to power, as well as indicating an ultimate ruling will.[53] The term *ba'al* is not limited to the husband–wife relationship: it also includes the male's ultimate authority over animals (Exod 21:28, 29, 36; 22:10; 2 Sam 1:6; Isa 1:3), property (Exod 21:34; Eccles 5:12), and the household in general (Exod 22:7; Judg 19:22, 23). But it is also not an abstract term. It does not accord an absolute status of control to the male. The male as *ba'al* is not an isolated despot but rather a will exerted in relationship to others.

A recent study by Tosato of Hebrew marriage[54] (partly motivated by the current Marxist critique of the institution of marriage) emphasizes the juridical nature of marriage in ancient Israel. The use of *ba'al* in several Pentateuchal texts seems to indicate a legal inequality between the spouses, with the wife unilaterally bound exclusively to the husband. However, such a judgment of the arrangement apparently comes from the bias of later biblical or postbiblical tradition. Tosato demonstrates that the husband owns neither his wife nor his possessions.[55] Nonetheless, the husband's position was clearly different from that of the wife, and the transmission of property patrilineally probably underlies the apparent male advantage.

Why should the male have this ultimate advantage or authority? The answer, speculative as it may be, perhaps lies in the dynamics of kinship in establishing continuity of land tenure. Because Israel reckoned its descent patrilineally, property disposition and transmission followed the male line. In practical terms, this meant that marriage arrangements involved female mobility and male stability. That is, the males (the chief heir or firstborn, and usually also his younger brothers who either shared in the inheritance or stood by to receive some or all of it should the father so decide or should the eldest die) remained in the family household. The females left the household and went to live in the domestic compounds of their husbands' families.

The dynamics of household life therefore required the female to adopt the technologies and cultural patterns of the husband's household. This was a significant matter, because of ancient Israel's marriage customs. Israel vacillated between patterns of endogamy (in which marriage was arranged within a prescribed kinship circle) and exogamy (in which marriages took place between Israelites and foreigners). At times both patterns existed, often with tension between them. Both patterns involved a difficult transition: a young woman had to adopt the cultural practices and values of the family of which she became a member.

It is easy to see the need for females to adopt a new cultural system with respect to exogamy, which was apparently present nearly throughout Israel's history. At various times, it actually seems to have been essential that Israelites take foreign wives, because the higher female mortality rate meant shortages of marriageable women. The premonarchic period especially is associated with exogamous marriage. The Beth Baal Peor incident described above (pp. 70–71), for example, reflects a situation in which there was an advantage to sparing certain Moabite virgins regardless of a strong sense that the whole contaminated enemy ought to meet death (Num 25:1–8; 31:9–18). These "daughters of Moab" were the very females who had led Israelites astray, causing them to acknowledge Moabite gods; yet, ironically, they were allowed to survive in order to become wives for Israelites.

The Moabite story probably reflects an early stage in Israelite history, as does also the notice in Judges 3:5–6, which records that "the Israelites lived among the Canaanites, the Hittites, the Perizzites, the Hivites, and the Jebusites; and they took their daughters to themselves for wives, and their own daughters they gave to their sons; and they served their gods." Note the routine reporting of marriage with foreigners. And note too the statement that the daughters, going to live with foreign families, adopted the gods of the people among whom they dwelled.

But what about the foreign daughters joining Israelite households? It was evidently not easy for women to put aside the patterns of their own families and people. Along with apparent acceptance of exogamy, there was understandably also strong resistance to it. Exodus 34:11–16 warns against arrangements of any kind with those various groups inhabiting the neighboring lowlands of Palestine; in particular this passage warns against taking the foreign daughters as wives, lest they bring foreign customs and idolatry (read cultural systems and values) into Israelite households. This Exodus text does *not* deal with Israelite women going to foreign families. A similar and probably later passage in Deuteronomy (7:3–4) does abjure both male and female exogamy. However, the reason given concerns *only* the males, that their sons' way of life might be countermanded or threatened by foreign wives unable to give up the ideas and practices of their youth.

This treatment of exogamy is interesting on several counts. It shows that the male's household is dominant with respect to cultural patterns: someone coming into it is expected to adopt its ways. However, it also shows that this was not easily achieved. Females did not easily relinquish their cultural traditions. Furthermore, it demonstrates that foreign females exerted considerable power within their new households. The texts warning against their corrupting influence make no sense unless the foreign wives were in fact maintaining foreign values or practices.

These biblical texts all cast the warnings about foreign women in religious terms. The daughters of Canaanites are said to have brought their gods with them; and the sustained popularity of Baal worship throughout Israelite history, as evidenced in the prophetic outrage against it (e.g., Hos 2:17; Jer 23:13; 1 Kgs 18; Zeph 1:4; see Mal 2:11–

12; Ezra 9–10; Neh 10:31 and 13:23–27), attests to the ongoing problem. Religious ideology and cult, as we pointed out in Chapter 1, were not autonomous features of human existence. Rather, they were an integral part of a cultural system. The threat of foreign gods, introduced by foreign women, must be seen as a clash between cultural systems. Worshipping foreign gods in fact represented a threat to the whole social, economic, and political fabric of the culture.

In exogamous arrangements, male authority can be recognized as filling an ideological or cultural need. But there also would have been a functional need for male authority operating on a pragmatic and technological level. This becomes clearer with consideration of the functional aspect of male authority in situations of endogamy, or in-group marriage, in which the ideological dimension of a non-family member entering a household would not have been operative.

The preference for in-group marriage over a "mixed" exogamous marriage is certainly understandable in a kinship-based society. Even today we recognize the psychological advantages to a relationship in which the partners have a common background on which to build their future interactions and express their values. In an agrarian setting, the closer the families of bride and groom, the more likely the bride would have learned the techniques of household labor that would best serve the new household. "Closer" here means spatially as well as relationally. To explain this, the ecological factor again merits consideration.

Ancient Israel, as we have seen in Chapter 3, occupied ecological niches that posed challenges to subsistence. True, hill cultivation required specialized techniques and knowledge, but it would be a mistake to assume that such techniques and knowledge were uniform throughout the hill country. On the contrary, the highlands of Palestine represent perhaps the most fractured, complex combination of ecosystems in the world. The overall agricultural potential is rather uniform. However, the network of hills and valleys, of rain shadows and wind patterns, is extraordinarily complex and diverse.[56] Consequently, only the individual farmers, knowing intimately the conditions of their own land (e.g., soils, rainfall, temperature ranges), can make the minute yet essential adjustments in agricultural technique that can mean the difference between want and plenty. Plowing and seeding times, the layout of fields, the pruning or plucking, and many other aspects of agricultural life called for the daily decisions that affected the economic viability of a household.

Because of the complexity of Palestine's highland ecology, a farmer in one village may have developed a strategy that differed in significant ways from that of a farmer in a nearby village. The gross technology and crop selection would be the same, but subtle and vital variants would have evolved according to the ecology of each village. Women from the broader kinship groups, from nearby villages, were the wives in an endogamous system. Yet, they too would have had to learn the management of their husband's household. The husband's authority in establishing household practices suitable to the local ecology thus had a strong functional advantage.

In light of these considerations of male authority, the role of the husband as *ba'al* (master) appears to have been operant in maintaining household efficiency when outsiders, whether from near or far, were brought into the compound. Such authority would have been shared by the senior female to the extent that she had long experience with the operation of the household domain. If the male held the authority to determine the method of completing household tasks as well as the means of integrating behavior into a cultural system, he did so because of his prior tie to the land that was the source of the household's survival.

But male behavior in this regard should not be generalized to all aspects of household life. Much of daily life and technology were uniform throughout the hill country and even the Levant as a whole. However, the division of labor according to gender may have followed a pattern that had males (growing up and remaining in a particular household) responsible for tasks most sensitive to the nuances of the local ecosystem. It is no wonder that the management of plow agriculture, the part of the household economy for which understanding environmental variables is most important, largely falls to males in a patrilineal inheritance system.

One other important aspect of the patrilineal, patrimonial system is relevant to this discussion of male authority. Marriage was conceptually and legally a part of the inheritance, or property transmission, system of ancient Israel. As such, it involved negotiations, arrangements, and legal considerations that transcended the household group. Whether marriages were secured endogamously (with related kin groups) or exogamously (from distant or foreign peoples), the contractual dimension meant interaction in what might be legitimately called the public sphere. Males secured marital contracts for their sons or daughters and therefore had a legally recognized role—an authoritative position—in the public world.

Be that as it may, this authority in arranging marriages was tempered informally by the wishes and desires of the females involved. Two biblical tales bear this out, although one of them comes from the problematic narratives of Genesiṣ. In the story of Rebekah's betrothal to Isaac, she is asked if she will go to become Isaac's wife (Gen 24:5–8). And the account of Samson's marriage to a Philistine woman relates how Samson approaches both his mother and his father in expressing his marital desires, although it was apparently the father who made the arrangements (Judg 14:1–3).

It is clear that ultimate male authority existed in the households as well as in public interaction. But we reiterate that such authority must always be qualified in terms of its functional role. Furthermore, our contemporary notions of family hierarchy are not adequate to describe the situation of gender relationships in a society where the family household was the determinative institution and in which women were essential to both subsistence tasks and group survival. Anthropologists are right in warning that it is inappropriate to generalize authoritative behavior in one category to all categories, or even to assume that the concept of dominance always existed and meant the same as it does in our industrial, urban world.[57]

The structural authority of the male in the Israelite household cannot be separated from the considerable female involvement in the economic and other aspects of household life. Family dynamics were naturally radically different from those in the present-day western family, which is a "non-producing collectivity of consumers."[58] As long as the household remained the central institution of the villages and tribes, the critical role of the female in sharing the labor, bearing and socializing children, and managing vital subsistence procedures offset the hierarchical potential of formal male authority. The decentralized and difficult village life of premonarchic Israel provided a context for gender mutuality and interdependence, and of concomitant female power. Male authority existed in certain spheres but there was no connotation of misogyny, the oppression of females, or the notion of female inferiority.

In Chapter 2 (pp. 43–44), we listed the components of a situation (as outlined by Rogers) in which male dominance is characterized as a "myth." As we have discovered in this work, those components existed in early Israel. Therefore, male dominance did not exist in the formative stages of Israel.

When social and political conditions changed dramatically, as they did during the centuries after the monarchy was established, the repercussions were pervasive for the fabric of communal life. It is difficult to know how rapidly household life changed once the kings began to rule. For better or for worse, the household was recreated and reshaped as the result of both inward trajectories and outward influences.

evitably changed (along with the changes in her household
the locus of power shifted to a nation-state. And the new
nder the monarchy left us the texts that suggest patriarchy
subservience. But the premonarchic period remains the formative period in Israel's long history. If the egalitarian values and patterns that prevailed during those prestate centuries are to have any
meaning for later generations, including our own, this recovery of Everywoman Eve's life and context should make the nonhierarchical position of women a visible and enduring model, as are the other widely
acclaimed theological and social innovations and accomplishments, of
early Israel.

Epilogue:
The Monarchy and Beyond

The Eve of the premonarchic era has become visible: the peasant woman now seen is hardly the exploited, subservient creature imagined by those who have been influenced by the androcentricity of the biblical canon and by the misogyny of much of the postbiblical tradition. What happened to her? Why did she become hidden behind the cultural legacy of a male-dominated society? One reason it is so difficult to accept the idea of a powerful Eve, working interdependently with her mate to establish a nonhierarchical society with Yahweh alone as the sovereign force, is that the traces of that pristine balance of gender relationships have been nearly erased by the documents left by succeeding generations. Yet they have not been completely removed, and here and there a biblical passage preserves a sense of the parity of the early generations. Those passages have been teased out and given context with the help of archaeological materials and anthropological analogies.

Parity did not endure. It was eroded (at what speed it is impossible to determine) by the complex forces that accompanied the formation and development of the Israelite state at the end of the eleventh century BCE. Israel's survival was threatened because internal growth had stretched the meager resources of the land. At the same time external military pressures—especially from the Philistines—threatened Israel's ability to maintain territorial integrity using only local militias. Only a centralized mechanism for redistributing resources and for establishing a strong military presence could sustain Israel through the demographic, economic, and political crises that threatened the very existence of the tribal groups in the waning decades of the early Iron Age.[1]

The formation of the monarchy was perhaps the most significant change in the millennium-long history of ancient Israel's national existence. Even before socioeconomic analysis became a prominent concern of the study of ancient Israel, scholars recognized the dramatic changes brought about by state formation: "The monarchy, owing to its nature and its effects, was the most radical revolution in ancient Israel. It aimed to give Israel an international status, . . . to industrialize the country, and to develop the city at the expense of the village."[2] More recently the establishment of the monarchy as a powerful force effecting widespread changes and as being a watershed event in the creation of hierarchies in ancient Israel has been similarly evaluated: "A hierarchical structure, such as the monarchic state requires, means a complete break with the social, political, and economic principles on which tribal society is based."[3]

The rise of the state meant the gradual end of a society in which the household was the dominant social unit. The locus of power moved from the family household, with its gender parity, to a public world of male control. The establishment of a nation-state meant the growing prominence of the military and of state and religious bureaucracies controlling economic development. These institutions are typically public and male controlled; whenever they become an important part of a society's organization, female prestige and power recede.[4]

State formation meant a radical disruption of the social fabric of the clan and tribal levels of social organization. It is no accident that Solomon established a viable tax base and a public support for the imperial power of Jerusalem that involved a territorial redistricting of the kingdom. He broke down old kinship connections and loyalties in order to secure new loyalties to the court-appointed bureaucrats of the newly created administrative districts.[5] It is difficult to know how, and how quickly, the new public organization affected the internal dynamics of family households. Nonetheless, we can assume that changes eventually occurred. The rise of male-controlled military, civil, and religious bureaucracies, and the concomitant breakup of kinship-based social organizations must have taken a toll on gender relations.

The observations of social scientists bear this out. Conkey and Spector, for example, discuss the effects of state formation on gender in these terms: "The suppression of the kinship base that is so powerful an organizer of social relations in pre-state society undoubtedly triggered important changes in gender status and gender relations."[6] State formation created hierarchical relationships and robbed females of their customary equality or interdependence with males.[7] The rise of a public world dichotomized the social structure (see Chapter 2) and led to male preeminence.

Israel surely retained many of the ideals of its formative period such as a monolatrous religious orientation and concern among some for social justice and economic security; yet, like the surrounding nation-states, it developed the aforementioned public institutions—all of them in the hands of men. To be sure, an elite class never fully arose in an official political sense, at least if the lack of a vocabulary for it in the biblical record is to be taken seriously. Unlike other ancient Semitic literatures, the Hebrew Bible has no explicit term for human overlords or seigniors. But on a pragmatic and economic level, an elite class de facto came into existence.

The formation of the nation-state and the emergence of bureaucratic elites went hand in hand with a gradual demographic shift from country to city. Urban development, limited as it may have been in actual percentage of the population directly involved, characterized the monarchic period. This shift had implications for female roles and status, because women probably remained economically productive in rural areas, but became less productive or even nonproductive as urban wives of bureaucrats. Women in such positions became less essential to the household economy as their husbands gained access to resources external to the household. Also, if their husbands accumulated wealth under such circumstances, the wives' contributions became nominal except for their reproductive role. The wives of bureaucrats, largely though not exclusively in urban contexts, thus had the leisure and boredom to become "loose women." Urban women became the chief referents for many of the negative images of women in the Bible, especially in Proverbs. But even for the less wealthy women, there would have been a loss of the relative parity that characterized male and female in agrarian village settings.[8]

The creation of bureaucracies and political hierarchies thus had one specific effect on women in elite groups. But what about the other women, the rural women, the Eves in the villages?

Despite the dominance of urban male institutions, Israel never became a homogeneous urban society, and rural village life continued.[9] Agriculture remained the basis of Israel's economy. The multiple-family compounds typical of the early settlements can still be spotted in archaeological remains of the monarchy.[10] Economic stratification emerged in the cities, where a growing differentiation of domestic quarters into villas and palaces on the one hand and hovels on the other can be seen in the archaeological record. However, such stratification was probably less pronounced in the small agricultural communities at least as long as families retained control of their ancestral land holdings.

Thus, social homogeneity in economic matters and in gender valuation was probably sustained in places outside the urban centers for some time. Later on in the monarchy, prophecy and the call for social justice emerged from rural contexts (Amos 7:14; 2 Kgs 1:8–9). This aspect of prophecy provides some justification for the possibility that egalitarian ideals were maintained in the countryside. However, it is questionable whether those egalitarian ideals included gender as well as property and economic viability. And even the economic viability of household units evidently eroded during the centuries of the monarchy.

Analysis of the gradual transformation of the economic structure of Israelite life in the Iron II period is only now beginning.[11] Although reviewing the problems and complexities of this transformation is not appropriate here, consideration of some of the economic changes can shed light on changes in female roles and status.

The rise of the monarchy brought about the increasingly centralized control of production. It also brought the development of foreign markets. Archaeology reveals the presence of imported ceramics and an increase in luxury items during the period of the monarchy. This was certainly the case in the major cities, and it also is noticeable in the smaller settlements. A decline in the household-based economy, the inevitable result of such a shift, would inevitably have weakened the female's voice in household economic decisions.[12]

With the control of economic life becoming ever more centralized, family households, where they endured, became less self-sufficient. Eventually their very existence was threatened. The market economy, along with the burden of taxation and the inexorable ecological risks of the Palestinian environment, all strained the fragile household economy beyond what it could bear in many cases.

The struggle of households for survival is reflected in the expansion of the earlier legal handling of debt in the biblical laws by the eighth or seventh century BCE. Deuteronomic law deals extensively with debt servitude. Such legal attention indicates an increase of debt servitude as households either failed or took desperate measures to remain viable. The increase of the indenture of persons is a consequence of problems of self-sufficiency in the household economy and is typically related to the growth of commerce and production outside traditional family or "lineage" modes of production.[13]

These strains on the family production system brought about by the formation of a state led to the dissolution of many household units. Small landowners inevitably had to relinquish lands that had been transferred within families for generations. Large landholders emerged, and the peasants lost control of their means of subsistence and consequently of their social and economic power.[14] This process perhaps culminated in the events of the seventh century BCE, when the crown appears to have broken whatever remnants of the lineage system and of the economic self-sufficiency of household units had survived the earlier centuries of monarchic domination.[15] Royal policies between Hezekiah and Josiah (715–609) imposed a new economic and social order and created, perhaps for the first time, such a dramatic concentration of population in urban centers that the traditional underpinnings of Israelite life were irrevocably disrupted.

Certainly, then, the monarchy meant changes in the entire fabric of society. We have only alluded to the complexity of the social, political, economic, and religious changes. Yet, there was also continuity, and the evidence for the enduring forms and values during the monarchy are likewise manifold and complex and hence beyond the scope of this work. Thus, the specific effects of both the change and the continuity in gender relationships during the centuries of monarchic life cannot be ascertained here.

Nevertheless it is apparent that the general changes noted earlier must have figured in an erosion of female power and status even in isolated and relatively intact village settings. The eventual disruption of the lineage system certainly reinforced social and political hierarchies, which would have contributed to gender hierarchies. Furthermore, the development of a market economy would probably have exaggerated the division of labor along gender lines with more prestige and control going to the males dominating the extradomestic economic life.

Demographic changes also affected the structure and values of Israelite society. The strategy of increasing the population was necessary and effective in the early stages of tribal Israel. It succeeded to the extent that, over the centuries as the population and its territorial base expanded, the frontier was closed. Even marginally arable lands were settled, and there were no further lands available for the still-growing population.

This problem, along with the external threat of a similarly expanding Philistine population, led to the call for a monarchy that could command and balance resources on regional and national levels. A centralized government also created bureaucratic positions that could be filled by a growing number of young men who, once the frontier was closed, would have been closed out of agricultural household lineages by the land limitations. A land shortage in a patrilineal society like ancient Israel meant that difficulties arose when a portion of land had to be divided among several sons.[16] The division of land into ever smaller plots creates ineffective farm lands as well as family tensions. Laws of primogeniture, a preferential double portion for the oldest male (Deut 21:15–17), became important under such conditions. Similarly, bureaucratic options for sons with a limited inheritance helped alleviate the problem of land shortage. "In ancient Israel," Stager notes, "as in medieval Europe and many other cultures, this 'safety valve' for young unmarried males involved careers in the military, government or priesthood."[17]

These measures were part of, or contributed to, the general intensification of the value placed on productive property that accompanies population increase. Social scientists have long pointed out the association between population density and agricultural intensification on the one hand, and emphasis on property and the ownership of land on the other. Under such conditions, the transgenerational transmission of land becomes highly formalized and restrictive. The implications of gender differentiation are enormous when property inheritance is reckoned patrilineally. The problem of establishing proper heirs becomes critical, and the sexual behavior of females becomes restricted.[18] The double standard in treatment of females in terms of extramarital or premarital sexual activity is first a pragmatic response to this situation of inheritance legalities and only later a matter of morality.

Under these conditions of decreasing territorial resources, marriage and controlled maternity become part of a strategy for transmitting land. The legal arrangements for marriage tend to become highly formalized, and the autonomy of females—and of males—in selecting mates becomes greatly restricted. Our comments in Chapter 8 (pp. 183–186) about marriage patterns as part of extrahousehold relationships is related to this point. Consequently it becomes irrelevant to criticize as sexist the male-oriented marriage patterns visible in biblical law and narrative. In a preindustrial agrarian society in which land is the chief resource and especially when it is an increasingly scarce resource, the existence of marriage strategies safeguarding the inheritance of property has essential functional value.

Monarchic rule no doubt curtailed Eve's power, but there were qualifying influences that should be considered. First, the monarchy or state as an institution dominated by males should not be blamed for the deterioration in the role and status of females. The nation-state took shape, at least partially, in response to ecological limitations. Ironically, the very success of territorial and population expansion ultimately mandated the end of the relatively egalitarian and noncentralized system. It seems that the conditions under which women and men acted interdependently could not be sustained indefinitely.

Second, despite all the forces that may have operated under the monarchy to limit female power and autonomy, Eve's power in fact never completely disappeared. Never in the Hebrew Bible are women deemed inferior as a class. Thus, differential treatment of women in many of the laws of the Pentateuch should not be separated from their functional role: dealing with problems of adultery, divorce, betrothal, inheritance, etc. Such laws are not inherently discriminatory within their own social context and in view of territorial problems and patrilineal structures.

Third, many of the forces that restricted female power were likewise damaging to male power and autonomy. The loss of household properties meant the economic and political subservience of males as well as females. Certain options and opportunities were probably foreclosed in such situations for women and not for men, yet the fact remains that many freeholding peasants were forced into wage labor and to the disenfranchised status resulting from the loss of property. The "poor" and the "stranger" join the "widow" and "orphan" in prophetic and Deuteronomic literatures as landless groups that are economically vulnerable and are in need of special protection.

Fourth, most of the information about the rural population indicates that the radical changes just mentioned, involving loss of property and disruption of lineage systems, did not reach acute proportions until the eighth and seventh centuries BCE. That is, the household units remained relatively intact structurally (though not in terms of their role in society as a whole) until well into the monarchy. The household would have continued as a fundamental unit of society even when it ceased to be the locus of political, social, and economic power.[19] This being the case, many of the norms, values, and functions characteristic of premonarchic family households would have continued despite radical changes in the public world.

The destruction of the northern kingdom (in 722 BCE) meant a large influx of refugees to the south. Jerusalem only then became a major urban center, and the other cities of Judah likewise had to cope with the arrival of landless "sojourners." Before this time, Israelite and Judean cities were relatively small. With the concentration of population in the urban centers, urban life became the prevailing mode. The age old pattern of agricultural hinterlands around small, walled settlements gave way to a state dominated by one enormous urban center, Jerusalem, and a number of satellite cities. Urban life with its androcentric character finally overpowered traditional rural values and folkways, the ones not readily visible in the canonical record.

Fifth, despite the many influences leading to the emergence of male dominance in local as well as national settings, women still appear in occasional leadership roles even in the biblical record. Those women should be viewed not as the exceptions but rather as the representation of perhaps a larger group of publicly active females whose identity was lost because of the male-controlled canonical process. The female prophets and wisdom figures could not have found their paradigmatic though limited place in the canon if they were not part of an intrinsic acknowledgment of female worth and even authority.

Finally, one must give due weight to the survival of strong female images in the Hebrew Bible. The very existence of the Song of Songs (with its gender mutuality and associations of females with power) as well as the presence of a figure such as female Wisdom are not chance aberrations. Rather they provide testimony to the ongoing reality of what these materials represent.

The ultimate displacement of females from the early parity they held with males in the premonarchic period and well into the monarchy in many rural quarters could not have come until the late preexilic period. Even then, the exile and the reemergence of pioneer conditions in the early postexilic period might have slowed down the process leading to Eve's loss of power and status. So perhaps one must look for the causes of the changes in Eve's fortunes even beyond the monarchy, to the next radical transition in the history of Israel: the superimposition of Greco-Roman thought and cultural forms on the biblical world and the subsequent emergence of Judaism and Christianity from the embers of Israelite national life.

Greco-Roman culture brought a dualistic way of thinking to the Semitic world: pairs such as body and soul, evil and good, female and male became aligned. Eve was the victim of this alignment: female was linked with body and evil. Relegated to a position of decreasing power as the household lost its prominence, she then became associated with negative aspects of life. The misogynist expansions of the Eden story in early Christian and Jewish literature begin to emerge. A new concept of Eve associated with sin, death, and suffering is superimposed so indelibly on the assertive and productive figure of the Eden narrative that we can hardly see the original woman of Genesis 2–3. But now, with the help of a wide range of scholarly and analytical tools, we have begun to rediscover and reclaim the pristine Eve.

NOTES

CHAPTER 1

1. For the views of William Foxwell Albright (1841–1971), see Albright (1940). A translation of representative essays by Albrecht Alt (1883–1956) appears in Alt (1968).
2. See, e.g., O'Barr (1988) and DuBois *et al.* (1985).
3. Pointed out by Crumbine (1983); *see also* Gifford (1985).
4. See the summary in Rogers (1978), pp. 123–128.
5. The most comprehensive such study to date is Gottwald (1979).
6. Flanagan (1985), p. 309.
7. Leach (1982), p. 130.
8. Gottwald (1979) focuses on the premonarchic period.
9. Not all archaeologists agree on these dates. Many followers of Albright, for example, continue Iron I for another century or until the end of the United Monarchy in 922 BCE. See Lance (1981), pp. 97–98.
10. Albright (1949).
11. As in Binford and Binford (1968). For a more recent treatment see Renfrew (1984).
12. Bass (1982), p. 9.
13. Flannery (1972).
14. Geertz (1973), pp. 167–172.

CHAPTER 2

1. Russell (1985a).
2. Russell (1985b), pp. 11–12.
3. Sakenfeld (1985), pp. 55–56.
4. Ibid., p. 64.
5. Exum (1985), pp. 74, 77.
6. Ruether (1985), p. 119.
7. Rowbotham (1979), p. 970; cf. the definitions in Lerner (1986), pp. 238–242.
8. Beechey (1979).
9. Millett (1970).
10. Engels (1972).

11. DuBois *et al.* (1985), pp. 92–95.

12. Rowbotham (1979), p. 970.

13. See our discussion of Israelite demography in Chapter 3, pp. 62–71.

14. See the discussion of these issues in Rosaldo (1980).

15. Leacock, in (1981) and other works, is a leading proponent of this view.

16. E.g., by Binford (1979).

17. Cronin (1977), p. 91. Similar presence of female autonomy and power in an overtly "patriarchal" system has been recognized in Chinese society; see M. Wolf (1972).

18. Cronin's identification [(1977), pp. 88–92] of the circumstances that placed extraordinary demands on both women and men in order for them to achieve subsistence reveals a set of conditions strikingly similar to the challenge besetting the highland farmers in earliest Israel. See our description of those challenges in Chapter 3.

19. Lamphere (1977).

20. See Quinn (1977).

21. The classic formulations of this dichotomizing model are reviewed and criticized by DuBois et al. (1985), pp. 113–125, and by Rosaldo (1980), 396–401; 407–409.

22. In addition to the works cited in note 21, see Tilly (1978), pp. 167–168, and Nicholson (1982), pp. 734–735.

23. Schlegel (1977b), pp. 17–18.

24. Rosaldo (1980), p. 407.

25. See the discussion in Gould (1980), p. 464.

26. Lefkowitz (1983), pp. 31–32.

27. Whyte (1978).

28. Ibid., p. 10.

29. See ibid., pp. 167–184.

30. Ibid., p. 170.

31. Schlegel (1977b), p. 20.

32. See our discussion in Chapter 8 (pp. 170–171) of the age–sex valuations set forth in Leviticus 27.

33. Millett (1970), pp. 46–47.

34. Bird (1974), p. 54.

35. Douglas (1966), p. 142; Schlegel (1972), pp. 89–90, 93. Cf. the discussion in Stack *et al.* (1975), pp. 150–151.

36. Bachofen (1861); Morgan (1877); Engels (1972). References to feminist readings and critiques of Engels can be found in Rosaldo (1980), note 22.

37. Schusky (1974), pp. 11–15.

38. Schlegel (1972).

39. Martin and Voorhies (1975), pp. 286–290.

40. McLennan (1865). This influential book and the evolutionary theory it proposed were taken up by social scientists such as Herbert Spencer and Lewis Morgan (see note 36 above) as well as by biblical scholars.

41. W. R. Smith (1885).
42. As in Mace (1953), pp. 35–43, 76–94; cf. Gottwald (1979), p. 305.
43. Wilson (1985b), pp. 970–971.
44. Weber (1947).
45. Edited by Rosaldo and Lamphere (1974).
46. Rosaldo (1974), pp. 21–22.
47. Ibid., p. 21.
48. Rogers (1975), p. 729.
49. Leach (1969).
50. Rogers (1975), p. 729.
51. Ibid., 729–730.
52. E.g., Fuchs (1985).
53. Gould and Kern-Daniels (1977), p. 183.
54. Ibid., p. 184.

CHAPTER 3

1. Gottwald (1979) exemplifies this approach, as already noted in Chapter 1. Another recent example is Frick (1985).
2. Friedl (1975).
3. Ibid., p. 7.
4. Ibid., pp. 7–8.
5. Gottwald (1979), p. xxv.
6. Thompson (1979), pp. 39–50.
7. Aharoni (1979), p. 241.
8. Stager (1981).
9. This reconstruction of Israelite beginnings was first suggested in a landmark article by Mendenhall (1962). Its most developed exposition is in Gottwald (1979). Reviews, critiques, and further utilization of sociopolitical models for early Israel are now voluminous: see, for example, the articles in Freedman and Graf (1983).
10. Lenski (1980).
11. We are assuming that the term Israelites can be used for the Iron Age settlers of the hill country, although skeptics are admittedly right in pointing out that the archaeological evidence from the new Iron Age hill country settlements does not provide proof of the ethnic, social, or political identity of the inhabitants.
12. Zohary (1982), pp. 28–33.
13. Hopkins (1983), p. 180.
14. Albright (1949), p. 113.
15. Callaway (1984), p. 56.
16. Wampler (1947).
17. Callaway and Cooley (1971), p. 10.
18. Waldbaum (1978), pp. 41–42: Tables IV.1,2; Figs. IV.1,2.
19. Friedl (1975), p. 53.

20. Sanday (1974), pp. 194 ff; Meyers (1983c), pp. 573–575.

21. Friedl (1975), pp. 8, 26, 48, 137.

22. Draper (1975), pp. 78–91.

23. E. R. Wolf (1966), pp. 19–34.

24. Hopkins (1985), p. 178.

25. Such as Boserup (1976).

26. Stager (1976), pp. 11–12.

27. Callaway (1969), p. 16: Figs. 10, 11; Callaway and Cooley (1971).

28. Stager (1985), p. 6.

29. Ibid., p. 9.

30. Stager (1982), pp. 115–117.

31. See the discussion in Hopkins (1985), pp. 173–187.

32. Ron (1966), p. 34, and Borowski (1987), p. 17; but cf. Hopkins (1985), p. 268.

33. Hopkins (1985), p. 181.

34. Edelstein and Gat (1980), p. 73. See also Borowski (1987), pp. 31–44.

35. Peltzer (1945), p. 67.

36. Hopkins (1985), p. 183.

37. Hareuveni (1980), p. 37.

38. Hopkins (1985), p. 189.

39. Rossi (1977), p. 22.

40. Boserup (1970), p. 15.

41. Ibid., p. 35.

42. Sandars (1978) examines the disastrous state of affairs in the eastern Mediterranean at the end of the thirteenth century.

43. McNeill (1975), pp. 13–14.

44. Ibid., pp. 1–3, 199–216.

45. The Epic of Gilgamesh XI:185–186. Translation of E. Speiser in Pritchard (1955). The composition of Gilgamesh has been dated to the end of the third millennium BCE.

46. Atrahasis Epic I:352 f.; cf. II:1–8. Translation of Lambert and Millard (1969). This epic poem was composed early in the second millennium BCE.

47. McNeill (1975), p. 284. For example, dysentery during the Crimean War (1854–1856) claimed ten times more British soldiers than did battle wounds.

48. Hare (1954), pp. 37–66.

49. McNeill (1975), pp. 166–170.

50. Mendenhall (1973), p. 109, notes 17, 18.

51. Ibid., p. 109. The Hittite word for fire, *paḫura,* underlies Greek *pyr* and English "fire." In Semitic mythology, fire divinities (such as Reshef) are closely connected to plague.

52. Amarna Letter 244. Translation of W. F. Albright in Pritchard (1955).

53. Translations of A. Goetze in Pritchard (1955).

54. The problems of attributing destruction are summarized in Gottwald (1979), pp. 261–269.

55. Meyers (1978), pp. 96–97.

56. Hare (1954), pp. 150–152.

57. Angel (1972), p. 93 and Table 28.

58. Friedl (1975), p. 100.

CHAPTER 4

1. Koestler (1959), p. 334.

2. Opere XI: 192 f.; cited in Koestler (1959), pp. 435–436.

3. Ecclesiasticus 25:24. This translation is that of Trenchard (1981), p. 58; cf. idem, pp. 81–82.

4. Malina (1969), pp. 22–24.

5. Vita Adae et Evae 35:2–3. Translation of L. S. A. Wells, in Charles (1913), vol. 2, p. 142.

6. Apocalypsis Mosis 32:2. Translation of L. S. A. Wells, in Charles (1913), vol. 2, p. 149.

7. Barr (1982) p. 268; cf. Clark (1986).

8. O'Brien and Major (1982), p. 95.

9. Hanson (1972), pp. 41–42.

10. For a sampling of works on Genesis, see the bibliography for that Book in Childs (1979), pp. 136–138.

11. See her discussion of methodology: Trible (1978), pp. 8–11.

12. Trible (1973a); for a more popular version, see idem (1973b).

13. Selected from the partial listing of eleven "consensus" items in Trible (1978), p. 73.

14. Higgins (1976).

15. Quoted in Terrien (1985), p. 8.

16. Sproul (1979), p. 27; see also Sproul's general discussion of creation myths, in idem, pp. 1–30.

17. Terrien (1985), pp. 8–9.

18. Sproul (1979), p. 27.

19. Maass (1974), p. 75.

20. Speiser (1964), p. 16.

21. Plöger (1974), pp. 90–92.

22. Verses 8 and 9 are included in this unit, although some literary critics arrange it differently. See Coats (1983), pp. 49–60.

23. The word for bush (śiah) has the sense of noncultivated plants in the three other places (Gen 21:15; Job 30:4, 7) in which it is used.

24. Ottosson (1974), pp. 393–399.

25. Described by Trible (1973a), pp. 35–37.

26. The earth-centered narrative of Genesis 2 omits mention of cosmic features (light/darkness and heavenly luminaries) that are beyond the exercise of human dominion.

27. Stanton (1895), part 1, pp. 14–15.

28. Bird (1981).

29. The last verse of Genesis 2 (2:25) is usually placed with the next chapter as part of the first scene (3:1–8) of the episode presented in Genesis 3.

30. See Naidoff (1978), pp. 2–3.

31. Alter (1981), p. 88.

32. See Walsh (1977), p. 177 and Trible (1978), pp. 82–87.

33. From vol. 2 (*Schriften zur Bibel*), p. 1131 of Buber's collected works. The translation is by Alter (1981), p. 93.

34. For a brief description of wisdom literature and its subgenres, see Murphy (1981), pp. 1–12.

35. Lieberman (1975), pp. 156–157.

36. E.g., Scott (1974), p. xxii; Mendenhall (1974); Blenkinsopp (1983), pp. 6–7.

37. Suggested long ago by Albright (1919–1920).

38. Especially Proverbs 8; see Camp (1985).

39. Notably in 2 Samuel 14 and 20. See Camp (1981) and (1985), pp. 120–124.

40. See Speiser (1964), pp. xvii–xviii for a discussion of the putative literary sources of Genesis.

41. So G. E. Wright (1960), pp. 24–25 and von Rad (1961), p. 98, among others.

42. Mendenhall (1974), p. 320.

CHAPTER 5

1. See the discussions in Chapter 4, pp. 72–78.

2. Author's translation. See the comments of Barr (1982), p. 270. Barr notes that the word rendered "under the power of" (*sub potestate*) is a word that Jerome knew well and translated properly in Gen 4:7, where Latin *appetitus* ("strong desire") comes much closer to representing the nature of the Hebrew word. See below, pp. 110–113.

3. Orlinsky (1966), p. 9.

4. Fishbane (1986), p. 153.

5. Alter (1985), pp. 3–26; Kugel (1981).

6. Alter (1985), p. 19.

7. Speiser (1964), p. 24; cf. idem, p. LXX.

8. Fabry (1980), p. 190.

9. Ibid., p. 189.

10. Ottosson (1978), p. 458.

11. Freedman (1972), p. xxvii.

12. Alter (1985), pp. 27–28.

13. This use of the verb '*ṣb* may in fact derive from a separate root related to an Arabic word for "cut." The verse in Eccles 10:9 would then read: "Whoever removes stones would be cut by them; and he who chops wood shall be endangered by this."

14. Speiser (1964), p. 24 points out that the translation "curse" for the He-

brew root *'rr* is seldom appropriate. When followed by the preposition "from," as it is in Gen 2:14 and 17, "curse" is altogether incorrect. Rather, it means that the serpent and the earth are each "restrained" or "held back" in some way.

15. Greenberg (1971), p. 1320 and Meyers (1987b).

16. Consider also the little-noticed counterpart to the fourth (Sabbath) commandment: "Six days shall you labor . . ." (Exod 20:9; Deut 5:13). The divine charge to rest on one day follows and is consequent upon the divinely ordained command for six days of work.

17. "Pregnancies" is actually singular in Hebrew. However, the preceding verbal form implies a collective plurality, and a simple English plural seems the best way to express that.

18. Alter (1985), p. 33 points out that departure from syntactic parallelism can be a way to heighten meaning. Such an explanation would surely be relevant here.

19. Translation mine. The other four passages are Prov 5:10; 10:22; Isa 58:3; Ps 127:2. The last citation refers explicitly to agricultural labor, or at least to "bread" as a symbol of earnings produced by long, hard days of toil.

20. 1 Chron 4:9 is a strained etymology of the name Yabez, whose mother is said to have given birth "with *'eseb.*"

21. The technical term for this is comitative.

22. Cf. Alter (1985), pp. 62–65, who cites Lotman (1977), pp. 126–127.

23. Bratsiosis (1974), pp. 223–224.

24. So Trible (1973), pp. 42–47 and (1978), pp. 144–165.

25. Ullendorf (1978), p. 428.

26. See Speiser (1964), pp. 32–33 for a discussion of sin as demon.

27. See Genovés (1969) and Goldstein (1969).

28. See Hughes (1965) for Jericho, Giles (1953) and (1958) for Lachish, and P. Smith *et al.* (1981) for Meiron.

29. Genovés (1969), pp. 441–443; Goldstein (1969), p. 486.

30. von Rad (1961), p. 90.

31. E.g., Fuh (1974–1975); cf. references cited by Fuh.

32. Vawter (1977), p. 85.

33. Ullendorf (1978), pp. 428–429. Ullendorf cites Rashi, Ibn Ezra, and also the Talmud (Erub 1006).

34. Culver (1980), p. 534.

35. Meyers (1983a), p. 347.

36. Offen (1984) presents an excellent analysis of the intersection of nationalism, depopulation, and feminism.

37. In an article published in *Le journal des femmes* in 1982; cited in ibid., p. 656.

38. Mendenhall (1974), p. 327.

39. E.g., von Rad (1961), p. 89 and Westermann (1974), p. 98.

40. Cowgill (1975), p. 516. Note, too, the statement of Levine and Levine (1985), p. 30, that "customary beliefs and practices promoting fertility . . . are

fundamental to the adaptive strategies by which agrarian parents maintain the family food supply and obtain both current support and long-term personal security. . . ."

41. Atrahasis Epic III vii 1, translation of Lambert and Millard (1969).
42. Kilmer (1972), pp. 171–172.
43. Freedman (1978), pp. 65–66.

CHAPTER 6

1. Pedersen (1926), pp. 99–181; 245–259.
2. Ibid., pp. 259, 263.
3. E.g., Wolff (1974).
4. See the discussion in Gottwald (1979), pp. 239–243.
5. The exceptions are Ephraim and Manasseh, the so-called Joseph tribes, which are the "grandsons" of Jacob.
6. Meyers (1983b).
7. The inaccuracy of "thousands" has been demonstrated by Mendenhall (1968). Cf. Gottwald (1979), pp. 257–278.
8. See Andersen (1970), pp. 32–33, Table 2.
9. Wilson (1985a), p. 302.
10. E.g., Netting, Wilk, and Arnould (1984b), p. xiii. Yanagisako (1979) provides a helpful review of the issues and problems involved in defining the structure and function of household and family.
11. Mayes (1985), p. 49.
12. Wrigley (1977), p. 72.
13. Wilson (1985a), p. 302.
14. Herlihy (1985), p. 4.
15. Ibid., p. 3.
16. Ibid., p. 5.
17. Bender (1967), p. 493; cf. Yanagisako (1979), pp. 162–163.
18. Gelb (1967), p. 5.
19. Reprinted by Laslett (1972), whose anthology (Laslett and Wall, 1972) seeks to redress that imbalance.
20. Laslett (1972), pp. 2–10; cf. Goody (1972).
21. See Wilk and Netting (1984).
22. Netting, Wilk, and Arnould (1984b), pp. xiv–xv.
23. Ibid., p. xix.
24. Rapp, Ross, and Bridenthal (1979), p. 181.
25. For the difficulties of seeing residential propinquity as a universal quality of households, see Goody (1972), pp. 106–110.
26. Callaway (1969, 1970); Callaway and Cooley (1971).
27. Kempinski and Fritz (1977).
28. Stager (1985).
29. For this definition of nuclear family and related groupings mentioned below, see Laslett (1972), pp. 28–34 and Table 1.1.

30. Translation is that of Gottwald (1979), p. 291.
31. Stager (1985), p. 22.
32. Goody (1972), p. 122; cf. Shorter (1973).
33. Porter (1967).
34. See ibid., pp. 1–5 for a review of the various positions that have been taken on these passages.
35. Ibid., p. 6.
36. Mayes (1985), p. 49.
37. Pasternak, Ember, and Ember (1976, p. 121) comment on the difficulties of extended family life.
38. E.g., Shiloh (1980).
39. See the critique of Stager (1985), p. 18.
40. Burch (1972).
41. Netting, Wilk, and Arnould (1984b), p. xvii.
42. Davis (1981), using an average of 10 liters a day for a 180-day dry season, estimates the cisterns could sustain households of ten to twelve individuals.
43. Pasternak, Ember, and Ember (1976), p. 121.

CHAPTER 7

1. See Mayes (1985), p. 81.
2. Mazar (1981), p. 16.
3. Renfrew (1974); Peebles and Kus (1977).
4. Goody (1972), p. 106.
5. Ibid.
6. Wilk and Netting (1984), pp. 5–15.
7. Ibid., p. 5.
8. See the summary in Hopkins (1985), p. 252.
9. Sahlins (1968), p. 75.
10. Herlihy (1985), pp. 2–4; cf. Gelb (1967), p. 6.
11. Ibid., p. 2.
12. Callaway (1983), p. 47.
13. See the summary in Stager (1985), pp. 12–15.
14. E.g., Jäger (1912), pp. 24–26.
15. Stager (1985), p. 17.
16. Yadin (1972), pp. 129–130.
17. Bridenthal and Koonz (1977), p. 6.
18. Ibid.
19. Goody (1972), p. 106; (1982), pp. 40–70.
20. Whyte (1978), p. 68.
21. Harris (1982).
22. Whyte (1978), pp. 66–68.
23. Goody (1982), p. 70.
24. Oral communication, based on ethnographic research, by K. Seger, University of Arizona.

25. Cf. Wrigley (1977), p. 72.

26. See the summary in Murphy (1985).

27. The postbiblical term *horim* (masc. pl.) is unattested in the Hebrew Bible. Genesis 49:26 may be an exception but the text is corrupt; see Speiser (1964), p. 369. Two other instances (Cant 3:4; Hos 2:7) are in the feminine singular and mean "mother" in the biological sense, as the one who has conceived a child; cf. Pope (1977), pp. 412, 421.

28. Bird (1974), p. 57.

29. Wolff (1974), p. 178.

30. So de Vaux (1961), p. 43, and Wolff (1974), pp. 121, 178, although the evidence is indirect; cf. 1 Sam 1:21–28 and 2 Chron 31:16.

31. See the extensive discussion by Chodorow (1978).

32. Boserup (1970), p. 140.

33. But now see Camp (1985).

34. Crenshaw (1985).

35. Kramer (1963), pp. 228–232.

36. Albright's remarks were made in a symposium on cultural development in the ancient Near East held at the Oriental Institute in Chicago in 1953. His comments on literacy were part of the discussion, recorded in Kraeling and Adams (1960) pp. 94–123, on "Scribal Concepts of Education."

37. Lemaire (1981) has conveniently gathered the inscriptional evidence for early literacy, but he does so for the dubious purpose of suggesting that schools existed already in premonarchic times.

38. Crenshaw (1985), pp. 614–615.

39. See the discussion in Mendenhall (1954).

40. So Phillips (1973), p. 350.

41. C. J. H. Wright (1979).

42. Ibid., pp. 104–105.

43. Hsu (*The Myth of Chinese Family Size,* 1943), as cited by Burch (1972), pp. 91–92 in a discussion of various reasons for the relatively small size of families cross-culturally.

44. Herlihy (1985), pp. 2–3.

45. Pritchard (1955), p. 175, translation of T. J. Meek.

46. Mayes (1985), p. 78.

47. LeVine and LeVine (1985), p. 31.

48. E.g., Meyers (1981).

49. Dever (1983), p. 578.

50. Myers (1975), p. 139.

51. Dever and Paul (1973), p. 267; cf. Rachel's theft of the teraphim, Gen 31:34.

52. Although no Israelite temples predate the monarchy, some Israelite sites built on Canaanite cities apparently reused parts of Canaanite shrines; and some open-air structures, outside of villages, have been excavated and identified by some as shrines. See Dever (1987), pp. 232–233.

53. Boling (1975), p. 257.

54. Ibid., p. 7, and Poethig (1985), p. 185.

55. Poethig (1985), p. 185.

56. Bird (1986) explores the domestic setting for women's religion as part of a forthcoming monograph on women in Israelite religion.

57. Recently and forthrightly stated by D. N. Freedman (1987) in his review of the evidence for goddess worship in ancient Israel in the preexilic period.

58. Negbi (1976), passim.

59. Cf. Pritchard (1943), pp. 83–87. See also the corroboration that these figures are not goddesses in Tigay (1987), especially note 116.

60. Ibid., p. 87.

61. Freedman (1987); but cf. Tigay (1987), pp. 163, 173–180, and nn. 84–104, 116; and McCarter (1987), pp. 143–149.

62. Meyers (1978).

63. Poethig (1985).

CHAPTER 8

1. Bird (1981), p. 153.

2. Mendenhall (1968).

3. Wilk and Netting (1984), pp. 14–15.

4. Tilly (1978), p. 167.

5. Rapp, Ross, and Bridenthal (1979), p. 182.

6. Bridenthal and Koonz (1977), p. 8.

7. Bender (1967), p. 498.

8. Laslett (1984), p. 368.

9. Gottwald (1979).

10. Gottwald (1985), pp. 285–286.

11. So Netting, Wilk, Arnould (1984b), pp. xxvi, xxxiii.

12. Sanday (1974), p. 199.

13. Ibid., pp. 199–200.

14. Noth (1977), pp. 203–204.

15. E.g., de Vaux (1961), p. 466.

16. For the internal and external evidence for the antiquity of this passage, see Meyers (1983c), pp. 584–585.

17. Graham (1979).

18. See the discussion in Chapter 2 (p. 36) on the relation between age and gender; cf. Boserup (1970), pp. 140–141.

19. See Meyers (1983c), pp. 585–587 for a more detailed analysis of the Leviticus data.

20. See Brown (1970), p. 1073, and Lenski and Lenski (1987), pp. 44–45.

21. See the review in Conkey and Spector (1984); cf. Schlegel (1977c), p. 354.

22. Datan (1977), pp. 330, 332.

23. Harris (1982).

24. Boserup (1970), p. 140.
25. Rosaldo (1980); cf. Conkey and Spector (1984).
26. Schlegel (1977c), p. 351.
27. Cf. Boorstin (1958), p. 348.
28. Whyte (1978), p. 135.
29. Friedl (1967).
30. Ibid., p. 92.
31. Pointed out by Rosaldo (1980), p. 404.
32. Cf. Gottwald (1985), pp. 175–178.
33. Ginsberg (1857).
34. Pope (1977), p. 140; cf. pp. 136–141, 200–210.
35. The various suggestions for dating the Song of Songs are reviewed in ibid., pp. 22–23.
36. Albright (1963).
37. Thus Trible (1978), pp. 144–165.
38. Ibid.
39. These images are fully explored in Meyers (1987a).
40. Cf. ibid. for the way the other ten or so faunal creatures are associated with the male and/or the female.
41. E.g., Pritchard (1954), nos. 470–474, 522, 525, 526, 537, 685, 704.
42. Most recently Lyons (1987).
43. Camp (1985), p. 91.
44. McKane (1970), p. 669.
45. Gottwald (1985), pp. 549–550.
46. Bridenthal and Koonz (1977), p. 6.
47. Friedl (1967), p. 107; Rogers (1978), pp. 148–153; Yanagisako (1979), p. 191.
48. Camp (1985), pp. 139–140.
49. But see Rosaldo (1980), pp. 390–393.
50. Amiran (1969), p. 112; cf. Gottwald (1979), pp. 489–503.
51. Going back to the early third millennium—thus, Lerner (1986); cf. Borowski (1987), pp. 22–25.
52. Datan (1977), p. 326.
53. Pedersen's discussion (1926, pp. 62–63) is still valuable.
54. Tosato (1982).
55. Ibid., pp. 121–125.
56. This is especially true in Galilee; see Meyers (1983b), pp. 49–53.
57. Reiter (1975), p. 15.
58. Bridenthal and Koonz (1977), p. 5.

EPILOGUE

1. See Frick (1985).
2. Neufeld (1960), p. 37.
3. Mayes (1985), p. 90; cf. Gottwald (1985), pp. 323–325.

4. Schlegel (1977c), p. 355.

5. G. E. Wright (1967).

6. Conkey and Spector (1984), p. 6.

7. Muller (1977), p. 7; Rapp (1977).

8. Cf. Blumberg (1979).

9. Mayes (1985), p. 66.

10. Stager (1985, p. 22) has identified them at Tell Farah (North), Tell Beit Mirsim, and Tell en-Nasbeh; cf. Halpern (1986).

11. E.g., by Elat (1977) and Silver (1983).

12. Harris (1982).

13. Zagarell (1986), p. 416.

14. Chaney (1985); Hopkins (1983), p. 193.

15. Halpern (1986).

16. Stager (1985), pp. 25–28.

17. Ibid., p. 25.

18. Wilk and Netting (1984), p. 11; cf. Whyte (1978), p. 164, and P. E. L. Smith (1972). Sexual restriction of both males and females can also be seen as serving the needs of a centralized government; thus, Steinberg (1986).

19. Cf. Netting, Wilk, and Arnould (1984b), p. xxx.

BIBLIOGRAPHY

Aharoni, Y.
1979   *Land of the Bible,* 3rd edition (trans. A. Rainey). Philadelphia: Westminster.
Albright, W. F.
1919–1920 The Goddess of Life and Wisdom. *American Journal of Semitic Languages* 36:258–294.
1940   *From the Stone Age to Christianity.* Baltimore: Johns Hopkins Press.
1949   *The Archaeology of Palestine.* Baltimore: Penguin Books.
1963   Archaic Survivals in the Text of Canticles. In *Hebrew and Semitic Studies,* eds. D. W. Thomas and W. D. McHardy, pp. 1–7. Oxford: Clarendon Press.
Alt, A.
1968   *Old Testament History and Religion* (trans. R. A. Wilson). Garden City, N.Y.: Doubleday.
Alter, R.
1981   *The Art of Biblical Narrative.* New York: Basic Books.
1985   *The Art of Biblical Poetry.* New York: Basic Books.
Amiran, R.
1969   *Ancient Pottery of the Holy Land.* Jerusalem: Massada Press Ltd.
Andersen, F.
1970   Israelite Kinship Terminology and Social Structure. *Biblical Translator* 20:29–39.
Angel, J. L.
1972   Ecology and Population in the East Mediterranean. *World Archaeology* 4:88–105.
Bachofen, J. J.
1861   *Das Mutterrecht.* Stuttgart, Germany: Krais and Hoffman.
Barr, J.
1982   The Vulgate Genesis and St. Jerome's Attitude to Women. *Studia Patristica* 18:268–273.
Bass, D. C.
1982   Women's Studies and Biblical Studies: An Historical Perspective. *Journal for the Study of the Old Testament* 22:6–12.

Beechey, V.
1979   On Patriarchy. *Feminist Review* 1:66–82.
Bender, D. R.
1967   A Refinement of the Concept of Household: Families, Co-residence, and Domestic Functions. *American Anthropologist* 69:493–504.
Binford, S. R.
1979   Myths and Matriarchies. *Human Behavior* 8:63–66.
Binford, S. R. and Binford, L. R., eds.
1968   *New Perspectives in Archaeology.* Chicago: Aldine.
Bird, P.
1974   Images of Women in the Old Testament. In *Religion and Sexism,* ed. R. R. Ruether, pp. 41–88. New York: Simon and Schuster.
1981   "Male and Female He Created Them": Gen. 1:27b in the Context of the Priestly Account of Creation. *Harvard Theological Review* 77:129–159.
1986   The Place of Women in the Israelite Cultus: Prolegomena to a Reconstruction of Israelite Religion. Sociology of the Monarchy Seminar Paper, Society of Biblical Literature Annual Meeting, Atlanta.
Blenkinsopp, J.
1983   *Wisdom and Law in the Old Testament.* Oxford: Oxford University Press.
Blumberg, R. L.
1979   Rural Women in Development: Veil of Invisibility, World of Work. *International Journal of Intercultural Relationships* 3:447–471.
Boling, R. C.
1975   *Judges* (Anchor Bible 6A). Garden City, N.Y.: Doubleday.
Boorstin, D.
1958   *The Americans: The Colonial Experience.* New York: Random House.
Borowski, O.
1987   *Agriculture in Iron Age Israel.* Winona Lake, Ind.: Eisenbrauns.
Boserup, E.
1970   *Women's Role in Economic Development.* London: G. Allen and Unwin.
1976   Environment, Population, and Technology in Primitive Societies. *Population and Development Review* 2:21–36.
Bratsiosis, N. P.
1974   *'îsh;'ishshāh. Theological Dictionary of the Old Testament* I:222–235. Grand Rapids, Mich.: Eerdmans.
Bridenthal, R. and Koonz, C.
1977   Introduction. In *Becoming Visible: Women in European History,*

eds. R. Bridenthal and C. Koonz, pp. 1–11. Boston: Houghton Mifflin.

Brown, J.
1970   A Note on the Division of Labor. *American Anthropologist* 72:1073–1078.

Burch, J. K.
1972   Some Demographic Determinants of Average Household Size: An Analytic Approach. In Laslett and Wall (1972), pp. 91–102.

Callaway, J. A.
1969   The 1966 'Ai (et-Tell) Excavations. *Bulletin of the American Schools of Oriental Research* 196:2–16.
1970   The 1968–1969 'Ai (et-Tell) Excavations. *Bulletin of the American Schools of Oriental Research* 198:7–31.
1983   A Visit with Ahilud. *Biblical Archaeology Review* 9:42–53.
1984   Village Subsistence at Ai and Raddana. In *The Answers Lie Below,* ed. H. D. Thompson, pp. 51–66. Lanham, Md.: University Press.

Callaway, J. A. and Cooley, R. S.
1971   A Salvage Excavation at Raddana, in Bireh. *Bulletin of the American Schools of Oriental Research* 201:9–19.

Camp, C. V.
1981   The Wise Women of 2 Samuel: A Role Model for Women in Early Israel. *Catholic Biblical Quarterly* 43:14–29.
1985   *Wisdom and the Feminine in the Book of Proverbs.* Decatur, Ga.: Almond Press.

Chaney, M. L.
1985   Latifundialization and Prophetic Diction in Eighth Century Judah and Israel. Sociology of the Monarchy Seminar Paper, Society of Biblical Literature Annual Meeting, Anaheim, Calif.

Charles, R. H.
1913   *The Apocrypha and Pseudepigrapha of the Old Testament,* 2 volumes. Oxford: Clarendon Press.

Childs, B.
1979   *Old Testament as Scripture.* Philadelphia: Fortress Press.

Chodorow, N.
1978   *The Reproduction of Mothering.* Berkeley: University of California Press.

Clark, E.
1986   Heresy, Asceticism, Adam, and Eve: Intepretations of Genesis 1–3 in the Later Latin Fathers. In *Ascetic Piety and Women's Faith,* pp. 353–385. Lewiston, N.Y./Queenston, Ont.: Edwin Mellen Press.

Coats, G. W.
1983   *Genesis.* Grand Rapids, Mich.: Eerdmans.

Collins, A. Y.
1985   *Feminist Perspectives in Biblical Scholarship.* Chico, Calif.: Scholars Press.

Conkey, M. W. and Spector, J. D.
1984   Archaeology and the Study of Gender. In *Advances in Archaeological Method and Theory,* vol. 7, ed. M. Schiffer, pp. 1–38. New York: Academic Press.

Cowgill, G. I.
1975   On Causes and Consequences of Ancient and Modern Population Changes. *American Anthropologist* 77:505–525.

Crenshaw, J.
1985   Education in Ancient Israel. *Journal of Biblical Literature* 104:601–615.

Cronin, C.
1977   Illusion and Reality in Sicily. In Schlegel (1977a) pp. 67–93.

Crumbine, N.
1983   Religion and the Feminist Critique of Culture. Working Paper no. 16 of the Wellesley College Center for Research on Women, Wellesley, Mass.

Culver, R. D.
1980   *Māshal* III, rule, have dominion, reign. *Theological Wordbook of the Old Testament* I:534–535. Chicago: Moody Bible Institute.

Datan, N.
1977   Ecological Antecedents of Sex-Role Consequences in Israel. In Schlegel (1977a), pp. 326–343.

Davis, J. B.
1981   Hill Country Dry Farming: A Revolutionary Development of Iron I. Paper presented at Society of Biblical Literature Regional Meeting, Atlanta.

Dever, W. G.
1983   Material Remains and the Cult in Ancient Israel: An Essay in Archaeological Systematics. In *The Word of the Lord Shall Go Forth,* eds. C. L. Meyers and M. O'Connor, pp. 571–587. Philadelphia: American Schools of Oriental Research.
1987   The Contribution of Archaeology to the Study of Canaanite and Early Israelite Religion. In Miller, Hanson, and McBride (1987), pp. 209–248.

Dever, W. G. and Paul, S., eds.
1973   *Biblical Archaeology.* Jerusalem: Keter.

Douglas, M.
1966   *Purity and Danger.* London: Routledge and Kegan Paul.

Draper, P.
1975   !Kung Women: Contrasts in Sexual Egalitarianism in Foraging and

Sedentary Contexts. In *Toward an Anthropology of Women,* ed. R. R. Reiter, pp. 77–109. New York: Monthly Review Press.

Dubois, E. C. *et al.*
1985   *Feminist Scholarship: Kindling in the Groves of Academia.* Urbana: University of Illinois Press.

Edelstein, G. and Gat, Y.
1980   Terraces around Jerusalem. *Israel—Land and Nature* 6:72–78.

Elat, M.
1977   *Economic Relations between the Lands of the Bible* (c. 1000–539 BCE). Jerusalem: Magnes (Hebrew).

Engels, F.
1972   *The Origin of the Family, Private Property, and the State,* ed. E. Leacock. New York: International Publishers (originally published in 1884).

Exum, J. C.
1985   "Mother in Israel": A Familiar Story Reconsidered. In Russell (1985a), pp. 73–85.

Fabry, H. S.
1980   *ḥbl* IV; *chēbel. Theological Dictionary of the Old Testament* IV:188–192. Grand Rapids, Mich.: Eerdmans.

Fishbane, M.
1986   The Academy and the Community. *Judaism* 35:147–154.

Flanagan, J. W.
1985   History as Hologram: Integrating Literary, Archaeological, and Comparative Sociological Evidence. In *Society of Biblical Literature Seminar Papers,* pp. 291–314. Atlanta: Scholars Press.

Flannery, K.
1972   The Cultural Evolution of Civilization. *Annual Review of Ecology and Systematics* 3:399–426.

Freedman, D. N.
1972   Prolegomenon. In *The Forms of Hebrew Poetry,* ed. G.B. Gray, pp. vii–lvi. New York: Ktav.
1978   Psalm 113 and the Song of Hannah. *Eretz Israel* 14:56–69.
1987   Yahweh of Samaria and His Asherah. *Biblical Archaeologist* 50:241–249.

Freedman, D. N. and Graf, D. F., eds.
1983   *Palestine in Transition.* Sheffield, England: Almond Press.

Frick, F.
1985   *The Formation of the State in Ancient Israel.* Sheffield, England: Almond Press.

Friedl, E.
1967   The Position of Women: Appearance and Reality. *Anthropological Quarterly* 40:47–108.

1975   *Women and Men: An Anthropologist's View*. New York: Holt, Rinehart and Winston.

Fuchs, E.
1985   The Literary Characteristics of Mothers and Sexual Politics in the Hebrew Bible. In Collins (1985), pp. 117–136.

Fuh, S.
1974–1975 What Is Woman's Desire? *Westminster Journal of Theology* 37:376–383.

Geertz, C.
1973   *The Interpretation of Cultures*. New York: Basic Books.

Gelb, I. J.
1967   Approaches to the Study of Ancient Society. *Journal of the American Oriental Society* 87:1–7.

Genovés, S.
1969   Estimation of Age and Mortality. In *Science and Archaeology,* eds. S. Brothwell and E. Higgs, pp. 440–452. London: Thames and Hudson.

Gifford, C. DeS.
1985   American Women and the Bible: The Nature of Women as a Hermeneutical Issue. In Collins (1985), pp. 11–34.

Giles, M.
1953   The Human and Animal Remains. Appendix A, pp. 405–412 in *Lachish III: The Iron Age,* ed. O. Tufnell. London: Oxford University Press.

1958   The Human and Animal Remains. Appendix B, pp. 318–322 in *Lachish IV: The Bronze Age,* ed. O. Tufnell. London: Oxford University Press.

Ginsburg, C. P.
1857   *The Song of Songs* (trans. S. Blank). New York: Ktav (reprinted in 1970).

Goldstein, M. S.
1969   The Paleopathology of Human Skeletal Remains. In *Science and Archaeology,* eds. S. Brothwell and E. Higgs, pp. 480–489. London: Thames and Hudson.

Goody, J.
1972   The Evolution of the Family. In Laslett and Wall (1972), pp. 103–124.

1982   *Cooking, Cuisine, and Class*. Cambridge: Cambridge University Press.

Gottwald, N. K.
1979   *The Tribes of Yahweh*. Maryknoll, N.Y.: Orbis.
1985   *The Hebrew Bible*. Philadelphia: Fortress Press.

Gould, M.
1980   Review Essay: The New Sociology. *SIGNS* 5:459–467.

Gould, M. and Kern-Daniels, R.
1977   Toward a Sociological Theory of Gender and Sex. *American Sociologist* 12:182–189.

Graham, P.
1979   The Perspectives of Leviticus 25 and 27 on Real Property: A Comparative Study. Paper given at Society of Biblical Literature Southeast Regional Meeting, Atlanta.

Greenberg, M.
1971   Labor in the Bible and Apocrypha. *Encyclopedia Judaica* 10:1320–1322.

Halpern, B.
1986   Israelite History, Iron Age. Paper given at Society of Biblical Literature Annual Meeting, Atlanta.

Hanson, R. S.
1972   *The Serpent Was Wiser*. Minneapolis: Augsburg Publishing House.

Hare, R.
1954   *Pomp and Pestilence: Infectious Disease, Its Origins and Conquest.* London: Victor Gollancy.

Hareuveni, N.
1980   *Nature in Our Biblical Heritage*. Kiryat Ono, Israel: Neot Kedumim Ltd.

Harris, O.
1982   Compensation and Commodities: The Organization of Subsistence in the High Andes. Paper given at a seminar on women and food in developing countries, Oxford University.

Herlihy, D.
1985   *Medieval Households*. Cambridge, Mass.: Harvard University Press.

Higgins, J.
1976   The Myth of Eve the Temptress. *Journal of the American Academy of Religion* 44:639–647.

Hopkins, D.
1983   The Dynamics of Agriculture in Monarchic Israel. In *Society of Biblical Literature Seminar Papers,* ed. K. H. Richards, pp. 177–202. Chico, Calif.: Scholars Press.

1985   *The Highlands of Canaan*. Sheffield, England: Almond Press.

Hughes, D. R.
1965   Report on Metrical and Non-metrical Aspects of E.B.–M.B. and Middle Bronze Human Remains from Jericho. In K. Kenyon, *Excavations at Jericho,* vol. 2, pp. 664–685. London: British School of Archaeology in Jerusalem.

Jäger, K.
1912   *Das Bauernhaus in Palästina*. Göttingen, Germany: Vandenhoeck and Ruprecht.

Kempinski, A. and Fritz, V.
1977   Excavations at Tell Masos (Khirbet el-Meshâsh), Preliminary Report on the Third Season. *Tel Aviv* 4:136–158.

Kilmer, A.
1972   The Mesopotamian Concept of Overpopulation and Its Solution as Represented in the Mythology. *Orientalia* 41:160–177.

Koestler, A.
1959   *The Sleepwalkers*. New York: Macmillan.

Kraeling, C. H. and Adams, R. M., eds.
1960   *City Invincible*. Chicago: University of Chicago Press.

Kramer, S. N.
1963   *The Sumerians*. Chicago: University of Chicago Press.

Kugel, J. L.
1981   *The Idea of Biblical Poetry: Parallelism and Its History*. New Haven, Conn.: Yale University Press.

Lambert, W. G. and Millard, A. R.
1969   *Atra-ḫasīs: The Babylonian Story of the Flood*. Oxford: Clarendon Press.

Lamphere, L.
1977   Review Essay: Anthropology. *SIGNS* 2:612–627.

Lance, H. D.
1981   *The Old Testament and the Archaeologist*. Philadelphia: Fortress Press.

Laslett, P.
1972   Introduction: The History of the Family. In Laslett and Wall (1972), pp. 1–90.
1984   The Family as a Knot of Individual Interests. In Netting, Wilk, and Arnould (1984a), pp. 359–379.

Laslett, P. and Wall, R, eds.
1972   *Household and Family in Past Time*. London: Cambridge University Press.

Leach, E. R.
1969   *Genesis as Myth and Other Essays*. London: Jonathan Cape.
1982   *Social Anthropology*. Glasgow: Fontana.

Leacock, E. B.
1981   *The Myth of Male Dominance*. New York: Monthly Review Press.

Lefkowitz, Mary R.
1983   Wives and Husbands. *Greece and Rome* 30:31–47.

Lemaire, A.
1981   *Les écoles et la formation de la Bible dans l'ancien Israël*. Göttingen, Federal Republic of Germany: Vandenhoeck and Ruprecht.

Lenski, G.
1980   Review of N. K. Gottwald, *The Tribes of Yahweh. Religious Studies Review* 6:275–278.

Lenski, G. and Lenski, J.
1987   *Human Societies,* 5th edition. New York: McGraw Hill.
Lerner, G.
1986   *The Creation of Patriarchy.* New York: Oxford University Press.
LeVine, S. and LeVine, R.A.
1985   Age, Gender, and the Demographic Transition: The Life Course in
        Agrarian Societies. In *Gender and the Life Course,* ed. A. S. Rossi,
        pp. 29–42. New York: Aldine.
Lieberman, S. R.
1975   *The Eve Motif in the Ancient Near East and Classical Greek Sources.*
        Dissertation, Boston University.
Lotman, Jo
1977   *The Structure of the Artistic Text* (trans. R. Vroom). Ann Arbor:
        University of Michigan.
Lyons, E. L.
1987   A Note on Proverbs 31:10–31. In *The Listening Heart,* eds. K. G.
        Hoglund *et al.,* pp. 237–246. Sheffield, England: Journal for the
        Study of the Old Testament Press.
McCarter, P. K., Jr.
1987   Aspects of the Religion of the Israelite Monarchy. In Miller, Han-
        son, and McBride (1987), pp. 137–156.
McKane, W.
1970   *Proverbs: A New Approach.* Philadelphia: Westminster Press.
McLennan, J. F.
1865   *Primitive Marriage.* Edinburgh: A. and C. Black.
McNeill, W. H.
1975   *Plagues and Peoples.* Garden City, N.Y.: Doubleday.
Maass, F.
1974   *'ādhām. Theological Dictionary of the Old Testament* I:75–87. Grand
        Rapids, Mich.: Eerdmans.
Mace, D. R.
1953   *Hebrew Marriage: A Social Study.* London: Epworth Press.
Malina, B. J.
1969   Some Observations on the Origin of Sin in Judaism and St. Paul.
        Catholic Biblical Quarterly 31:18–34.
Martin, M. K. and Voorhies, B.
1975   *Female of the Species.* New York: Columbia University Press.
Mayes, A. D. H.
1985   *Judges.* Sheffield, England: Journal for the Study of the Old Testa-
        ment Press.
Mazar, A.
1981   Giloh: An Early Israelite Settlement Site near Jerusalem. *Israel Ex-
        ploration Journal* 31:1–36.

Mendenhall, G. E.
1954   Law and Covenant in Israel and the Ancient Near East. *Biblical Archaeologist* 17:22–46, 49–76.
1958   The Census Lists of Numbers 1 and 26. *Journal of Biblical Literature* 77:52–66.
1962   The Hebrew Conquest of Palestine. *Biblical Archaeologist* 25:66–87.
1973   *The Tenth Generation*. Baltimore: Johns Hopkins University Press.
1974   The Shady Side of Wisdom: The Date and Purpose of Genesis 3. In *Light unto My Path*, eds. H. N. Bream, R. D. Heim, and C. A. Moore, pp. 319–334. Philadelphia: Temple University Press.

Meyers, C.
1978   Roots of Restriction: Women in Early Israel. *Biblical Archeologist* 41:91–103.
1981   The Elusive Temple. *Biblical Archeologist* 45:33–42.
1983a   Gender Roles and Genesis 3:16 Revisited. In *The Word of the Lord Shall Go Forth*, eds. C. Meyers and M. O'Connor, Philadelphia: American Schools of Oriental Research.
1983b   Of Seasons and Soldiers: A Topological Appraisal of the Pre-Monarchic Tribes of Galilee. *Bulletin of the American Schools of Oriental Research* 252:47–60.
1983c   Procreation, Production, and Protection: Male–Female Balance in Early Israel. *Journal of the American Academy of Religion* 51:569–593.
1987a   Gender Imagery in the Song of Songs. *Hebrew Annual Review* 10:209–223.
1987b   ʿāṣab II. *Theologishes Wörterbuch zum Alten Testament* VI:298–302. Stuttgart, Federal Republic of Germany: Verlag W. Kohlhammer.

Miller, P. D., Jr. Hanson, P. D., and McBride, S. D., eds.
1987   *Ancient Israelite Religion*. Philadelphia: Fortress Press.

Millett, K.
1970   *Sexual Politics*. Garden City, N.Y.: Doubleday.

Morgan, L. H.
1877   *Ancient Society*. New York: World Publishing.

Muller, V.
1977   The Formation of the State and the Oppression of Women. *Review of Radical Political Economics* 9:7–21.

Murphy, R.
1981   *Wisdom Literature*. Grand Rapids, Mich.: Eerdmans.
1985   Wisdom. *Harper's Bible Dictionary*. San Francisco: Harper and Row.

Myers, J.
1975   The Way of the Fathers. *Interpretation* 29:121–140.

Naidoff, B. D.
1978   A Man to Work the Soil: A New Interpretation of Genesis 2–3. *Journal for the Study of the Old Testament* 5:2–14.

Negbi, O.
1976   *Canaanite Gods in Metal.* Tel Aviv: Tel Aviv Institute of Archaeology.

Netting, R. McC., Wilk, R. R., and Arnould, E. J.
1984a   (eds.) *Households: Comparative and Historic Studies of the Domestic Group.* Berkeley: University of California Press.
1984b   Introduction. In Netting, Wilk, and Arnould (1984a), pp. xiii–xxxviii.

Neufeld, E.
1960   Emergence of a Royal-Urban Society in Ancient Israel. *Hebrew Union College Annual* 31:31–53.

Nicholson, L. J.
1982   Comment on Rosaldo's "The Use and Abuse of Anthropology." *SIGNS* 7:732–735.

Noth, M.
1977   *Leviticus,* 2nd edition (trans. J. E. Anderson). Philadelphia: Westminster Press.

O'Barr, J., ed.
1988   *Gender and Cultural Contexts.* Madison: University of Wisconsin Press.

O'Brien, J. and Major, W.
1982   *In the Beginning.* Chico, Calif.: Scholars Press.

Offen, K.
1984   Depopulation, Nationalism, and Feminism in Fin-de-siecle France. *American Historical Review* 89:648–674.

Orlinsky, H. H.
1966   The Rage to Translate: The New Art of Bible Translation. Introduction to *Genesis:* The N.J.V. Translation. New York: Harper and Row.

Ottosson, M.
1974   *'erets. Theological Dictionary of the Old Testament* I:390–405. Grand Rapids, Mich.: Eerdmans.
1978   *hārāh; hāreh; hērāyôn; hēron. Theological Dictionary of the Old Testament* III:458–461. Grand Rapids, Mich.: Eerdmans.

Pasternak, B., Ember, C. R., and Ember, M.
1976   On the Conditions Favoring Extended Family Households. *Journal of Anthropological Research* 32:109–123.

Pedersen, J.
1926   *Israel: Its Life and Culture,* 2 volumes. London: Oxford University Press.

Peebles, C. and Kus, S.
1977   Some Archaeological Correlates of Ranked Societies. *American Antiquity* 42:421–448.

Peltzer, K. L.
1945   *Pioneer Settlement in the Asian Tropics.* New York: American Geographical Society.

Phillips, A.
1973   Some Aspects of Family Law in Pre-exilic Israel. *Vetus Testamentum* 23:349–361.

Plöger, J. G.
1974   *'adhāmāh. Theological Dictionary of the Old Testament* I:88–98. Grand Rapids, Mich.: Eerdmans.

Poethig, E.
1985   *The Victory Song Tradition of the Women of Israel.* Dissertation, Union Theological Seminary, New York.

Pope, M. H.
1977   *Song of Songs* (Anchor Bible 7c). Garden City, N.Y.: Doubleday.

Porter, J. R.
1967   *The Extended Family in the Old Testament.* London: Edutext Publications.

Pritchard, J. B.
1943   *Palestinian Figurines in Relation to Certain Goddesses Known Through Literature.* New Haven, Conn.: American Oriental Society.
1954   *The Ancient Near East in Pictures.* Princeton N.J.: Princeton University Press.
1955   ed., *Ancient Near Eastern Texts,* 2nd edition. Princeton: N.J.: Princeton University Press.

Quinn, N.
1977   Anthropological Studies on Women's Status. *Annual Review of Anthropology* 6:186–198.

von Rad, G.
1961   *Genesis* (trans. J. H. Marks). Philadelphia: Westminster Press (originally published in 1956).

Rapp, R.
1977   Gender and Class: An Archaeology of Knowledge Concerning the Origins of the State. *Dialectical Anthropology* 2:309–316.

Rapp, R., Ross, E., and Bridenthal, R.
1979   Examining Family History: Household and Family. *Feminist Studies* 5:174–200.

Reiter, R. R.
1975   Introduction. In *Toward an Anthropology of Women,* ed. R. R. Reiter, pp. 11–19. New York: Monthly Review Press.

Renfrew, C.
  1974   Beyond a Subsistence Economy: The Evolution of Social Organiza-
          tion in Prehistoric Europe. In *Reconstructing Complex Societies,* ed.
          C. B. Moore, pp. 69–88. Cambridge, Mass.: American Schools of
          Oriental Research.
  1984   *Approaches to Social Anthropology.* Cambridge, Mass.: Harvard
          University Press.

Rogers, S. C.
  1975   Female Forms of Power and the Myth of Male Dominance: A Model
          of Female/Male Interaction in Peasant Society. *American Ethnolo-
          gist* 2:727–756.
  1978   Women's Place: A Critical Review of Anthropological Theory. *Com-
          parative Studies in Society and History* 20:123–162.

Ron, Z.
  1966   Agricultural Terracing in the Judean Mountains. *Israel Exploration
          Journal* 16:33–49, 111–122.

Rosaldo, M. Z.
  1974   Women, Culture, and Society: A Theoretical Overview. In Rosaldo
          and Lamphere (1974), pp. 17–42.
  1980   The Use and Abuse of Anthropology: Reflections on Feminism and
          Cross-Cultural Understanding. *SIGNS* 5:389–417.

Rosaldo, M. Z. and Lamphere, L., eds.
  1974   *Women, Culture, and Society.* Stanford, Calif.: Stanford University
          Press.

Rossi, A.
  1977   A Biosocial Perspective on Parenting. *Daedalus* 106:1–31.

Rowbotham, S.
  1979   The Trouble with Patriarchy. *New Statesman* (December 21/28), pp.
          970–971.

Ruether, R. R.
  1985   Feminist Interpretation: A Method of Correlation. In Russell
          (1985a), pp. 111–124.

Russell, L. M.
  1985a   (ed.) *Feminist Interpretation of the Bible.* Philadelphia: Westminster
          Press.
  1985b   Introduction: Liberating the Word. In Russell (1985a), pp. 11–18.

Sahlins, M.
  1968   *Tribesmen.* Englewood Cliffs, N.J.: Prentice-Hall.

Sakenfeld, K. D.
  1985   Feminist Uses of Biblical Materials. In Russell (1985a), pp. 55–
          64.

Sandars, N. K.
  1978   *The Sea Peoples.* London: Thames and Hudson.

Sanday, P. R.
 1974   Female Status in the Public Domain. In Rosaldo and Lamphere (1974), pp. 189–206.

Schlegel, A.
 1972   *Male Dominance and Female Autonomy: Domestic Authority in Matrilineal Societies.* New Haven, Conn.: Human Relations Area Files Press.
 1977a   (ed.) *Sexual Stratification: A Cross-Cultural View.* New York: Columbia University Press.
 1977b   Toward a Theory of Sexual Stratification. In Schlegel (1977a), pp. 1–40.
 1977c   Overview. In Schlegel (1977a), pp. 344–357.

Schusky, E. L.
 1974   *Variation in Kinship.* New York: Holt, Rinehart and Winston.

Scott, R. B. Y.
 1974   *Proverbs and Ecclesiastes* (Anchor Bible 18). Garden City, N.Y.: Doubleday.

Shiloh, Y.
 1980   The Population of Iron Age Palestine in the Light of a Sample Analysis of the Urban Plans. *Bulletin of the American Schools of Oriental Research* 239:26–35.

Shorter, E.
 1973   Kinship and Family Size in History. *History of Childhood Quarterly* 1:342–347.

Silver, M.
 1983   *Prophets and Markets.* Boston: Kluwer-Nijhoff Publishing.

Smith, P. *et al.*
 1981   Human Skeletal Remains. Chapter 7.2 in E. Meyers, J. Strange, and C. Meyers, *Excavations at Ancient Meiron,* Cambridge, Mass.: American Schools of Oriental Research.

Smith, P. E. L.
 1972   Land-use, Settlement Patterns, and Subsistence Agriculture: A Demographic Perspective. In *Man, Settlement and Urbanism,* eds. P. J. Ucko, R. Tringham, and G. W. Dimbleby, pp. 409–425. Cambridge, Mass.: Schenkman Publishing Company.

Smith, W. R.
 1885   *Kinship and Marriage in Early Arabia.* Cambridge: Cambridge University Press.

Speiser, E.
 1964   *Genesis* (Anchor Bible 1). Garden City, N.Y.: Doubleday.

Sproul, B. C.
 1979   *Primal Myths: Creating the World.* San Francisco: Harper and Row.

Stack, C. B. *et al.*
 1975   Review Essay: Anthropology. *SIGNS* 1:147–159.

Stager, L. A.
  1976   Agriculture. *The Interpreter's Dictionary of the Bible* Supplementary
            Volume: 11–13. Nashville: Abingdon.
  1981   Highland Life in Palestine Three Thousand Years Ago. *Oriental
            Institute Notes and News* 69:1–3.
  1982   The Archaeology of the East Slope of Jerusalem and the Terraces of
            the Kidron. *Journal of Near Eastern Studies* 41:111–121.
  1985   The Archaeology of the Family in Ancient Israel. *Bulletin of the
            American Schools of Oriental Research* 260:1–36.
Stanton, E. C.
  1895, 1898 *The Woman's Bible* (2 parts). New York: European Publishing Com-
            pany (reprinted 1974, as *The Original Feminist Attack on the Bible*,
            with introduction by B. Welter). New York: Arno Press.
Steinberg, N.
  1986   Gender Roles in the Monarchy. Sociology of the Monarchy Seminar
            Paper, Society of Biblical Literature Annual Meeting, Atlanta.
Terrien, S.
  1985   *Till The Heart Sings*. Philadelphia: Fortress Press.
Thompson, T. L.
  1979   *The Settlement of Palestine in the Bronze Age. Beihefte zum Tübinger
            Atlas des vorderen Orients,* Reihe B, no. 34. Wiesbaden, Federal
            Republic of Germany: Dr. Reichert Verlag.
Tigay, J.
  1987   Israelite Religion: The Onomastic and Epigraphic Evidence. In
            Miller, Hanson, and McBride (1987), pp. 157–174.
Tilly, L.
  1978   The Social Sciences and the Study of Women: A Review Article.
            Comparative Studies in Society and History 20:163–173.
Tosato, A.
  1982   *Il matrimonio israelitico* (Analecta Biblica 100). Rome: Biblical Insti-
            tute Press.
Trenchard, W. C.
  1981   *Ben Sira's View of Women*. Chico, Calif.: Scholars Press.
Trible, P.
  1973a   Depatriarchalizing in Biblical Interpretation. *Journal of the Ameri-
            can Academy of Religion* 41:30–48.
  1973b   Eve and Adam, Genesis 2–3 Reread. *Andover Newton Quarterly*
            13:251–258.
  1978   *God and the Rhetoric of Sexuality*. Philadelphia: Fortress Press.
Ullendorf, E.
  1978   *The Bawdy Bible*. Oxford: Oxford Centre for Postgraduate Hebrew
            Studies.
de Vaux, R.
  1961   *Ancient Israel* (trans J. McHugh). New York: McGraw-Hill.

Vawter, B.
1977   *On Genesis: A New Reading.* Garden City, N.Y.: Doubleday.
Waldbaum, J. C.
1978   *From Bronze to Iron: Transition from Bronze Age to Iron Age in the Eastern Mediterranean* (Studies in Mediterranean Archaeology, 54). Göteborg, Sweden: Paul Aström.
Walsh, J. T.
1977   Genesis 2:4b and 3:24: A Synchronic Approach. *Journal of Biblical Literature* 96:161–177.
Wampler, J. C.
1947   Some Cisterns and Silos. In *Tell en-Naṣbeh* I, ed. C. C. McCown, pp. 129–147. Berkeley: Pacific School of Religion.
Weber, M.
1947   *The Theory of Social and Economic Organization* (trans. and ed. T. Parsons). New York: Free Press (originally published in 1922).
Westermann, C.
1974   *Creation* (trans. J. Scullion). Philadelphia: Fortress Press.
Whyte, M. K.
1978   *The Status of Women in Pre-industrial Societies.* Princeton, N.J.: Princeton University Press.
Wilk, R. R. and Netting, R. McC.
1984   Households: Changing Forms and Functions. In Netting, Wilk, and Arnould (1984a), pp. 1–28.
Wilson, R. W.
1985a   The Family. In *Harper's Bible Dictionary,* pp. 302–303. San Francisco: Harper and Row.
1985b   Sociology of the Old Testament. In *Harper's Bible Dictionary,* pp. 968–973. San Francisco: Harper and Row.
Wolf, E. R.
1966   *Peasants.* Englewood Cliffs, N.J.: Prentice-Hall.
Wolf, M.
1972   *Women and the Family in Rural Taiwan.* Stanford, Calif.: Stanford University Press.
Wolff, H. W.
1974   *Anthropology of the Old Testament* (trans. M. Kohl). Philadelphia: Fortress Press.
Wright, C. J. H.
1979   The Israelite Household and the Decalogue: The Social Background and Significance of Some Commandments. *Tyndale Bulletin* 30:101–121.
Wright, G. E.
1960   The Nature of Man: An Exposition of Genesis 3. *The Rule of God.* Garden City, N.Y.: Doubleday.
1967   The Provinces of Solomon. *Eretz Israel* 8:58–68.

Wrigley, E. A.
    1977   Reflections on the History of the Family. *Daedalus* 106:71–85.

Yadin, Y.
    1972   *Hazor* (1970 Schweich Lectures). London: Oxford University Press for the British Academy.

Yanagisako, S. J.
    1979   Family and Household: The Analysis of Domestic Groups. *Annual Review of Anthropology* 8:161–205.

Zagarell, A.
    1986   Trade, Women, Class, and Society in Ancient Western Asia. *Current Anthropology* 27:415–430.

Zohary, M.
    1982   *Plants of the Bible*. Cambridge: Cambridge University Press.

Index of Scriptural References

229

General Index

Abel, city of, 160
Abraham, 100, 102, 166, 176
Adam, 3–4, 75, 77, 79, 87, 121
'adam/'adamah, 81–83, 86, 89
Adam and Eve, Books of, 3, 75
'adon, 182
Age groups, 36, 171
Agrarian life, 12, 16, 34, 38, 47, 57, 185
Agriculture, 31, 38, 48, 54–55, 57–63,
    146, 148, 191
Aharoni, Y., 52
'Ai, 55, 59, 132
Akkadian, 152
'kl, 89
Albright, W. F., 6, 17, 54, 153
Alexander, 16
Alphabet, 52, 153
Alt, A., 6
Alter, R., 88–89
Amarna, 68
American Colonies, 53
American Indians, 65
Anat, 162
Androcentrism. *See* Patriarchy
Angel, J. L., 70
Anthropology. *See* Social science
Apocalypse of Moses, 75
Apocryphya and Pseudepigrapha, 3, 72,
    75
Archaeology, 15–20, 44, 48, 51–52, 55,
    69–70, 97, 112, 122, 132–34, 140,
    143–44, 147, 152, 157–58, 161, 182,
    189, 191–92
Archetype, 80
Aristotle, 113, 142
Asherah, 162
Asymmetry, gender, 29, 31, 34, 44, 181–
    82
Athaliah, 5
Atrahasis, 65–66

Authority, 41–43, 45, 155–57
    female, 44, 157, 174–75
    male, 36, 157, 168, 175, 181
Authorized Version. *See* King James Version
Azariah, 85

ba'al, 182–86
Babylonians, 48, 80, 143, 153
Bachofen, J. J., 37–38, 131
bayit, 142
Ben Sirah, 75
bet 'ab, 39, 128–30, 179–80
bet 'em, 179–80
betah, 179
Beth Baal Peor, 67, 69–70, 183
Biblical studies, 11, 19–23
Bilhah, 106
Binford, L. R., 18
Biological determinism, 28, 48
Boserup, E., 62–63
Bridenthal, R. and Koonz, C., 167
Bronze Age, 15, 51–52, 54, 64, 66, 68–
    70, 140, 144, 162, 182
Buber, M., 90
Burial, 112

Cain and Abel, 87–88, 111
Callaway, J. A., 132
Canaan, Canaanites, 9, 15, 48, 50–52,
    67–69, 140, 162–63, 165, 182, 184
Capitalism, 28–29
Catch-22, 69
Census, 129, 166
Ceramics, 82, 148, 192
Childbirth, 46, 49, 62, 78–79, 95–96,
    100–103, 105–6, 108, 113, 116, 167,
    171

233